A Parent's Guide™ to
San Francisco

Written by
Paul Otteson

A Parent's Guide™ to
San Francisco

Text and Maps © Mars Publishing 2001
Photos by Paul Otteson and Mary Hagemann, except as noted.
ISBN: 1-931199-03-5

© 2001 Mars Publishing, Inc. All rights reserved. No part of this publication may be reproduced, stored in a retrieval system or transmitted in any form by any means electronic, mechanical, photocopying, recording, or otherwise, except for brief extracts for the purpose of review, without written permission of the publisher and copyright holder.

Mars Publishing and the Mars Publishing Logo, Parent's Guide and the Parent's Guide logo are trademarks of Mars Publishing, Inc.

The authors and Mars Publishing have tried to make the information in this book as accurate as possible. We accept no responsibility for any loss, injury, or inconvenience sustained by anyone using this book.

This book, and all titles in the Parent's Guide series, are available for purposes of fund raising and educational sales to charity drives, fund raisers, parent or teacher organizations, schools, government agencies and corporations at a discount for purchases of more than 10 copies. Persons or organizations wishing to inquire should call Mars Publishing at 1-800-549-6646 or write to us at *sales@marspub.com*.

At the time of publication of this book, all of the information contained within was correct to the best of our knowledge. If you find information in this book that has changed, please contact us. Even better, if you have additional places to recommend, please let us know. Any included submissions to the new edition of this book will get the submitter a by-line in the book and a free copy of any Mars publication.

Please contact us at *parentsguides@marspub.com*

Dedicated to Maxwell Strider, born to explore.

parent's guide press

Edwin E. Steussy, CEO and Publisher
Lars J. Peterson, Project Editor
Michael P. Duggan, Graphic Artist

A Parent's Guide to San Francisco

Contents

Introduction 1

Chapter One:
San Francisco – Young at Heart 3
    Getting around the Bay 6
        Rail 6
        Bus 6
        Ferry 7
        By Car 7
    Getting into and out of San Francisco 8
        From Marin 9
        From the East Bay 9
        From the Peninsula 10
    Driving and Parking in San Francisco 10
    What Should We See? 11

Chapter Two: San Francisco 13
    Introduction & Map 14
    Sites 15

Chapter Three: Marin & the North Bay 60
    Introduction & Map 61
    Sites 62

Chapter Four: The East Bay 89
    Introduction & Map 91
    Sites 92

A Parent's Guide to San Francisco

Contents

Chapter Five: The Peninsula & South Bay 121
Introduction & Map 122
Sites 123

Chapter Six: Within 100 Miles 149
Introduction & Map 150
Sites 151

Appendices 173
A Kid's San Francisco Calendar 174
Index 179

Introduction

Kid Stuff

Kids? Where did *they* come from? Wasn't it just yesterday that all your worldly belongings fit in a shoe box and you were trying to decide between joining the Peace Corps or hitchhiking to Guatemala? Well guess what—they're here and they're yours. Adorable as bunnies one minute, demanding as the IRS the next, your imp or imps look to you for all things. It's an astonishing responsibility.

Fortunately, you have allies. Whether you reside in the Bay Area or are just passing through, you are immersed in a rich network of destinations, organizations, institutions, and businesses that have something to contribute to your multi-year venture of child-rearing. Some exist in service to youth, community, and humanity. Others just want to make a buck. Either way, you are wise to know about them as you invent your children's lives, deciding day by day what they will experience.

As parents, we have our own set of needs. We want convenience when it comes to locations, opening hours, transit, parking, and more. When it's time to pay up, we'd rather give the cashier a couple of fives than a couple of twenties. If we hand control of our young ones over to a guide or teacher, we want the peace of mind that comes with knowing they are competent. Perhaps more than anything else, we want to "do the right thing," choosing wisely and well for those we love so much.

How can you make sure you "do the right thing" when designing adventures and excursions for your children? Sometimes you can measure success in smiles, hugs, or an uttered, "Thanks, Pop." On other occasions, success is less obvious, but you sense somehow that your child grows a bit—they gain understanding or confidence; their eyes open to something new; their worlds expand. And sometimes you know you've done well if they've simply spent pent up energy in a constructive way. You can smile as they snooze in the backseat on the way home from a healthful activity.

A Parent's Guide to San Francisco

Introduction

While there are no guarantees when taking young ones out into the world, kids are pretty predictable—you know yours well enough to embarrass them for the rest of their lives. Trust your instincts, use common sense, and consider the following tried-and-true guidelines for activity planning. Some may seem to be mutually contradictory, but that's because matching kids and activities is not a hard science. Besides, most of the time you'll just throw them in the car and go, and all this guideline business will be forgotten:

Prepare them: Do siblings need to have safety rules reviewed before a trip to the amusement park? Will a discussion of dinosaurs put junior into museum mode? If your daughter researches driving directions on the web, will she be better able to weather the long car trip? Preparation pays. In general, if kids feel involved in an excursion, it will go a lot better.

Surprise them: This one can be tricky. I find that it's best to be very casual and low key about whatever surprise I have in mind. It's a bad idea to over-inflate expectations, and you should nip any false hopes they express in the bud. On longer trips, it may help to have a few hints or clues that you can dole out periodically, keeping their anticipation on track. Even jaded teens like to be surprised, though they would rather die than appear impressed.

Dim the context to brighten the content: If you want the experience you plan for your child to stand out in mind and memory, try to frame it with calm. When my son is wired and over-excited, it's hard for him to focus or assimilate new information. On your drive to the exhibit, class, event, park, farm, etc. consider relaxing your child with mundane conversation, mild music, a favorite story, or the like.

The younger the kids, the less ambitious the trip: If your children are in the toddler through pre-school set, plan on one fun destination that can be casually enjoyed and exited easily (like a zoo). Keep the car time short and build in a chance for rest and free play. Elementary age kids can last longer and make additional stops, especially if they are motivated by a carrot-on-a-stick promise of a treat when all is done.

When kids get older, friends, and siblings matter more: While adolescents can be impressed, entertained, and educated by the options listed ahead, they may offer a greater planning challenge to parents. The secret, I think, is to know who to bring along. Invite the wrong friend or sibling, and you may find your teen resistant, bored, disdainful, or just too cool to care. Make the correct match and your double-digit offspring will be energized and engaged. Make it a duo—just you and your teen—and you may rekindle a closeness that you thought was fading away.

So much more could be said, but talk is cheap. The key thing is that you head out and do something together. When they're thirty-something, they'll thank you.

San Francisco:
Young at Heart

San Francisco—what a city! Pause to watch the fog caressing the Golden Gate Bridge, and you'll quickly forget the minor hells of traffic, parking, and cost-of-living. Those who live here can barely contemplate living elsewhere. Those who don't wish they did.

For starters, the San Francisco Bay Area is visually stunning. Its beauty centers around the Golden Gate—not the bridge, but the gap in the Coast Range through which fierce tides ebb and flow, and the waters from half of California drain to the sea. West of the mile-wide gate are the cold, endless miles of the Pacific. East is placid San Francisco Bay, surrounded by the homes of millions. North are the wild headlands of the Marin Coast. South is the bold city of San Francisco. Bridging the gate itself is the west's equivalent of the Statue of Liberty: the incomparable Golden Gate Bridge.

As if all that wasn't enough, the region is a hotbed of arts, ingenuity, and culture. Young rising stars flock here from lesser places around the globe to add their talents to the mix. Natives and long-timers know that they're a part of an elite assemblage of humanity, and it shows. Yet potential arrogance is tempered by the general niceness of a place where tolerance rules and the political sentiment is left of center.

"So what?" spouts your middle child after you've told him how lucky he is to live in this wondrous area. "I'm bored!"

A Parent's Guide to San Francisco

Chapter One
San Francisco: Young at Heart

Whether you're a resident or visitor, kids change everything. Suddenly, "visually stunning" and "hotbed of arts, ingenuity, and culture" are meaningless expressions. For junior, the attractions you explore together need to be "fun," "cool," or... (plug in the latest popular adjective). You, on the other hand, must pay attention to education value and the will-they-like-it factor.

Fear not. The Bay Area is rich in options for kids of all ages that are fun, cool, *and* educational (as well as a few that are just fun and cool). Like most large metro areas, there are plenty of hands-on museums, libraries, historic sites, zoos, amusement attractions, etc. Unlike others, the bay is blessed with huge park and wild lands that provide numerous options for outdoor recreation and education.

The hills that host most of the parklands ring the Bay Area and channel its growth. While suburbs and ex-urbs sprawl beyond the hills for dozens of miles, the heart of the region is compressed in a belt around the bay shores. Because of this layout, many people find it easier to navigate around the region than elsewhere. There are only a few freeways and other major arteries to learn, and many destinations are located along logical transit corridors.

The weather is also amazingly kid-friendly. Cool and sunny are the common conditions around the Golden Gate; warm and sunny dominate the surrounding region. You can target your efforts throughout the year so your young ones don't get too cold on the one hand, or sweaty and cranky on the other. While you'll need to watch for the two scourges of the hills—poison oak and ticks—there are few mosquitoes or biting flies to bother your gang.

The one weather phenomenon that can ruin the best laid plans is *fog*. Throughout the summer and less often during other times of year, fog banks will jam up against the Pacific coast, shrouding the valleys that drain to the sea in a chill, dank grayness. You may drive through bright sunshine on your way to Ocean Beach, Anō Nuevo, the Marin Headlands, or Point Reyes, only to find your destination socked in. Sure, there's a mysterious beauty to the fog, but try selling that to an under-dressed kid with a bucket and shovel who wants to play in the sand. You can check ahead, take your chances, or save the outer coast activities for the fall.

A Parent's Guide to San Francisco

Chapter One
San Francisco: Young at Heart

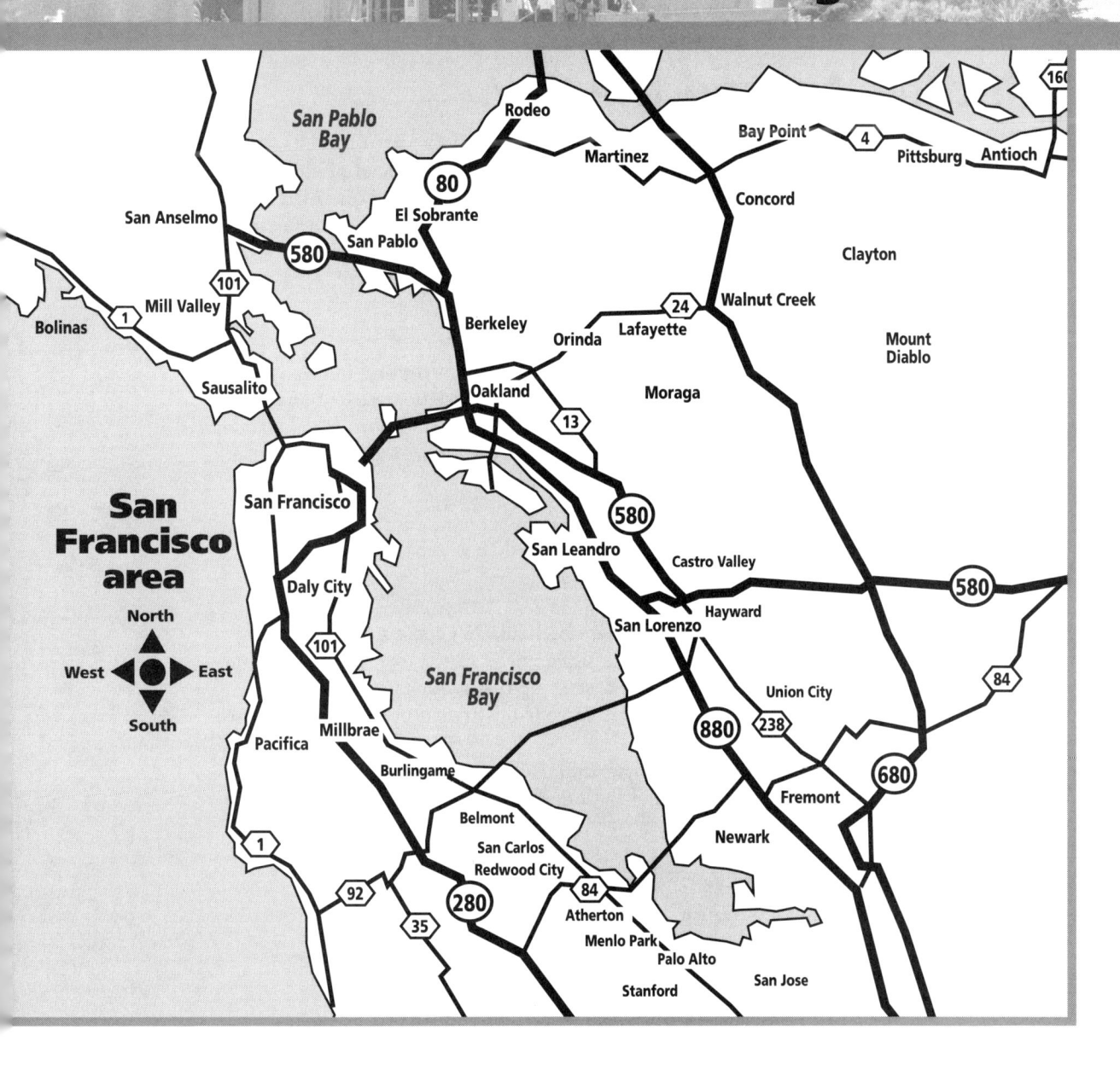

A Parent's Guide to San Francisco

Chapter One
San Francisco: Young at Heart

Getting Around the Bay

Crowded, bustling, megalopolis that it is, the San Francisco Bay Area can challenge the sanity of anyone trying to get from Point A to Point B with a carload of children. A twenty minute connection on the map might be an hour-long ordeal on the road. Freeways slow to a crawl at all the predictable rush hours, but they also seem to jam up at odd times for no apparent reasons. And parking? Don't get me started. The secret, of course, is not to drive.

Rail

BART (Bay Area Rapid Transit) and CalTrain offer convenient routing for many excursions, especially those involving downtown San Francisco, the East Bay, and the Peninsula town centers between San Francisco and San Jose. If some sort of rail station is convenient to a site listed in the book, I note it in the directions. Routing and schedule information is available here:

BART 650/992-2278, www.bart.gov
CalTrain 800/660-4287, www.caltrain.com

Bus

Bus systems link up with all rail stations, with particularly good connections at major centers and endpoints. Almost every site listed ahead can be reached by bus, but the routings and schedules are so varied that describing the options is beyond the scope of this book. For quick accurate answers to your bus transit questions, use these resources:

San Francisco: MUNI, 415/673-6864, www.sfmuni.com (Consider buying a MUNI "Passport" for $6, allowing unlimited riding for a day on San Francisco's buses, light rail trains, street cars, and cable cars).
East Bay: AC Transit, 415/817-1717, www.actransit.dst.ca.us
Peninsula: SamTrans, 800/660-4287, www.samtrans.com/samtrans
Marin County: Golden Gate Transit, 415/455-2000, www.goldengate.org
Contra Costa County (East Bay), 925/676-7500, www.cccta.org
Santa Clara County (South Bay), 408/321-2300, www.vta.org

A Parent's Guide to San Francisco

Chapter One
San Francisco: Young at Heart

Ferry

Ferry services offer another great way to cross the bay. All of them connect with bus, rail, or street car lines where they dock:

Alameda/Oakland Ferry (service linking Oakland's Jack London Square, Alameda Main Street, San Francisco Ferry Building, and Pier 41, plus seasonal Angel Island service): 510/522-3300, www.eastbayferry.com

Angel Island—Tiburon Ferry: 415/435-2131, www.angelislandferry.com

Blue & Gold Fleet (service between Fisherman's Wharf and Tiburon, Angel Island, or Sausalito, and between the S.F. Ferry Building and Tiburon): 415/773-1188, www.blueand-goldfleet.com

Golden Gate Ferry (service between S.F. Ferry Building and Larkspur or Sausalito), 415/455-2000, www.goldengate.org

Harbor Bay Ferry (service between Alameda and S.F. Ferry Building): 510/769-5500, www.harborbay.com/hbm/pages

Red & White Fleet (service between Fisherman's Wharf and U.S.S. Hornet in Alameda): 415/447-0597, www.redandwhite.com

Vallejo Baylink Ferry (service between Vallejo and S.F. Ferry Building with runs to Fisherman's Wharf and Angel Island): 707/64-FERRY, www.baylinkferry.com

For More Information

The best resource of all is **TravInfo**. They can give you the optimal connections for just about any trip in the Bay Area. Dial **817-1717** from any local area code (415, 650, 408, 510, 925, and 707). The top total transit web source is the similarly excellent San Francisco Bay Area Transit Information site: **www.transitinfo.org**

To build some 'transit consciousness' in your offspring, let them help you research the most efficient routes. If they can handle it, put them in charge of navigating your journey. When they're busy guiding you onto and off of the proper trains and buses at the correct stops, your time-in-transit will be easy. Riding bus, train, or trolley, you might even catch up on some light reading as they pore over notes, schedules, and maps.

By Car

Unfortunately, many destinations cannot be reached easily, cheaply, or quickly via public transit. What if you do have to drive? Well, you're a parent already and you know what's involved. Some kids take to car rides easily, chatting happily for minutes on end, or losing themselves in a book or electronic game. For others, strapping them in a car is like parking them on an ant hill.

I have certain rules of thumb about driving in and around the Bay Area. The rules would work for everyone if kids were robots, traffic was logical, and your routes and schedules were simple. As it is, you'll need to adapt them to suit your situation.

A Parent's Guide to San Francisco

Chapter One
San Francisco: Young at Heart

Out at 10, Home by 3 – On weekdays, traffic is tolerable between the rush hours. This period also offers warmth for outdoor activities and the right timeframe for a picnic. Note that Saturday also has some rush hour traffic, and that people flood *into* San Francisco on Friday and Sunday afternoons and evenings.

Don't Join the Herd – If you need to drive during rush hours, plan it so you can watch the traffic jam in one lane as you cruise along in the opposite direction. While the patterns are complex, you'll generally do best if you head away from San Francisco or the San Jose/Silicon Valley area in the morning, toward them in the afternoon.

Read the Events Calendar – Bay Area cities are frequently the scene of big parades, celebrations, sporting events, and other crowded gatherings. During the events, significant areas of town may be nearly impossible to get around. Before and after, freeways and other major arteries may be plugged for a time. Of course, you might be taking your offspring to these very events! When doing so, my general policy is to arrive early and leave early.

Have an Odd Weekend – Every Friday afternoon, thousands of weekenders squeeze along the Bay Area's exit roads on their way to ski slopes, vacation cabins, campgrounds, B&Bs, and grandma's house. Every Sunday evening, they squeeze back in to bring the regional population back up over the six million mark. If you can frame your weekend differently, you'll miss the squeeze.

Park and Walk – Why spoil a smartly planned drive with a frustrating search for a good parking spot when you arrive? Instead, lower your standards and take a "bad" spot. The kids will get to stretch their legs after being cooped up in the car. When the activity is done, the walk to the car will drain the last of their energy, preparing them for a quiet homebound trip.

Getting into and out of San Francisco

San Francisco isn't the most populous city in the Bay Area—that honor belongs to San Jose. It is, however, one of the most challenging cities in the nation to get into, out of, and through. If you aren't familiar with the city, make sure you have a detailed map or *very* good directions before hitting the city streets. Most of the driving directions included with the San Francisco listings refer back to the following instructions on how to reach key areas of the city (key words in *italics*).

A Parent's Guide to San Francisco

Chapter One
San Francisco: Young at Heart

From Marin County

All drivers will enter the city via US-101 by crossing the Golden Gate Bridge. To reach the *Golden Gate Bridge*, *Presidio*, and surrounding area, take the first right-hand exit immediately after the toll booths, then turn right and right again to pass back under the bridge to the bridge visitor parking area. One more right puts you on Lincoln Boulevard, the Presidio's main drag.

For most destinations, stay to the left as you come off the bridge, continuing on US-101. Choose the left-hand Marina Boulevard fork to hug the waterfront for the *Marina* and *Fort Mason*. The right-hand, Lombard Street fork will keep you on US-101 for a more direct route to *Fisherman's Wharf*, *Chinatown*, the *Financial District*, *Tourist Zone* attractions, the *Mission District*, *South of Market*, and points east and south.

For *Golden Gate Park, Ocean Beach*, all of *Western San Francisco*, and destinations on the Peninsula, stay to the right and be ready for the quick, easy-to-miss right-hand exit after the toll booths for CA-1 / 19th Avenue.

From Oakland, Berkeley, and the East Bay

Your point of entry will be the Bay Bridge via Interstate 80. For the *Financial District, Chinatown, Fisherman's Wharf, North Beach*, and the basic *Tourist Zone*, take the first right-hand exit (Howard Street) at the west end of the bridge.

For *Fort Mason*, the *Presidio*, the *Golden Gate Bridge*, and other northern city attractions, take the US-101 North exit from I-80. Follow US-101 North which becomes Van Ness Avenue.

For *Golden Gate Park, Ocean Beach*, and *Northwestern San Francisco*, take the US-101 North exit from I-80, but then stay to the left until you are dropped onto Fell Street. Fell shoots you west on a timed-light one-way. (NOTE: The Fell Street exit is expected to close at some point. The city has promised to make access to Fell easy and clear with new signage. Carry a map!)

For the zoo, *Fort Funston*, and *Western San Francisco* attractions, stay left on I-80 as it becomes US-101 south, bear right onto I-280.

For the *South of Market* and *Mission District* area, stay to the left coming off the Bay Bridge and take the left-hand, 5th Street exit, unless otherwise specified in the listings.

A Parent's Guide to San Francisco

Chapter One
San Francisco: Young at Heart

From the Peninsula and Points South

Two major freeways access the city from the south—US-101 on the east or bay side, I-280 through the hills to the west. The two meet in case you're on one and want the other. They are also linked by I-380 near the airport, south of the city.

For most city destinations, US-101 is the route you'll want. For *Mission District*, *South of Market*, and *Financial District* destinations, you'll take the Cesar Chavez, Vermont Street, 7th Street, or 4th Street exit (I specify which in the listings). Miss the 4th Street exit (the last before the Bay Bridge) and you'll have to reverse course on Yerba Buena Island.

For the *Tourist Zone*, *Fisherman's Wharf*, *Chinatown*, *Fort Mason*, the *Presidio*, *the Golden Gate Bridge*, and other northern attractions, stay to the left as US-101 forks with I-80, following US-101 North as it turns from freeway to Van Ness Avenue.

For the *Pacific Ocean shoreline*, *San Francisco Zoo*, *Ocean Beach*, *Golden Gate Park*, *Golden Gate Bridge*, and all of *Western San Francisco*, approach the city on I-280 or take I-280 South from US-101. Follow the signs for CA-1 North/19th Avenue.

Driving and Parking in Downtown San Francisco

If "Don't do it!" doesn't scare you off, be prepared. Here's some advice for the novice:

Use a City Map – They're for sale at bookstores, convenience stores, supermarkets, and elsewhere. Get one that shows *all* of the city streets. I can't emphasize this one enough. With the ability to read street signs at an intersection, and the patience to read your map, you can find any San Francisco destination and escape its traffic traps (there are many of both).

Keep it Simple – From long experience, San Franciscans know all sorts of time-saving ways to zip through the city. Visitors, however, should stick to main drags like Van Ness, Mission, the Embarcadero, Lombard, and others. Be the turtle: slow and steady.

Avoid Left Turns – There are many places where they are hard to make, legal only at certain times, or always illegal. If you need to turn left and see a lot of no-left-turn signs ahead, take three rights instead.

Stay off Market Street – Market traps the unwary. It's slow, confusing, and darn near impossible to get off of if you need to turn left. You can only cross Market on certain streets: from south to north, use 3rd, 5th, 7th, 9th, Van Ness, or Valencia Streets. From north to south, use Bush, Battery, Hyde, Van Ness, or Gough. If you try to cross using many other streets, you'll be forced to turn right onto Market and will find yourself unable to exit the trap with a left turn for many blocks.

A Parent's Guide to San Francisco

Chapter One
San Francisco: Young at Heart

Expect to Walk – Sharp-eyed drivers willing to circle the block for a bit may find what is often called, "rock star parking." The rest of us should just take the first available spot within a few blocks of our goal.

Pay to Park – Yeah, it's stunningly expensive to park in a pay lot or structure, but who wants to interrupt a family walkabout to feed a meter? It's even worse to find a ticket on your windshield, or to find that windshield and the rest of the vehicle at an impound lot.

Don't Do It – I'll say it one more time: take BART, then continue on a bus, trolley, cable car, taxi, or your feet.

If you carry a map, read street signs, and are able to recover after getting trapped by one-way streets and no-left-turn intersections, you'll be fine. Be brave and go forth!

What Should We See?

When our son was ready to start eating solid food, one book advised us to begin with bland cereals, move next to bland vegetables, and later introduce not-so-bland bananas. The theory, of course, is that once babies experience the sweet wonder of a banana, they won't be interested in trying less inspiring foods. We started with bananas anyway, and the boy ate everything we sent his way.

What's the lesson here? Is it that kids are all different and that few theories work for all of them? Or that parental mistakes need not prove disastrous? Or perhaps that kids can sometimes be trusted to know what's good for them? Yes to all, but I think the bigger lesson is that all kids like bananas.

Every listing in this book was chosen for its banana-like quality. Your child may love to walk in the park, but I've only chosen parks where you'll find hang gliders soaring, lakes to swim in, canoes to paddle, or giant trees to hide behind. There are dozens of museums in and around the Bay Area, but dusty artifacts and historic photos aren't enough to make the cut here. Instead, I looked for hands-on science, live animals, bright colors, and cartoons.

As you explore the options on the pages ahead, ask yourself how each would rate on your child's "banana meter." Your mature, quiet 10 year-old may be content on a two-hour drive to a half-banana attraction, but your fidgety five year-old or jaded teen may need five-banana excitement for the excursion to be a success. Only you know what will work for your family. When in doubt, think color, motion, speed, volume, and thrills.

A Parent's Guide to San Francisco

Chapter One
San Francisco: Young at Heart

"But what about the education value?" you may wonder. Don't worry—except for a handful dedicated to pure fun, all the selections offer educational value in the areas of science, nature, history, culture, art, etc. Remember, however, that the deepest lessons kids will learn with any choice you make are those of family and values. By doing something with your kids instead of putting them in the care of toys or television, they come to see you as a top source of fun and wonder—as, in other words, their best guide to the world.

Remember that it's *always* a good idea to contact your chosen attraction before setting out. Offerings vary, prices go up, and hours change. Road construction may temporarily alter the ideal driving directions. Attractions may be closed for special holidays, the off-season, renovations, changing exhibits, family emergency, fumigation, bad hair days, whatever. Indeed, an attraction may be gone altogether! It's the guidebook writer's curse.

Remember, too, that there is no perfect choice. Sometimes, your hopes for an amazing day will be dashed by a sudden rain, an earache, or a kid who just doesn't see it your way. Other times, you'll be stunned when your wee ones are thrilled by an excursion you thought would fall flat. Regardless of the uncertainties, go—shelve your doubts, your fatigue, and their resistance, and take them out to meet their planet.

San Francisco

Even though I'm an urban guy, veteran traveler, and full-fledged adult, I'm sometimes reluctant to venture into the crowded heart of San Francisco. It's a busy, sometimes frenzied place with a somewhat confusing maze of streets and tough, expensive parking. The public transit system is darn good, but not always fast or convenient. I can walk many places from my home in the Mission District, but most walks are long enough to be called hikes. That's just me—put my son into the plan and I'm tempted to just stay home and play in the yard. You might feel a similar temptation.

Well, fight it! My son isn't the least bit intimidated by urban adventures, which is just what my wife and I want for him. We work to see that he feels at home on the planet—willing to go just about anywhere, unafraid of skyscrapers or wilderness. When children spend time in the city, their minds are opened and stretched, and they grow comfortable with human activity at its most intense.

A Parent's Guide to San Francisco

Chapter Two
San Francisco

While fewer than 15% of Bay Area residents actually live in San Francisco, nearly a third of the listings in this book are located within the city limits—more than a third if you ignore the listings for destinations beyond the accepted limits of the Bay Area. Why so many? Part of the reason is that San Francisco is the area's centerpiece, and the namesake of both the region and this guide. Mainly, though, it's that San Francisco truly does concentrate an astonishing array of excellent options for families.

In several areas of the city, the concentrated nature of the sights allows you to park once and visit several places. The best are Fisherman's Wharf, Golden Gate Park, Yerba Buena Gardens, and Ocean Beach. If your kids are good walkers, the general downtown area is walkable, including the Yerba Buena area, Civic Center, Financial District, and Chinatown/North Beach. BART-based trips have similar advantages, especially if you extend your range via streetcar, cable car, or bus lines.

Please note that most of the driving directions get you to the site involved, but not necessarily to a place you can park. If you use directions alone, you may find yourself driving right by the destination in a search for parking. Use the directions in conjunction with a good city map to plan your approaches with care.

A Parent's Guide to San Francisco

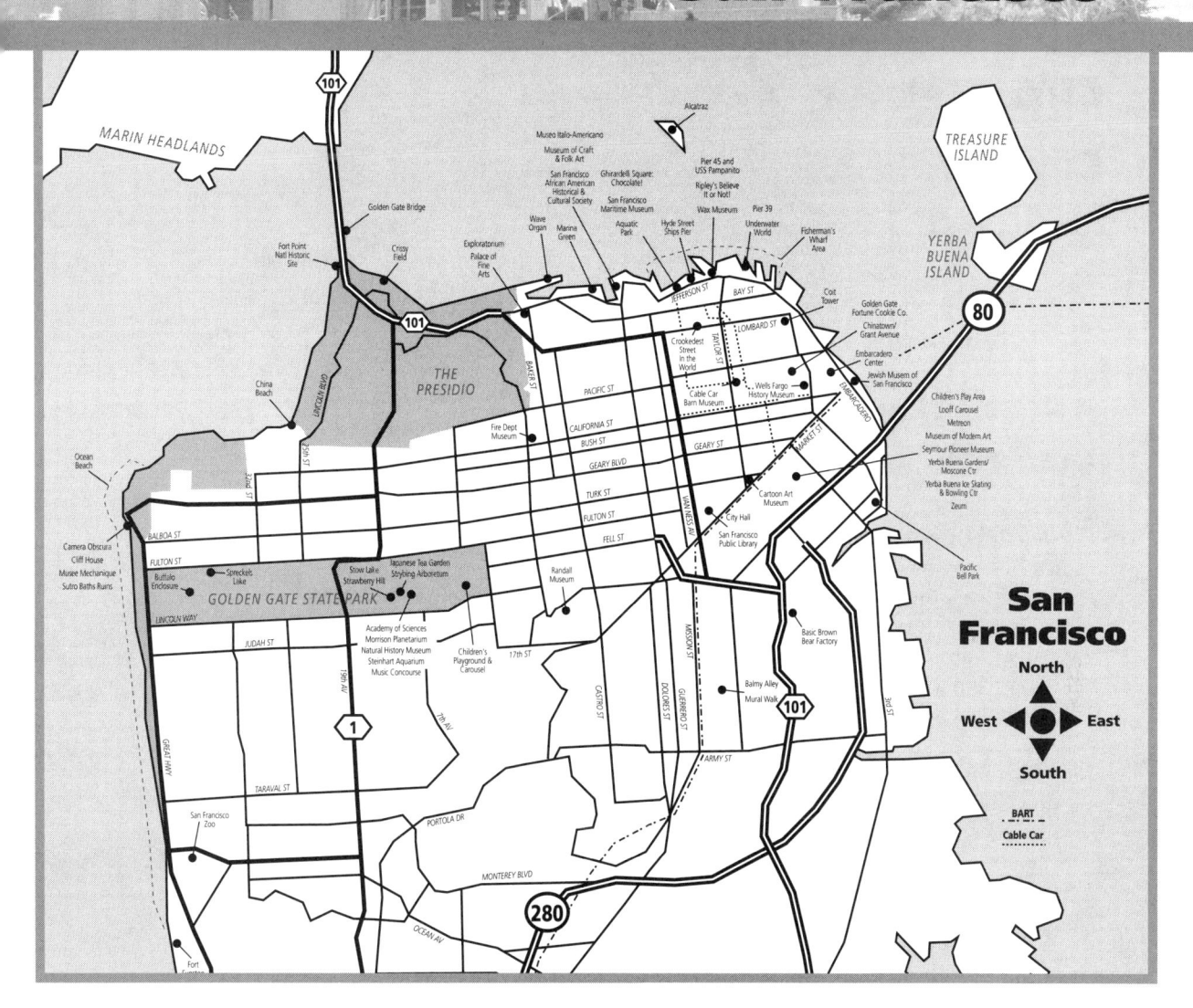

Chapter Two: San Francisco

A Parent's Guide to San Francisco

Chapter Two
San Francisco

Civic Center

City Hall

Van Ness between Grove and MacAllister, San Francisco
415/554-5780 • www.ci.sf.ca.us/cityhall

Hours: Open Monday – Friday, 8:00 a.m. to 8:00 p.m., and weekends from noon to 4:00 p.m. Tours are offered Tuesday – Friday at 10:00 a.m., noon, and 2:00 p.m., and on weekends at 12:30 p.m. A combined art and public tour is offered Mondays at noon and 2:00 p.m. Evening tours are offered the 2nd and 4th Wednesday of every month at 6:30 p.m.

Admission: Free.

Directions: If at all possible, take BART to the Civic Center station and walk. Drivers find and follow US-101 onto Van Ness to the block between Grove and MacAllister, just north of Market.

While hardly oriented towards young visitors, City Hall is still a pretty cool place. Known by many as the "crown jewel" of classical architecture in America, the huge structure covers the better part of two city blocks. City Hall's dome is one of the world's largest, lofting more than 300' above Civic Center Plaza, which sprawls across Polk Street from the main entrance. Other impressive edifices surround hall and plaza, including the public library, state and federal buildings, the Opera House, Symphony Hall, War Memorial building, and others.

If the architecture doesn't impress the young ones, they may be wowed by the limos along Polk Street, or by sight of very well-dressed, intense people coming and going up and down the entrance steps. Inside the door, stern guards keep an eye on things, and everyone passes through metal detectors. Walk on past cool stone columns and staircases into the vast rotunda…

Then let them shout to see if there's an echo! Sometimes, City Hall needs a little lightening up. Besides, if you're a resident, you own the place. "Junior," you'll say, "all these people work for us."

If yours are particularly studious or enjoy gallery browsing, head downstairs to see what's currently hanging on the wall. You can also sign up for a tour—just stop in at the Docent Tour Kiosk by the Van Ness entrance.

A Parent's Guide to San Francisco

Chapter Two
San Francisco

San Francisco Public Library

100 Larkin Street, San Francisco
415/557-4400 • sfpl.lib.ca.us

Hours: Open 10:00 a.m. to 6:00 p.m. Monday and Saturday; 9:00 a.m. to 8:00 p.m. Tuesday – Thursday; noon to 6:00 p.m. Friday; noon to 5:00 p.m. Sunday. Tours are offered at 2:30 p.m., Wednesday, Friday, and Saturday.

Admission: Free.

Directions: Take BART to the Civic Center station – the library entrance is just north of Market on Grove Street. Drivers stay with US-101 onto Van Ness and turn east on Grove.

San Francisco's new library is a beauty; it's fun just to explore with no thought of reading in mind. As you would expect, all typical library services are available, but the main library also offers special resources for young people, including an "Electronic Discovery Center" that features a dozen computers with special software for kids. Regular activities and special events for children include preschool storytimes, family craft sessions, infant/toddler "lap sits" with music and stories, puppet shows, performers, Spanish language storytimes, and more. Branch libraries duplicate and extend the offerings to suit neighborhood interest. The Summer Reading Club includes guests like "The Lizard Lady," "The Bubble Lady," folk singers, clowns, and scientists. Check the library web site or call for the current schedule.

Financial District

Embarcadero Center

Along Sacramento between Clay and Drum Streets, San Francisco
415/772-0700 • www.embarcaderocenter.com

Hours: Hours vary. Many shops are open only during the business day while the theaters and restaurants go late.

Admission: Free to enter, but plenty of places to spend money. Basic parking in the underground garages is about $9/hour on weekdays, $3/hour evenings and weekends.

Directions: Take BART to the Embarcadero Station and walk north on Drum, Davis, or Front. Drivers use Chapter 1 Financial District directions. From Marin, turn left on Clay from Van Ness. From the East Bay, turn left on Fremont from the I-80 Howard exit, cross Market, continue straight on Front. From the Peninsula, bear left on Bryant from the I-80 4th Street exit, left on 3rd, right on Mission, left on Fremont, cross Market, continue straight on Front.

Have a shopper in your brood? If you'd like to dazzle them with upscale retailers and splendid architecture, head to downtown San Francisco. At the base of the four, famous Embarcadero Center buildings are 125 shops and restaurants. The complex is a wondrous maze of wide passages, spacious plazas, and changing levels. A 5-screen theater offers the chance to trade retail for entertainment.

Access is helped by the presence of underground parking garages beneath the center with 4 hours worth of ticket validation offered on weekends by several stores, eateries, and the theater. Best of all, it's all a short walk from the Embarcadero BART station.

A Parent's Guide to San Francisco

Chapter Two: San Francisco

Wells Fargo History Museum

420 Montgomery Street, San Francisco
415/396-2619 • www.wellsfargohistory.com

Hours: Open Monday – Friday, 9:00 a.m. to 5:00 p.m., every day that the bank is open.

Admission: No charge.

Directions: Go north on Montgomery from the Montgomery Street BART station. Drivers use Chapter 1 Financial District directions. From Marin, turn left from Van Ness onto Clay, right on Montgomery. From the East Bay, left on Fremont from the I-80 Howard Street exit, cross Market, straight on Front, left on Sacramento, left on Montgomery. From the Peninsula, bear left on Bryant from the I-80 4th Street exit, left on 3rd, cross Market, straight on Kearny, right on Clay, right on Montgomery.

While it may not be worth a trip by itself, stop in at the Wells Fargo Museum if you're exploring the area—especially since it's free! As a knowledgeable area resident might expect, the museum is located in the San Francisco's main Wells Fargo Bank building in the Financial District. Exhibits include gold rush artifacts and a vintage stagecoach, clearly visible from the street through the big plate glass windows (thus making it worth a walk-by even when the museum is closed).

Chinatown/North Beach

Cable Car Ride

San Francisco
415/474-1887 • www.sfcablecar.com

Hours: Cable cars run daily from 5:45 a.m. to 1:00 a.m.

Admission: No matter how far you ride, tickets are $2. Buy tickets from the vending machines at the turnarounds (endpoints), or onboard from the conductor.

Directions: Cable car turnarounds are: 1) on Powell at Market – by the Powell BART station, 2) on California at Market – by the Embarcadero BART station, 3) on California at Van Ness, 4) on Taylor at Bay above Fisherman's Wharf, and, 5) in Aquatic park at Hyde and Beach. Use Financial District (1,2,3) or Fisherman's Wharf (4,5) directions in Chapter 1.

From Marin, follow CA-101 to Van Ness. Turn left on Van Ness, right on Bay, then straight to Taylor for 4 or left on Hyde for 5. Or turn right on Van Ness, then straight to California for 3 or left on Clay; from Clay turn right on Powell for 1 or right at the end on Drum for 2.

From the East Bay, turn left on Fremont from the I-80 Howard exit. Cross Market, right on California for 2 or left for 3. Or turn left on Howard, right on 5th, cross Market, right on Eddy for 1. Or turn right on Folsom, left on The Embarcadero, left on Bay to Taylor for 4, continue and right on Hyde for 5.

From the Peninsula, take US-101. Continue on US-101 onto Van Ness, to California for 3 or turn right on Bay, straight to Taylor for 4 or left on Hyde for 5. Or bear right on to I-80, take 4th Street exit, bear left on Bryant, left on 3rd, cross Market; immediate left on Geary and left on Powell for 1, or straight on Kearney and right on California for 2.

Cable cars operate by a simple, elegant system. To travel ahead, the car operator engages a clutch, which grabs a steel cable that is in constant motion under the street. To stop, the clutch is released and the brakes applied. Before the 1906 earthquake, dozens of cable car lines crisscrossed the city. The system was devastated in the quake, never recovering its past glory. Only three routes ultimately survived and were restored—two running from Powell Street and Union Square to the Fisherman's Wharf area via Hyde and Mason, the third stretching up and down California Street from Market Street to the top of Nob Hill.

A Parent's Guide to San Francisco

Chapter Two
San Francisco

Today, cars are spaced about 5 minutes apart on each of the routes. While you can wait in line for as much as an hour to ride on cars that serve Union Square and Fisherman's Wharf, you may be able to board the first car you see on the California Street line. If a car isn't packed full—and the Union Square based lines often are packed—you can board a car mid-route and pay the conductor.

Be a bit cautious when boarding at points other than the turnarounds. The steps onto the cable cars can be awkwardly spaced in relation to the street, making stumbles common. Vehicles may pass close to the cars in certain areas, so remind junior to "look both ways." Once you're safely onboard, the kids will love the steep hills, clanging bell, and rickety ride.

Consider a BART trip to the Embarcadero Station, a cable car ride up California Street, and a mostly downhill walkabout that takes in the Cable Car Museum and Chinatown. You'll be back at the Embarcadero BART station in 2 to 3 hours.

Cable Car Barn Museum

1201 Mason Street, San Francisco
415/474-1887 • www.cablecarmuseum.com

Hours: Open daily, 10:00 a.m. to 6:00 p.m. from April through October, 10:00 a.m. to 5:00 p.m. November through March.

Admission: Donations are accepted.

Directions: Follow the Chapter 1 Tourist Zone directions onto Van Ness. Turn east on Washington from Van Ness, left on Mason.

At pretty much the midpoint of all three cable car lines, you'll find the Cable Car Barn. The museum features exhibits on the history of the cable car system while the cars themselves are garaged here at night and for repairs. Three 500 horsepower engines are also housed here, one for each of the cables needed for the three operating routes. The engines keep the cables moving at 9 miles per hour; that, obviously, is the maximum speed of the cars. You and the kids can watch them operate, envisioning the stresses on the blocks-long cables as they haul the cars up some of the steepest hills in the city. Related displays round out the museum's offerings.

A Parent's Guide to San Francisco

Chapter Two

San Francisco

Coit Tower

East end of Lombard Street, San Francisco
415/362-0808

Hours: Tower open daily, 10:00 a.m. to 8:00 p.m., 10:00 a.m. to 6:00 p.m. in the winter. Park accessible at all times.

Admission: The ride to the top is $3.75. Viewing the murals in the tower base is free.

Directions: Use Tourist Zone directions in Chapter 1. From the East Bay, turn left on Fremont from the I-80 Howard Street exit, right on Mission, left on Embarcadero, left on Broadway, right on Columbus, an immediate right onto Grant, then right on Lombard. From Marin, stay on Lombard all the way. From the south, take Van Ness to Lombard and turn right.

Most children love getting to the tops of things, perhaps for the vertigo as much as the view. They can't help but enjoy a visit to Coit Tower, built in 1934 and rising 210 feet above the summit of Telegraph Hill. Lillie Coit commissioned the structure to honor San Francisco's fire fighters. Inside the base are some wonderfully leftist murals by local artists, depicting work and life in the early part of the century. An elevator takes you to the top for a 360° view of the historic heart of the city. A persistent rumor states that the tower resembles the nozzle of a fire hose. Some authorities dismiss the idea, but ask the kids what they think.

Outside the tower is small Pioneer Park, crowning the summit of Telegraph Hill. Your daring offspring will enjoy walking atop the wall that circles the tower parking area while you enjoy views out over North Beach and Fisherman's Wharf. If you've walked up via the steps of Filbert Street (see Hidden Stairways below), you'll be glad it's all downhill from here.

Coit Tower is easily visible atop Telegraph Hill at the west end of Lombard Street, near its intersection with Grant. Avoid driving to the tower, especially on weekends. Unknowing tourists often find themselves waiting in line on Lombard Street (the only access road) for a spot in the small parking lot, often for many minutes. Expect an uphill walk if you use public transit or choose not to drive to the summit.

A Parent's Guide to San Francisco

Chapter Two

San Francisco

Crookedest Street in the World
West end of Lombard Street, San Francisco

Hours: Always open when not under repair.

Admission: Free.

Directions: Use Tourist Zone directions in Chapter 1. From Marin, follow US-101 onto Lombard and continue straight ahead. From the East Bay or Peninsula, get on or stay with US-101 north onto Van Ness, right on Lombard.

The name says it all. Lombard Street drops from Hyde Street down to Leavenworth Street in a narrow, zig-zagging line of brick. As one of San Francisco's signature attractions, the route is sometimes subject to a continuous parade of cars driving from top to bottom, as well as to a fair number of heartier tourists walking the same stretch. It's a cheap thrill, but the kids should like it.

This stretch of Lombard is one-way (downhill, eastbound only). You can't turn onto it from Hyde, so you must approach Lombard from a block or two west.

Hidden Stairways
Filbert Street and other locations, San Francisco

Hours: Public access to the stairways at all times.

Admission: Free.

Directions: For Filbert Street, use Tourist Zone directions in Chapter 1. For the western approach, use Coit Tower directions above, taking Grant south from Lombard or north from Broadway, and turning east on Filbert.

For the eastern Filbert steps: From Marin, follow Lombard, left on Van Ness, right on Bay, right on Embarcadero, right on Battery, walk up Filbert. From the East Bay, left on Fremont from the I-80 Howard exit, right on Mission, left on Embarcadero, left on Broadway, right on Sansome to Filbert. From the Peninsula, turn right on Clay from Van Ness, left on Sansome to Filbert.

If your kids would take pride in earning a summit with a little exercise, you can avoid the Coit Tower parking hassle and walk up. Two notable stairways climb Telegraph Hill. The shorter set begins at the corner of Kearney and Filbert to the west. Another set ascends from Sansome at Filbert to the east. Both pass lovely gardens, interesting homes, and wonderful viewpoints.

Several other staircases pick up where the hills get too steep for streets. Pretend surprise when you come across them and let the kids feel like explorers. The Lyon Street steps link Green and Broadway, passing along the eastern boundary of the Presidio and among the mansions of Pacific Heights. The Macondray Lane steps connect Union and Green Streets, just off Leavenworth. Russian Hill features the Vallejo Street steps between Jones and Mason Streets, with access to little Coolbrith Park.

21

A Parent's Guide to
San Francisco

Chapter Two
San Francisco

Grant Street
Runs north from Market Street, San Francisco

Hours: Few area businesses are open late – when the tourists head to dinner, the shops close.

Admission: Grant is a public street.

Directions: Drivers follow the Financial District directions in Chapter 1. From Marin, follow US-101 onto Van Ness, turn left on Bush to Grant. From the East Bay, turn left on Fremont from the I-80 Howard exit, cross Market, left on California to Grant. From the Peninsula, follow US-101/Van Ness, right on Bush to Grant.

Once in awhile, people ask me what they should see in Chinatown. I don't really have an answer. There are a few special spots of interest to some, but the key thing is just to wander the lanes, soaking in the ambiance and responding to inspiration.

Grant Street between Bush and Broadway is the tourist heart of Chinatown. Genuine commerce is centered along Stockton Street, which parallels Grant a block to the west. To put your kids in the right frame of mind, enter the area through the elaborate gate at the intersection of Grant and California Street—perhaps after arriving via the California Street Cable Car from the turnarounds at Van Ness or Market Street—then walk north along Grant. Duck into intriguing shops for a look around. Head up side streets to discover narrow alleys to explore. Take in the song of the language and maybe grab lunch at a Dim Sum place. To squeeze an extra few minutes out of the experience, let the kids pick up a tacky souvenir at one of the many tourist shops.

Good walkers can start at the Powell Street BART stop and reach Chinatown via Union Square. You can also get off at the Embarcadero BART station and get to Grant via the California Street Cable Car.

Golden Gate Fortune Cookie Company
56 Ross Alley, San Francisco
415/781-3956

Hours: The shop is open 9:00 a.m. to midnight.

Admission: Customers are always welcome.

Directions: Tiny Ross Alley connects Jackson and Washington Streets, between Grant and Stockton. Follow Chinatown directions above.

"You will have success in a business venture." Ah, that it were true. Who can't crack a fortune cookie open without a spark of hope? Even the most jaded oldster harbors a secret wish that the cookie holds some magic. And kids? Well, they literally eat them up.

On your Chinatown walkabout, head up Jackson or Washington Street from Grant and duck into Ross Alley for a visit to see where dreams are made. There's not much to do at this little hole-in-the-wall but look and buy, which is enough.

A Parent's Guide to San Francisco

Chapter Two

San Francisco

Fisherman's Wharf

The Fisherman's Wharf Area and How to Get There

Jefferson and Beach Streets, from Embarcadero to Van Ness Avenue, San Francisco

Tourist central in San Francisco consists of a waterfront area stretching from Pier 39 along The Embarcadero, past Pier 45, and on west to Van Ness Avenue. Pier 45 is the actual Fisherman's Wharf, and is as close to the center of the area as you need. More city visitors come to Fisherman's Wharf than any other attraction—fully 83% of people who qualify as San Francisco tourists. Don't be surprised at the number of places to buy candy, t-shirts, and souvenirs.

There are pearls among the junk, though you may have to offer the young ones a little junk to get them interested in the pearls. The most educational offerings are collected in the San Francisco Maritime National Historic Park. Other touristy but good quality destinations include Underwater World, the new wax museum, the sea lions of Pier 39, the submarine *U.S.S. Pampanito*, and the Liberty Ship *U.S.S. Jeremiah O'Brien*. Best of all is a visit to Alcatraz Island.

Use the directions here to reach the Fisherman's Wharf area—those listed with the individual attractions ahead will complete the process. Drivers may find parking very difficult, though there are several expensive garages and lots near The Embarcadero between Pier 39 and 45, as well as elsewhere along the surrounding streets.

Here's how to get to the wharf area:

Via BART: Stop at the Embarcadero station, walk 3 blocks east down Market toward the waterfront Ferry Building. Head to the easy-to-spot trolley stop in the middle of The Embarcadero (the main waterfront boulevard), and take the first trolley heading left (northwest) along The Embarcadero. As you go, you'll pass all the odd numbered piers, including Pier 39. Get off at the end of the line.

By cable car: You have two choices from Powell at Market Street or nearby Union Square. The Hyde Street line drops you right in the heart of things a half block from the water at the base of Hyde Street. The Mason Street line leaves you with a 3 or 4 block walk at the intersection of Taylor and Bay (just follow Taylor straight down to Pier 45). Both are popular and crowded, though you'll probably wait longer to return via Hyde Street. The Powell Street Cable Car turnaround is just upstairs from the BART Powell Street station.

A Parent's Guide to San Francisco

Chapter Two
San Francisco

By Ferry: See Chapter 1 for ferry line options. Target Pier 41 or 43 1/2, or combine a ferry ride to the Ferry Building with a trolley ride up The Embarcadero.

Driving: Use the *Fisherman's Wharf* directions in Chapter 1. From Marin, follow Lombard to Franklin, left on Franklin, right on North Point, then left on Powell to reach parking (Pier 45 is to your left). From the East Bay, turn left on Fremont from the I-80 Howard Street exit, right on Mission, then left on The Embarcadero which ends at Pier 45. From the Peninsula, follow Van Ness more than two miles to the north end of the city (don't follow US-101 when it turns left onto Lombard). Turn right on North Point, then left on Powell to reach parking (Pier 45 is to your left).

Pier 39

Beach Street at The Embarcadero, San Francisco
415/705-5500 • www.pier39.com

Hours: Public access all day, shop hours vary.

Admission: You can walk the Pier for free, but everything along the way will cost you.

Directions: Use the Fisherman's Wharf area directions on page 23. As you face the water, the piers count down by odd numbers as you go right. Pier 39 is about 500 yards east of Pier 45 along The Embarcadero.

If your idea of happy children is best expressed by the saying, "like a kid in a candy store," Pier 39 is the place for you. Just get ready to empty your wallet to pay for the t-shirts, toys, and treats so readily available along this over-water tourist mall. Still, there's no doubt that young ones of all ages will be dazzled with the options for a time.

There are a few Pier 39 options that qualify as "activity" instead of plain "commerce." I take secret pleasure in the *Turbo Ride*—a simulation theater experience where specially animated films combine with shaking seats, blasts of air, and surround sound to take you on a short and wild journey through a fantasy world. The 10- to 15-minute features include "Secrets of the Lost Temple," "Smash Factory," "Dino Island," and "Aliens: Ride at the Speed of Fright." This one's for 6-and-overs (over 8 to be safe).

If any of your youngest tend to wander off, Pier 39 is a good place for hand-holding. Plan on finishing your visit with sugared up, over-stimulated kids on your hands.

A Parent's Guide to San Francisco

Chapter Two
San Francisco

UnderWater World

Pier 39, The Embarcadero, San Francisco
415/623-5300, 888/732-3483 • www.underwaterworldsf.com

Hours: Open 9:00 a.m. to 8:00 p.m. daily from Memorial Day through Labor Day, 10:00 a.m. to 6:00 p.m. the rest of the year. Closed only on Christmas Day.

Admission: Tickets are $13, $6.50 for ages 3 – 11 and those over 65, under 3 free. A family ticket (2 adults, 2 kids) is $30. Bring your trolley or bus coupon in for a $2 discount.

Directions: Use the Fisherman's Wharf area directions on page 23. Pier 39 is about 500 yards east of Pier 45 on the San Francisco waterfront.

While not cheap, this one's a sure hit with the young ones. Enter either of the two, 150' long acrylic tunnels that run beneath the water, and you'll find yourself surrounded by marine life of all kinds. There are also several marine life tanks and aquaria, including some where the kids can pet sharks, bat rays, and other harmless denizens of the deep. The facility hosts 11,000 animals representing 193 species.

While it strives to emphasize its educational offerings and scientific foundations, UnderWater World is primarily a tourist attraction—thanks mainly to its location. If you're looking for something more purely educational (and cheaper), opt for Steinhart Aquarium in Golden Gate Park.

Alcatraz

Tours from Pier 41, San Francisco
415/705-5444 (boat info), 415/705-5555 (reservations) • www.nps.gov/alca

Hours: Open every day but Christmas and New Year's Day. Blue & Gold Fleet boat departures vary, though the first usually leaves at 9:30 a.m. Many departures fill up well in advance, so reserve as far ahead of time as you can.

Admission: Boat fare is $9.25 per person, plus a $2.25 reservation fee for the group. The excellent tape-guided national park service tour is $3.25. Ride and tour are usually sold together, though may be purchased separately.

Directions: Use the Fisherman's Wharf area directions on page 23. Pier 41 is easy to find along the waterfront between Pier 39 and 45—just look for the Blue and Gold boats.

An excursion to Alcatraz Island is a San Francisco classic, and it's generally a good choice for kids. Short and exciting boat rides to and from the island nicely frame the slightly spooky mystery of the partially ruined prison. Children older than 7 or 8 should enjoy donning a walkman and headphones for the excellent tape-guided tour. Younger ones can race up and down the roads, balance on walls, and explore secret paths to hidden alcoves. Inside is all the chilling fascination of the lives of very bad men.

On the downside, there can be a good deal of waiting involved in an Alcatraz trip. If you haven't reserved your space on the boat in advance, you may find that your chosen departure time is filled with the next openings an hour or two (or more) away. In peak season, you should reserve days in advance. Arrive a half hour early to pick up tickets and join the line to board the boat. Another line awaits you on the island for the return trip.

25

A Parent's Guide to San Francisco

Chapter Two
San Francisco

When you board the first boat, there's a good chance a smiling photographer will try to pose your party and snap your picture in hopes that you'll buy the developed print on your return from the island. If you aren't in the market, feel free to refuse the initial shoot.

Tour boats operated by the Blue and Gold Fleet leave from Pier 41, which is positioned nicely between the various amusements of Pier 39 and Fisherman's Wharf. The piers count up by odd numbers as you proceed along The Embarcadero from the Bay Bridge, so Pier 41 is just northwest of Pier 39.

Bay Boat Tours and Ferries

Pier 43 1/2, Pier 41, or the Ferry Building, San Francisco
415/447-0597 (Red & White Fleet), www.redandwhite.com
415/705-5555 (Blue & Gold Fleet), www.blueandgoldfleet.com
707/643-3779 (BayLink Ferries), www.baylinkferry.com

Hours: Schedules vary widely—use the web or phone contacts to get current information.

Admission: Each company has a different fee structure. A 1-hour Bay tour should be about $14 for kids, $18 for adults, while a trans-bay ferry trip is in the $2 to $5 range.

Directions: Use the Fisherman's Wharf area directions on page 23. Pier 43 1/2, Pier 41, and Pier 39 line The Embarcadero a short walk east of Pier 45.

The waterfront Ferry Building is on The Embarcadero at the foot of Market Street, 3 blocks east of BART's Embarcadero station. Use *Financial District* directions in Chapter 1. From Marin, follow US-101, left on Van Ness, right on Bay, right on The Embarcadero. From the East Bay, turn left on Fremont from the I-80 Howard exit, right on Mission, and left on The Embarcadero. From the Peninsula, bear left on Bryant from the I-80 4th Street exit, turn left on 3rd, right on Mission, and left on The Embarcadero.

Several companies offer short cruises, water-based tour packages, and ferry trips on San Francisco Bay. Except for the commuter ferries that shuttle workers across the water, schedules tend to vary a fair amount throughout the year. It pays to call ahead or check current web information before heading down to the pier.

Blue & Gold Fleet boats depart from Pier 41, which is also in the Fisherman's Wharf zone. Besides being the only carrier to serve Alcatraz Island (see Alcatraz above), they offer 1-hour bay tours that go out as far as the Golden Gate Bridge. Additional land and water tour destinations include the Wine Country, Muir Woods, Monterey and Carmel, Yosemite, and more of San Francisco.

The Red & White Fleet is based close to the heart of the Fisherman's Wharf area at Pier 43 1/2. They also offer 1-hour boat tours along the waterfront, land/water tour packages to the Wine Country, and a trip to Yosemite.

A Parent's Guide to San Francisco

Chapter Two

San Francisco

BayLink offers a trip that connects the Ferry Building in downtown San Francisco with Six Flags Marine World in Vallejo. The Ferry Building is at the foot of Market Street, just a couple of blocks from The Embarcadero BART station. Can your offspring handle a long, adventurous day that includes BART, ferry and bus rides, as well as some hours at an amusement park? Go for it.

Pier 45 and the U.S.S. Pampanito

Pier 45, The Embarcadero, San Francisco
415/556-3002 • www.maritime.org

Hours: Open from the first weekend in October through Memorial Day, 9:00 a.m. to 6:00 p.m. Sunday – Thursday; 9:00 a.m. to 8:00 p.m. Friday and Saturday. Open the rest of the year from 9:00 p.m. to 8:00 p.m. daily, except Wednesday when it closes at 6:00 p.m.

Admission: $7; ages 6-12 $4; over 62 $5; under 6 free with an adult; and active duty military personnel $4. A family ticket costs $20 and is good for two adults and up to four kids.

Directions: Use the Fisherman's Wharf area directions on page 23. The Pampanito is moored on the right-hand side of Pier 45 as you face the water, beyond Alioto's and the outdoor crab stands.

Pier 45 is more or less the actual wharf referred to by "Fisherman's Wharf." There are still some active fishing businesses operating from the pier and some genuine fishing boats docked in its shadow, but these are only a remnant of the area's heyday as a bustling center of commercial fishing. Today, tourists enjoy sourdough bread and various crab dishes at a handful of restaurants while most of the pier remains closed to the curious.

Tucked away along the outer, northeast side of Pier 45 is a vintage World War II submarine, the *U.S.S. Pampanito*. The *Pampanito* saw action in the Pacific and has been lovingly maintained since. Visitors are given walkman and headsets for a decent, self-guiding audio tape tour through the boat. While navigating the sub-sized hatches and passages is no problem for little ones, taller folk will find themselves ducking a lot. The *U.S.S. Pampanito* is part of the San Francisco Maritime National Historic Park.

A Parent's Guide to San Francisco

Chapter Two
San Francisco

Liberty Ship Jeremiah O'Brien

Pier 45, The Embarcadero, San Francisco
415/441-3101 • www.ssjeremiahobrien.com

Hours: Open daily, 9:00 a.m. to 4:00 p.m. Closed New Year's Eve and Day, Easter, Thanksgiving, and Christmas Eve and Day.

Admission: $6; 65 and over $5; ages 6 – 13 $3; under 6 free.

Directions: Use the Fisherman's Wharf area directions on page 23 for a summer visit.

For a Pier 29 visit, use the Financial District directions in Chapter 1. From the East Bay, turn left on Fremont from the I-80 Howard exit, right on Mission, left on The Embarcadero. From Marin, stay on US-101 on to Lombard, left on Franklin, right on Bay, right on The Embarcadero. From the Peninsula, bear left on Bryant after the I-80 4th Street exit, left on 3rd, right on Mission, left on The Embarcadero.

During World War II, hundreds of Liberty Ships were built across the bay at shipyards in Richmond to transport troops and material for the war effort. All have been scrapped or mothballed, with the exception of the *Jeremiah O'Brien*. On the third Wednesday of the month (usually), the ship is brought to operational status with engines running, making it a great day for a visit.

The *O'Brien* is moored at Pier 45 from June to September (you can't miss it). The rest of the year, you *may* find it at Pier 29, about a mile southwest of Fisherman's Wharf and right on the trolley line. I say "may" because the ship has changed moorings a couple of times. Also, as a fully operational vessel with great historic significance, the *O'Brien* occasionally still sails on goodwill cruises. Call ahead to make sure it's in port, and where, exactly, "in port" is.

Ripley's Believe it or Not!

175 Jefferson Street, San Francisco
415/771-6188 • www.ripleysf.com

Hours: Open every day, 10:00 a.m. to 10:00 p.m. Sunday – Thursday; 10:00 a.m. to midnight Friday and Saturday.

Admission: $10; ages 5-12 $7; under 5 free.

Directions: Use the Fisherman's Wharf area directions on page 23. Ridley's and The Wax Museum are within a block of each other along Jefferson Street, just west of Pier 45.

They put it this way: "Two floors, 11 galleries, over 10,000 square feet of exhibits, state of the art interactive displays, illusions, and much more!" It's kid and tourist heaven. How can you resist the two-headed calf? How about an 8-foot long model of a cable car made of matchsticks, or a shrunken torso from ancient Ecuador? If they are in town on tour, are you up for explaining the uses of African Fertility Statues? All in all, it's a blast.

A Parent's Guide to San Francisco

Chapter Two
San Francisco

Wax Museum

145 Jefferson Street, San Francisco
800/439-4305 • www.waxmuseum.com

Hours: Open every day of the year, 9:00 a.m. to 11:00 p.m. weekdays, 9:00 a.m. to midnight on weekends.

Admission: Adults $13; ages 4 – 11 $7; 55 and over $11.

Directions: Use the Fisherman's Wharf area directions on page 23. Ridley's and The Wax Museum are within a block of each other along Jefferson Street, just west of Pier 45.

Recently reopened in a brand new facility, the wax museum rose a notch in respectability (and price). Still, like a good museum should be, the place is educational—the wax figures are exquisitely made, settings are true to their respective periods, and several worthy stories of California and San Francisco history are represented. The new place includes the flourishes of sound, light, and images that seem to be required to attract tourist dollars these days. The kids will love it.

Hyde Street Ships Pier

North end of Hyde Street, San Francisco
415/556-3002 • www.nps.gov/safr

Hours: Pier and ships are open daily, 9:30 a.m. to 5:30 p.m. year round.

Admission: Adult admission is $5; seniors and "juniors" $2; kids free.

Directions: Use the Fisherman's Wharf area directions on page 23. From Pier 45, walk west on Jefferson to the foot of Hyde.

This is a favorite of mine, and of kids. Hyde Street Pier extends into the bay from the bottom of Hyde Street (north end), and is managed by the park service as part of San Francisco Maritime National Historic Park. Marine history is the theme, and there's plenty of it.

Four old ships of note are moored at the pier, including the square-rigger *Balclutha*, schooner *C.A. Thayer*, tugboat *Hercules*, and ferryboat *Eureka*. Under normal circumstances, all four would be available for boarding and exploring, but restoration may be underway on one or more vessels when you visit. Even so, you'll be able to get on board something, and other historic maritime items along the pier are worth a look. Occasionally, extremely high tides can curtail all ship access, though this is rare. All in all, the kids will catch the feel of the sailing ships of yore, complete with the briny harbor smells, squawking gulls, and creaking timbers.

One event I highly recommend is the monthly sea shanty sing-along that usually takes place in the hull of a ship on the first Saturday of every month. A ranger leads the session with the support of an old salt or two and a couple local characters. Get there early to sit close to the singers, take cushions to sit on, a thermos of a hot drink, and maybe a blanket to stay warm. Plan on the chance that you'll want to leave early since it's not all that comfortable in the hulls of these old hulks. For current information, scheduling, and to leave your name to secure a reservation, call 415/556-6435.

A Parent's Guide to San Francisco

Chapter Two
San Francisco

Aquatic Park
North end of Van Ness Avenue, San Francisco
415/556-3002 • www.nps.gov/safr

Hours: Public access at all times.

Admission: Free.

Directions: Use the Fisherman's Wharf area directions on page 23. From Pier 45, walk west on Jefferson to the foot of Hyde, crossing onto the green and into the park.

The San Francisco Maritime National Historic Park and Golden Gate National Recreation Area manage most of the waterfront area between Fisherman's Wharf and Fort Mason, including the lawn along Beach Street, the Maritime Museum, Hyde Street Historic Ships Pier, and the graceful, curving Municipal Pier. "Aquatic Park" is most often used to refer to the free public access areas. The lawn is a favorite spot for basking and tourist watching. At its southeast corner, where Beach Street and Hyde Street intersect, visitors wait in line to ride the Hyde Street Cable Car. Walk all the way out to the tip of the Municipal Pier for the changing views, and for the fun of it. It's a great area to relax and play between shopping, museum visits, boat rides, or other amusements.

San Francisco National Maritime Museum
Corner of Polk Street and Beach Street, San Francisco
415/556-3002 • www.nps.gov/safr

Hours: Open daily from 10:00 a.m. to 5:00 p.m.; closed Thanksgiving, Christmas, and New Year's Day.

Admission: Donations are accepted.

Directions: Use the Fisherman's Wharf area directions on page 23. From Pier 45, walk west down Jefferson to its end and onto the green of Aquatic Park. The museum can't be missed—it's the only significant building in the park and it's right on the water.

Housed between Beach Street and the water in a wonderful art deco building shaped something like a ship's superstructure, the Maritime Museum has something to offer kids over 6 or 7. There are video and interactive exhibits on nautical history, the gold rush, and the whaling era, and a great selection of sailing ship models. Most will like the Steamship Room with its displays covering the evolution from wind to steam power. You'll also find the vessel, *Mermaid*—a one-man sailboat used by a Japanese adventurer for a solo crossing of the Pacific.

The museum is part of the San Francisco Maritime National Historic Park. As you piece together your half-day visit to the Fisherman's Wharf area, count on this for at least a 20-minute walkthrough.

A Parent's Guide to San Francisco

Chapter Two: San Francisco

Ghirardelli Square: Chocolate!

Larkin between North Point and Bay, San Francisco
415/775-5500 • www.ghirardellisq.com

Hours: The square is open to public access from 7:00 a.m. to midnight daily.

Admission: If you don't count what you'll spend on chocolate and other goodies, admission is free.

Directions: Use the Fisherman's Wharf area directions on page 23. The square occupies the block between Larkin, North Point, Bay, and Polk. Walk west down Jefferson from Pier 45, take Hyde up one block to Beach, continue along Beach to Larkin, and head up to the Square.

San Francisco's favorite souvenir, Ghirardelli chocolate, is indeed delicious. Though the company moved its chocolate-making operations years ago, the original factory was redeveloped into Ghirardelli Square, housing eateries, gift shops, galleries, and other upscale tourist businesses. While few of these will interest kids who aren't shopping-minded, the terraces, steps, and passages of the facility are fun to explore. Musical groups and performers of various sorts show their stuff in the courtyards. Then there's the annual *Chocolate Festival* in September. Mmmm.

The Ghirardelli Chocolate Manufactory and Soda Fountain operates in the clock tower, immediately inside the east entrance to the square. Inside, you'll find a delectable assortment of chocolate goodness, all made more enticing by the seductive aroma. While you wait in line to buy your chocolate of choice, the young ones can observe chocolate production on a small scale. Some of Ghirardelli's original chocolate-making machinery demonstrates the process from cocoa bean roasting through taste treat.

A Parent's Guide to San Francisco

Chapter Two

San Francisco

Fort Mason

Museo Italo-Americano

Landmark Building "C", Fort Mason, San Francisco
415/573-2200 • www.museoitaloamericano.org

Hours: Open Wednesday – Sunday, noon to 5:00 p.m.

Admission: Regular admission is $3; seniors and students $2; children under 12 free.

Directions: Use Fort Mason directions in Chapter 1. From Marin, bear left onto Marina from US-101, turn right at the end, then immediately left into the Fort Mason lot. From the East Bay and Peninsula, follow Van Ness (US-101), left on Bay, right on Laguna, and right into the Fort Mason lot.

Located on the San Francisco waterfront between Fisherman's Wharf and the Marina, Fort Mason is a somewhat awkward collection of old military warehouses, administration buildings, residences, and service facilities. Today, many of the spaces house non-profit and arts organizations, while others serve as venues for annual and one-time events. If your young one grows bored with the activity you've selected, you can head outside for a waterfront stroll.

The Museo Italo-Americano presents San Francisco's Italian heritage through art and historic items. They offer classes and special films, as well as changing exhibits that keep things fresh. Only a few kids will take to this one for any length of time, but it's free for under-12s and only $2 or $3 for you.

Museum of Craft and Folk Art

Landmark Building "A", Fort Mason, San Francisco
415/775-0991 • www.mocfa.org

Hours: Open Tuesday – Sunday, 11:00 a.m. to 5:00 p.m.; Saturday 10:00 a.m. to 5:00 p.m.; first Wednesday of the month from 11:00 a.m. to 7:00 p.m. Holiday hours in December are Monday 11:00 a.m. to 5:00 p.m.; Tuesday – Friday 11:00 a.m. to 6:00 p.m.; Sunday 11:00 a.m. to 5:00 p.m.

Admission: General admission is $3; families $5; 62 and over, students with ID, and ages 12 – 17 $1; under 12 free.

Directions: Use Fort Mason directions in Chapter 1. From Marin, bear left onto Marina from US-101, turn right at the end, then immediately left into the Fort Mason lot. From the East Bay and Peninsula, follow Van Ness (US-101), left on Bay, right on Laguna, and right into the Fort Mason lot.

Do you have one of those children who isn't swept up in the beeping, flashing, plastic, electronic fervor of the day? I don't want to generalize too much, but the Museum of Craft and Folk Art strikes me as a good place for quiet daughters of a certain age. Ever-changing exhibits highlight "…contemporary craft, 20th-century folk art, and art from traditional cultures home and abroad." Recent exhibitions have included paper hats by artist Moses, tattoo needlework, and traditional Japanese kimonos. Visit the web site or call for current offerings.

San Francisco African American Historical & Cultural Society

Landmark Building "C", Fort Mason, San Francisco
415/441-0640

Hours: Open Wednesday – Sunday, noon to 5:00 p.m.

Admission: Admission is $1 to $2, free the first Wednesday of every month.

Directions: Use Fort Mason directions in Chapter 1. From Marin, bear left onto Marina from US-101, turn right at the end, then immediately left into the Fort Mason lot. From the East Bay and Peninsula, follow Van Ness (US-101), left on Bay, right on Laguna, and right into the Fort Mason lot.

The Society's museum at Fort Mason features the work of African and African-American artists in a series of changing visual arts exhibits. Recent showings have included paintings and photo-watercolors by Hillary Younglove depicting the continuity of hairstyles from traditional Africa to contemporary America. Another exhibited Tony Hooker's photography, sculpture, and video work around the theme of the 1932 Tuskeegee Syphilis Experiment that victimized hundreds of black men. Your inquisitive 10-and-ups will find food for thought here.

A Parent's Guide to San Francisco

Chapter Two
San Francisco

Marina District

Palace of Fine Arts

Lyon Street at Beach Street, San Francisco
415/567-6643 (theater box office), www.palaceoffinearts.org

Hours: Public access to dome and grounds at all times. The schedules and types of events held in the arts venue vary widely—check the web site or call the box office for information.

Admission: Explore the grounds for free, pay plenty for events and performances.

Directions: Use Fort Mason directions in Chapter 1. From Marin, follow US-101, bear left onto Marina Boulevard. Take the first right for the parking lot, or the second for Baker Street. From the East Bay and Peninsula, follow US-101/Van Ness, turn left on Bay, right on Laguna, left on Marina, left on Baker.

In 1915, San Francisco hosted the Panama Pacific International Exposition, in part to celebrate the city's recovery from the devastating earthquake and fire of 1906. Nearly all that remains of the expo is the beautiful, restored dome-and-pillar structure by the Palace of Fine Arts. The "palace" itself is the semi-circular building behind the dome that houses the Exploratorium, performance, and arts spaces.

Kids will love playing hide-and-seek around the pillars and checking out the echo-producing qualities of the dome. A lovely reflecting pool hosts swans and other water-birds while a spacious lawn is great for parking a blanket. Don't be surprised to see wedding parties posing for photos amid the classic splendor. In all, it's a perfect place to rest and play after a morning in the Exploratorium.

Exploratorium

3601 Lyon Street, San Francisco
415/561-0360 • www.exploratorium.edu

Hours: Open Tuesday through Sunday, from 10:00 a.m. to 6:00 p.m. Memorial Day through Labor Day; 10:00 a.m. to 5:00 p.m. the rest of the year, and until 9:00 p.m. on Wednesdays all year long.

Admission: $9; seniors 65 and over and students with ID $7.50; ages 5 – 17 $6; under 5 free. Tactile Dome admission is $12, which includes basic admission.

Directions: Use Fort Mason directions in Chapter 1. From Marin, follow US-101, bear left onto Marina Boulevard. Take the first right for the parking lot, or the second for Baker Street. From the East Bay and Peninsula, follow US-101/Van Ness, turn left on Bay, right on Laguna, left on Marina, left on Baker.

A magnet for families and school groups, the Exploratorium is a world-class, hands-on, educational facility, guaranteed to interest the young and young-at-heart. Science, art, and human perception are central themes with over 650 exhibits roughly grouped in the following categories: light, color, sound and music, motion, animal behavior, electricity, heat and temperature, language, patterns, hearing, touch, vision, waves and resonance, and weather. All are carefully designed and arranged, though there may seem to be a lack of order to the untrained eye. Reservations are required for the ever-popular, crawl-through "Tactile Dome."

A Parent's Guide to San Francisco

Chapter Two
San Francisco

The Exploratorium also offers numerous web-based learning activities, including 50 live webcasts and links to Antarctica research, the Hubble Telescope, and the CERN particle accelerator. Check the web site or information line for a current list of special exhibits and programs, or just go and be amazed.

Marina Green
Marina Boulevard west of Laguna, San Francisco

Hours: Both green and jetty are open to public access at all times.

Admission: Free and free spirited.

Directions: Use the Fort Mason directions from Chapter 1. From Marin, bear left from US-101 onto Marina, taking the first left for Yacht Road or continuing on for Marina Green. From the East Bay and Peninsula, follow US-101 onto Van Ness, turn left on Bay, right on Laguna, and left on Marina, hugging the waterfront. Marina Green is to the right. Take the last right before the freeway begins for Yacht Road.

The popular Marina Green stretches from Fort Mason to the Presidio along the waterfront. Its expansive lawns and long walks are the scenes of jogging, strolling, kite flying, picnicking, basking, and general recreation. Bike riders and intrepid walkers can cover 3 miles from Fort Mason, along Marina Green, and on to Fort Point in the Presidio, all on designated trails that are safe from vehicle traffic. Those who are feeling less linear can park a blanket and let the kids run and tumble.

Wave Organ
Yacht Road from Marina Boulevard, San Francisco

Hours: Both green and jetty are open to public access at all times.

Admission: Free and free spirited.

Directions: Use the Fort Mason directions from Chapter 1. From Marin, bear left from US-101 onto Marina, taking the first left for Yacht Road or continuing on for Marina Green. From the East Bay and Peninsula, follow US-101 onto Van Ness, turn left on Bay, right on Laguna, and left on Marina, hugging the waterfront. Marina Green is to the right. Take the last right before the freeway begins for Yacht Road.

If you want to give your 4 to 12s a bit of an adventure, walk with them out to the tip of the jetty that shields the Saint Francis and Golden Gate Yacht Clubs' docks from the rougher waters of the Golden Gate. At the end you'll find the Wave Organ—a sculpted set of benches and terraces partly made of stone from a demolished cemetery. Twenty-five PVC "organ pipes" dive down into the bay waters, and are designed to turn the moving waters of wave and tide into musical sounds. They say the effect is supposed to be subtle; I've been out a couple of times and haven't heard a thing. Regardless, it's a lovely spot to rest wee legs for the walk back to your parking spot on Yacht Road.

A Parent's Guide to San Francisco

Chapter Two
San Francisco

The Presidio

Crissy Field

Mason Street, Presidio, San Francisco
415/561-4323 • www.nps.gov/prsf

Hours: Public access from dawn to dusk.

Admission: Free.

Directions: Use directions for The Presidio in Chapter 1. From Marin, turn left on Lincoln from the Golden Gate Bridge lot, follow it for just over a mile, turn left on Halleck to Mason. From the East Bay or Peninsula, follow US-101 onto Van Ness, turn left on Bay, right on Laguna, left on Marina along the waterfront, and straight ahead into the Presidio onto Mason (stay right, don't get onto the freeway on-ramp).

The transition of the Presidio from military base to a part of the Golden Gate National Recreation Area brought many improvements. The best has been the restoration of the waterfront area and Crissy Field, once an active military airstrip. Efforts included the re-creation of a wetland that was once blocked and filled, and the development of paths and picnic spots. Now, you can walk, bike, skate, jog, or otherwise propel yourself from Fort Mason to Fort Point through lovely, open parkland.

While there are modest attractions along the way—short piers, wetland, beach areas, etc.—this is really an area for play and exercise. Pack the kites, bikes, skates, sunhats, snacks, whatever, and head for the waterfront. Watch sailboats and windsurfers ply the waters with the Golden Gate Bridge, Marin Headlands, and bay islands as a backdrop.

Mason Street (not to be confused with Mason Street downtown) is essentially a westward extension of Marina Boulevard and follows the edge of Crissy Field. There are many places to park, unpack, and make your way to field and walkways.

Fort Point National Historic Site

End of Marine Drive, The Presidio, San Francisco
415/556-1693 • www.nps.gov/fopo

Hours: Public access to the area at all times. The fort is open Thursday through Monday, 10:00 a.m. to 5:00 p.m.

Admission: Free.

Directions: Use directions for The Presidio in Chapter 1. From Marin, turn left on Lincoln after the bridge visitor lot, then left on Long Avenue onto Marine. From the East Bay and Peninsula, stay on US-101, taking the exit just south of the Golden Gate Bridge tollbooths—the last exit before the bridge—turn right to Lincoln, left on Lincoln, left on Long Avenue and onto Marine.

Directly beneath the south end of the Golden Gate Bridge sits Fort Point—the name of both fort and point. Indeed, though it appears out of character with the rest of the structure, the designers of the bridge conceived a massive steelwork arch to save the fort from the wrecking ball. Fort Point was built between 1853 and 1861 to protect the mouth of San Francisco Bay from whoever might be crazy enough to attack by sea. No one ever tested its walls.

A Parent's Guide to San Francisco

Chapter Two
San Francisco

Today, there are old cannons to climb around, a couple of historic displays in dim rooms, and a set of stairs leading to rooftop views. Outside, a narrow walk lets you edge around the fort to get a view west and look more closely at the underside of the bridge. Besides offering a bit of military history, the fort is a good target for a waterfront walk from Crissy Field, or an even longer waterfront bike ride that takes in the Marina Green and Fort Mason.

Golden Gate Bridge

US-101, San Francisco and Marin County
www.goldengatebridge.org

Hours: The bridge may be viewed at any time. The east side is open for walking daily from 5:00 a.m. to 9:00 p.m. The west side is open only to bicyclists, 5:00 a.m. to 3:30 p.m. daily.

Admission: Free. Southbound drivers must pay a $3 toll to cross the bridge and reach the southside visitor area.

Directions: Find and follow US-101. Whether coming from the north or south, take the last exit before the bridge or the first exit after the bridge for one of the viewpoints. Parking areas and bridge walk are on the east or bay side of the bridge. Access to the south end is also possible from Lincoln Boulevard in the Presidio.

Not all must-see urban landmarks are fun for kids, but the Golden Gate Bridge is a sure winner. Other suspension bridges are longer, higher above the water, or have longer spans between towers, but nothing compares to the breathtaking wonder that this magnificent bridge inspires as it spans the Golden Gate, western gateway to the continent.

While viewpoints are many, you can't beat a walk out over the water. I think the south end is the best, though it hardly matters. If a young one says, "I want to walk all the way across!" you might answer with, "Well, let's get past that first tower and see what there is to see." It's nearly 1 ¼ miles from end to end. A nice option for families with two drivers is to send the hearty walkers across while the less inclined drive across to pick the others up.

A Parent's Guide to San Francisco

Chapter Two

San Francisco

Seacliff

China Beach

Seacliff Avenue, San Francisco
415/556-0560

Hours: Public access at all times.

Admissions: Free.

Directions: Follow Ocean Beach directions in Chapter 1. From Marin, follow CA-1 through the Presidio, right on California, right on 25th Avenue. From the East Bay, follow US-101 onto Van Ness, left on Geary, right on 25th Avenue. From the south, follow CA-1 from I-280, right on Clement, first left on 12th, left on California, right on 25th. All turn left on El Camino Del Mar from 25th, right on marked lane to beach.

Want a quiet beach with a view of the Golden Gate Bridge on the one hand, multi-million dollar Seacliff mansions on the other? Let the kids shovel sand and dip toes in the chilly water while you read some pulp fiction—though keep an eye out because there's no regular lifeguard protection. This is *not* one of those beaches where you are likely to see less-than-appropriately clothed people. Restrooms and showers are at hand. A grassy picnic area offers barbecues. No dogs allowed.

Laurel Heights

Fire Department Museum

655 Presidio Avenue, San Francisco
415/563-4630 • www.sffiremuseum.org

Hours: Open Thursday – Sunday, 1:00 p.m. to 4:00 p.m.

Admission: Free.

Directions: Use Tourist Zone directions in Chapter 1. From Marin, follow US-101, going only 1 1/2 blocks on Lombard before turning right on Divisadero, then right on Pine, left on Presidio Avenue. From the East Bay and Peninsula, follow US-101 along Van Ness, left on Pine, left on Presidio Avenue.

Even if none of your kids is in the, "I want to be a firefighter" stage, the focus of this basic history museum might catch their interest. Exhibits include old helmets, horse-drawn fire engine models, 1906 earthquake artifacts, historic fire extinguishers, paintings, and photographs. One of San Francisco's first three fire engines is here, dating to 1810, as are several other wagons, hose carts, and fire fighting hardware items.

Chapter Two

San Francisco

Outer Richmond

Cliff House

1090 Point Lobos, San Francisco
415/386-3330 • www.cliffhouse.com

Hours: Open every day of the year for breakfast, lunch, dinner, drinks, gifts, and snacks.

Admission: Free to walk in and use the restrooms, pricey to dine.

Directions: Use the Ocean Beach directions in Chapter 1. All sights are found where the Great Highway meets Point Lobos Avenue. From Marin, follow CA-1, turn right on Geary, bear right at 39th Avenue, Geary becomes Point Lobos. From the East Bay, follow Fell to Stanyan, right on Stanyan, left on Geary, bear slightly right at 39th Avenue, Geary becomes Point Lobos. From the Peninsula, follow I-280 to John Daly Boulevard, west on John Daly, right on Skyline (CA-35), left on the Great Highway.

While the Cliff House is indeed a famous tourist magnet, it isn't much of an attraction at all and barely deserves mention here. Once upon a time, the Cliff House was a large, ornate wooden structure that fit the image of landmark. Unfortunately, the original burned, as did its replacement. The third and current version was decidedly less ambitious in design. A fourth, due to be constructed soon, will supposedly return the Cliff House to its past glory.

Still—with its fine restaurant, less fine bar/café, and gift shop—the Cliff House provides an island of respite from the outdoor attractions all around. If the chill wind, dank fog, or blazing sun get to you on visits to Ocean Beach, Land's End, or the Sutro Baths, bring the gang here for a snack.

Sutro Baths Ruins

Point Lobos Avenue at the Great Highway, San Francisco
415/556-0560 • www.cliffhouse.com/history/sutro.htm

Hours: Open to public access from dawn to dusk.

Admission: Free.

Directions: See Cliff House above.

I wish I could have been around to experience the amusements of San Francisco earlier in the century when the Cliff House was a wonder, an amusement park backed Ocean Beach, and the Sutro Baths drew bathers from all around. The pools and structures of the baths were set near the water's edge in a modestly sheltered cove between Point Lobos and the promontory at the head of Ocean Beach. Today, all that remains are the broken foundations of the baths. Just north of the Cliff House, stairs and paths lead down to the site. Signs share history with visitors, but the kids will just want to explore the remains and test their boldness along the rocky shore.

A Parent's Guide to San Francisco

Chapter Two
San Francisco

Musee Mechanique

1090 Point Lobos, San Francisco
415/386-1170 • www.coin-opcollector.com/Musee.htm

Hours: Open 10:00 a.m. to 8:00 p.m. through the summer months; 11:00 a.m. to 7:00 p.m. the rest of the year.

Admission: Free, but you will want some coins to spend on the marvelous old machines.

Directions: See Cliff House above.

Don't enter this amazing little museum without a pocket full of change. Inside, you'll find dozens of old, coin-operated machines that offer all kinds of entertainments. Test your strength, measure your love, make the lady laugh, watch figures dance as the Mountain Boys play, or have your fortune told. Show the kids how their ancestors wasted money before the first transistor transisted. Tucked away behind the Cliff House, this one is a guaranteed winner—and it's free!

Camera Obscura

Point Lobos Avenue at the Great Highway, San Francisco
415/750-0415 • giantcamera.westphila.net

Hours: Open daily: weekdays from 11:00 a.m. to 6:00 p.m. (until 8:00 p.m. if the weather is sunny); weekends 11:00 a.m. to sunset.

Admission: $2; seniors and children $1.

Directions: See Cliff House above.

Ever want to get inside a camera? Neither have I, but when opportunity knocks, why not! Kids generally get a kick out of it, in any case. The Camera Obscura works like a regular camera, only on a much larger scale. Light enters through the lens and is projected onto a surface where the film would be in its smaller kin. Visitors in the darkened chamber can view the image and learn a thing or two about the behavior of light and lenses.

Though it was slated for destruction not too long ago in anticipation of the rebuilding of the Cliff House, the Camera was recently declared an historic landmark and will remain accessible into the future. Thanks go out to the small but loyal base of supporters that worked hard to save it.

A Parent's Guide to San Francisco

Chapter Two: San Francisco

Ocean Beach

Great Highway, San Francisco
415/556-0560 • www.nps.gov/goga

Hours: Public access to the beach at all times.
Admission: Free to all.
Directions: See Cliff House above.

Stretching 4 miles—from the Cliff House and Land's End in the north to the rising cliffs of Fort Funston to the south—Ocean Beach offers a vast, sandy playground to recreators of all sorts. It's a favorite with dog owners and joggers. Young parents with babies in backpacks stroll past busy shorebirds. Wet-suited surfers brave the cold Pacific waters to hone their skills in the generally modest waves.

Find a likely spot and park your family on a blanket for awhile. The kids can build sand castles, collect sundial shells, and dance at the edge of the surf. While the beach is a lot cleaner than similar urban beaches—and much less crowded—you may encounter areas with bits of litter that can cut feet, as well as the occasionally hot debris from the previous night's legal beach fires.

If the weather in the Bay Area is a mixed bag of warm, cool, sunny, and foggy, expect to find the least comfortable version at Ocean Beach. It's always good to be prepared for chilly, windy conditions.

A Parent's Guide to San Francisco

Chapter Two
San Francisco

Golden Gate Park

Golden Gate Park and How to Get There

Bounded by Lincoln Way, Stanyan, Fulton and the Great Highway, San Francisco
415/831-2700 • www.civiccenter.ci.sf.ca.us/recpark.nsf

Golden Gate Park is the crown jewel of the city's park system and one of the finest urban parks in the world. Much of the credit for its quality goes to the park's first and longest lasting superintendent, John McLaren, who served from 1887 to 1943. Over the years, McLaren took what were essentially wild dune lands and sculpted them into a lush, green retreat for area residents.

You could easily visit the park many times a year without exhausting its appeal for your kids. In addition to the special spots noted below, the park hosts dozens of wide lawns perfect for picnics and play. Miles of walks wind through gardens and groves. There's a golf course, fly casting pond, bowling green, polo field, stadium, tennis courts, archery field, and twelve lakes. Parking is free and generally easy. Walk, rest, eat, play, watch, and walk some more.

Use the *Golden Gate Park* directions in Chapter 1 to reach the general area. Two main drives wind from east to west through the park—John F. Kennedy (JFK) Drive through the north, Martin Luther King Jr. (MLK) Drive through the south. They will get you from point to point without hitting the city streets. All directions in the listings ahead are based on these two, most from MLK Drive, with only the Buffalo enclosure and Spreckels Lake from JFK Drive. Branch roads are not well signed, though there are signs for the major sights. It really pays to carry a good San Francisco map that shows park roads.

Note that the east half of JFK Drive is closed to vehicle traffic on Sunday, 6:30 a.m. to 5:00 p.m., when it is a great place to bike or skate safely.

To reach JFK Drive or MLK Drive, do the following:

From Marin: follow CA-1 through the Presidio, through the tunnel, and along Park Presidio Boulevard. Turn right on Balboa, left on 25th Avenue, and enter the park. Turn right on JFK for Spreckels and the Buffalo Enclosure. For MLK Drive, stay straight on Transverse Drive and cross the park, turning left for the other listed sights.

A Parent's Guide to San Francisco

Chapter Two: San Francisco

From the East Bay, follow Fell. Bear left with the main traffic in the last block of Fell and continue across Stanyan onto JFK Drive. For MLK, bear left onto Kezar Drive, winding around to the left, then turning right on MLK Drive. For western JFK Drive on Sunday, take MLK Drive across CA-1/Park Presidio, take the first right onto Transverse Drive, and turn left on JFK Drive.

From the Peninsula, follow CA-1 / 19th Avenue across Lincoln Way and into the park. Take the first right in the park (MLK Drive). For western MLK or to reach JFK, the easiest thing to do is to find a place for a safe U-turn on MLK, cross back over CA-1, and take the next right on Transverse Drive to JFK.

Children's Playground and Carousel

Golden Gate Park, San Francisco
415/831-2700 • www.parks.sfgov.org

Hours: Playground accessible all day, every day. The carousel operates daily, 10:00 a.m. to 5:00 p.m.

Admission: Playground free; carousel rides are $1 for adults, $.25 for kids.

Directions: Use the MLK Drive directions on page 42. Playground and carousel are just north of the intersection with Kezar Drive.

The biggest and best playground in Golden Gate Park is practically guaranteed to interest kids from toddlers to pre-teens for a good while. There are numerous pieces of apparatus, including slides, swings, and climbing structures. As with many urban playgrounds, the area is fenced to discourage animals and childless adults, and parents tend to contribute their monitoring skills to the larger group. The area is kept clean and free of threatening debris.

Right next to the playground is the wonderful Herschel-Spillman Carousel, built in 1912. Your little ones may find it hard to choose among the 62 handmade creatures circling this very merry merry-go-round, all beautifully restored and maintained.

43

A Parent's Guide to San Francisco

Chapter Two
San Francisco

Academy of Sciences

55 Concourse Drive, Golden Gate Park, San Francisco
415/750-7145 • www.calacademy.org

Hours: The Academy and all facilities are open 9:00 a.m. to 6:00 p.m. from Memorial Day to Labor Day, 10:00 a.m. to 5:00 p.m. the rest of the year.

The planetarium offers hourly star shows from 11:00 a.m. to 4:00 p.m. on Saturday, Sunday, the first Wednesday of the month, and holidays. Monday through Friday, there's one show daily at 2:00 p.m.

Admission: $8.50 for adults; $5.50 for ages 12 – 17, students with ID, and seniors 65 and over; $2 for kids 4 – 11; and free to children under 3. The Academy is free to all on the first Wednesday of every month, and is open until 8:45 p.m. on those days. Morrison Planetarium shows cost $2.50 for adults; $1.25 for ages 6 – 17 and seniors 65 and up—that's in addition to the basic admission price.

Directions: Use MLK Drive directions on page 42. The Japanese Tea Garden, De Young Museum, Music Concourse, and Academy of Sciences are very close to each other, just up a side road from MLK at Strybing Arboretum. Follow the signs.

Really three attractions in one, the Academy is a must-see for your inquisitive 6-and-ups. Earth, water, and heavens are represented in the Natural History Museum, Steinhart Aquarium, and Morrison Planetarium. It's actually a little much to explore the whole facility in one visit. Get out before the kids get tired to leave them wanting more.

The following trio is all in the same building complex, across the Music Concourse from the De Young Museum, a couple hundred yards from the Japanese Tea Garden. One admission fee gets you into both museum and aquarium, but you'll need to pay extra for a planetarium show.

Natural History Museum

55 Concourse Drive, Golden Gate Park, San Francisco
415/750-7145 • www.calacademy.org

Directions: See Academy of Sciences directions.

Dinosaurs! They're here to some extent in the "Life through Time" exhibit, leading the way in the museum's recounting of evolution. The kids will also like "Earthquake" where they can sit for a shake that simulates a California quake and watch an 11-minute film on all the big ones. Other child-enticing exhibits include the "Insect Room," "African Experience and Play Space," "Wild California," and a room that features cartoons by Far Side creator Gary Larson.

Some of the rooms are a bit dry for the young ones who may prefer the living creatures of the aquarium or sit-and-watch splendor of the planetarium. Come here first on your visit to the Academy, then head for the fish at the first fidget.

A Parent's Guide to San Francisco

Chapter Two
San Francisco

Steinhart Aquarium

55 Concourse Drive, Golden Gate Park, San Francisco
415/750-7145 • www.calacademy.org

Directions: See Academy of Sciences directions.

Thousands of living creatures of the deep are exhibited in 165 individual tanks and other wet habitat exhibits. The kids will be dashing from place to place, uttering some version of, "Mom, look at this!" over and over again. If you have more than one or two children in tow, you may find it hard to keep them all together. Just like you'd expect, the "Sharks of the Tropics" exhibit is a big hit. As you come to peer into the pit that holds the alligators and crocodiles, don't tell the kids what they are looking for. When they finally spot the huge gators lying still as stones, an "Ooooo!" will ensue.

The biggest tank—"Fish Roundabout"—is the scene of a marine frenzy when the 1:30 p.m. feeding comes along. Try to join the crowd. The goofy black-footed penguins, on the other hand, snack at 11:30 a.m. and 4:00 p.m. Additional tank feedings are scheduled throughout the day. Ask questions of the helpful staff so you don't miss a fun flurry of marine activity.

Morrison Planetarium

55 Concourse Drive, Golden Gate Park, San Francisco
415/750-7141 • www.calacademy.org

Directions: See Academy of Sciences directions.

With its 65' dome, 5000-pound main projector, and variety of supporting hardware, star shows at the Morrison offer a wondrous eye-opener to kids over about 4. The show creators know how to add just the right amount of theatrics to make the highly educational experience appealing throughout. Shows change every couple of months—call or check the web site for the latest offering.

A Parent's Guide to San Francisco

Chapter Two

San Francisco

Buffalo Enclosure

Golden Gate Park, San Francisco
415/831-2700 • www.parks.sfgov.org

Hours: The bison are always there, munching away. That stretch of JFK Drive is open to vehicles at all times.

Admission: They're big, but they won't ask for money.

Directions: Use JFK Drive directions on page 42. The bison are found between Spreckels Lake and the golf course in the west end of the park.

"Look, Mom, buffaloes!" Or to be strictly correct, *bison*.

Any outing that involves a drive through the west side of Golden Gate Park should include a stop at the Buffalo Enclosure (a.k.a. Bison Paddock). Inside this fenced, roadside parcel are a couple dozen bison, generally looking very bored. Why are there bison in San Francisco? Why not and who cares! When the attention of your children begins to stray, you'll know it's time to move on.

In case you're interested, animal protection groups like the SPCA have taken an interest in the Buffalo enclosure to make sure the habitat is suitable, and that the bison are not stressed—and believe me, these bison are not stressed.

Spreckels Lake

Golden Gate Park, San Francisco
415/831-2700 • www.parks.sfgov.org

Hours: Public access from dawn to dusk.

Admission: Free.

Directions: Use JFK Drive directions on page 42. The lake is on your right where JFK splits around "Rhododendron Island."

The toddler to 10 year-old set should enjoy the quiet pleasures of this classic urban pond. There's a walk all around with plenty of benches. Waterbirds are eager for tossed bread and crackers (bring something with you that's nutritious for birds). Other families provide a welcoming air, as do the smiling oldsters who come for peace, sun, and the nearby park senior center.

Best of all, perhaps, are the model yachts that are often found plying the waters. Just across the street from the lake is the Model Yacht Club House.

A Parent's Guide to San Francisco

Chapter Two
San Francisco

Stow Lake

Golden Gate Park, San Francisco
415/752-0347 • www.parks.sfgov.org

Hours: Lake and hill are accessible from dawn to dusk. Boats are rented daily from 10:00 a.m. to 4:00 p.m., weather permitting. Closed Christmas Day.

Admission: Rowboats $11/hour, paddleboats $15/hour, electric motorboats $18/hour, cash only.

Directions: Use the MLK Drive directions on page 42. A road circles lake and hill, connecting to MLK Drive just west of Strybing Arboretum. The boathouse is on the lake's north side where another short road connects with JFK Drive.

Here's a great place for an hour's worth of old-style family fun. You can think of Stow Lake as a small, doughnut-shaped body of water, or as a little lake with a big island in the middle. The boathouse rents paddle boats, rowboats, and very low power electric motorboats for circumnavigating the placid ring. If your daughter has her boyfriend along, you can pop them into one vessel and follow with the rest of the family in another, knowing that they can't get "lost."

It takes about a half-hour to do the loop at a moderate pace. Someone at least 16 or older must be on each boat. If kids younger than 11 or 12 are responsible for propelling a craft, consider going only as far as a bridge, then turning around. Head counterclockwise for the closest bridge. After your ride, you can get refreshments at the snack bar.

Strawberry Hill

Golden Gate Park, San Francisco
415/831-2700 • www.parks.sfgov.org

Hours: Lake and hill are accessible from dawn to dusk. Boats are rented daily from 10:00 a.m. to 4:00 p.m., weather permitting. Closed Christmas Day.

Admission: Rowboats $11/hour, paddleboats $15/hour, electric motorboats $18/hour, cash only.

Directions: Use the MLK Drive directions on page 42. A road circles lake and hill, connecting to MLK Drive just west of Strybing Arboretum. The boathouse is on the lake's north side where another short road connects with JFK Drive.

After being cooped up in one of the watercraft for a half-hour lake tour, stretch your legs by exploring Strawberry Hill—the island you just paddled around. Really more of a hill with a moat than an island, Strawberry Hill reaches over 400' above sea level and is the highest point in the park. It's accessible from north or south via footbridges. Trails give access to sights you saw from the water, including the small Taiwan Temple and Huntington Falls at the island's east end. There are several places to spy upon passing boaters. Golden Gate Park's two windmills once pumped water to fill the reservoir on top of the hill.

A Parent's Guide to San Francisco

Chapter Two
San Francisco

Japanese Tea Garden

Golden Gate Park, San Francisco
415/752-4227 • www.parks.sfgov.org

Hours: Open weekdays, 8:30 a.m. to 5:00 p.m. from November through February; 8:30 a.m. to 6:00 p.m. from March through October. Saturday, Sunday, and holidays year round from 10:00 a.m. to 5:00 p.m.

Admission: $3 for adults; $1.25 for seniors and ages 6-12; kids under 6 free. Tea and fortune cookies are $2.

Directions: Follow the MLK Drive directions on page 42. The Tea Garden is right on MLK, across from Strybing Arboretum.

A story only slightly better than rumor has it that fortune cookies were invented at the teahouse in this lovely garden in 1909. What is certain is that they are being served today, along with tea and a very short and austere menu of other items that rarely interest the young ones. What they almost certainly will enjoy is the wondrous garden itself, with its sculpted rockeries, winding paths, arching bridges, cool pools, and bright koi. It is particularly lovely when the cherry trees blossom in spring.

If the garden was less popular, you might hesitate to introduce energetic children to a scene that was clearly intended to offer peace and serenity. As it is, however, the garden rarely serves as a quiet place of contemplation, instead hosting a heavy load of tourists, many with loud voices and kids of their own. Don't hesitate to add another half hour to your park outing by including the garden in a visit to the Academy of Sciences, Steinhart Aquarium, Music Concourse, and Strybing Arboretum.

Music Concourse

Golden Gate Park, San Francisco
415/831-2700 • www.parks.sfgov.org

Hours: Public access at all times.

Admission: Free to all and sundry.

Directions: Use the MLK Drive directions on page 42. The Music Concourse is just to the east of the Japanese Tea Garden between the De Young Museum and Academy of Sciences. Park by Strybing Arboretum

This tree-dotted plaza between the De Young Museum and Academy of Sciences is fun with or without a performance in progress. Various events are scheduled for the big band shell at the plaza's southwest end. If you haven't checked local newspaper or web listings ahead of time, just follow your ears. When there's nothing going on, the kids can climb up on stage and express themselves as they see fit.

A Parent's Guide to
San Francisco

Chapter Two
San Francisco

Strybing Arboretum

Golden Gate Park, San Francisco
415/661-1316 • www.strybing.org

Hours: Open daily, 8:00 a.m. to 4:30 p.m.; weekends and holidays from 10:00 a.m. to 5:00 p.m. Free tours are given daily at 1:30 p.m.; Saturday and Sunday at 10:30 a.m. and 1:30 p.m.

Admission: Donations are gladly accepted.

Directions: Use the MLK directions on page 42. MLK forms Strybing's north boundary, just east of Stow Lake.

There are plenty of kid-friendly dimensions to this wonderful park-within-a-park with its splendid assemblage of plants from around the world. Narrow trails invite exploration and satisfy that peculiar desire of kids to follow lines. Hidden benches are nestled in groves of tall, cool redwoods. Inviting gazebos overlook still pools. Gulls and waterfowl are eager for tossed bread scraps at the classic duck pond. Wide lawns encourage running and tumbling.

For the education-minded caregiver, lessons are everywhere. The arboretum is nicely divided into botanical regions, featuring the bizarre succulents of South Africa, California native vegetation, trees of the Mediterranean, and many other ecosystems. A fragrance garden hosts dozens of species that boast intriguing aromas (though some may be subdued depending on the season).

Docent-led walks might be a good choice for older kids of a certain demeanor. Silliness and a picnic under a tree might be better for most.

A Parent's Guide to San Francisco

Chapter Two
San Francisco

Castro/Upper Market

Randall Museum

199 Museum Way, San Francisco
415/554-9600 • www.randallmuseum.org

Hours: Open Tuesday – Sunday, 10:00 a.m. to 5:00 p.m.

Admission: Donations gratefully accepted.

Directions: Use the Golden Gate Park directions in Chapter 1. From the East Bay, follow Fell, left on Divisadero, right on 14th Street, left onto Roosevelt Way, left on Museum Way. From Marin, turn right on Divisadero from Lombard, go 2.4 miles, turn right on 14th Street, left onto Roosevelt Way, left on Museum Way. From the south, take the CA-1/19th Avenue exit from I-280, stay right onto Junipero Serra which becomes Portola then Market Street, left on Clayton from Market, right on 17th, left onto Roosevelt, right on Museum Way.

Though the majority of tourists rarely notice it, the Randall is a standard school field trip destination and ranks as a must-see by parents in the know. As the staff puts it, the museum "…offers a unique haven where children and adults can explore the creative aspects of art and science and make discoveries about nature and the environment…" I agree.

The changing exhibits cover a wide range of science and art areas, with interactivity as a common component. A recent offering entitled, "Inviting Wildlife into Our City," featured projects by students from nine area schools, each of which had worked to create and restore neighborhood habitats for wildlife.

Long term offerings include an earthquake exhibit with a walk-through "refugee shack," and a recycling exhibit with the sniffable, "Let it Rot Spot." There's also a woodshop, arts and ceramic studios, darkroom, greenhouse, gardens, and more. The live animal exhibit is probably the most popular with the kids.

The Randall also offers a series of classes, programs, and workshops open to the public. Call or check the web site for the current slate, or just drop in on a Saturday when you'll be welcome to join in with whatever's going on. When you're through exploring inside, head outside into Corona Heights Park for a picnic and terrific views of the city. There are trails to walk and a decent playground.

A Parent's Guide to San Francisco

Chapter Two
San Francisco

Sunset District

Fort Funston
Skyline Boulevard (CA-35), San Francisco
415/556-0560 • www.nps.gov/goga

Hours: The park is open from dawn to dusk.

Admission: Free.

Directions: Use Western San Francisco directions in Chapter 1. From Marin, follow CA-1/19th Avenue, right on Sloat, left on Skyline. From the East Bay and Peninsula, take the John Daly Boulevard exit from I-280, west on John Daly, right on Skyline (CA-35).

For kids, there are two Fort Funstons. One features wind, lots of dogs and their owners, old gun emplacements, "dangerous" cliffs, and model airplane aficionados. That one is okay, but it's a whole different world when the hang gliders show up. Even in this I've-seen-it-all world, no child can resist the excitement of watching a winged daredevil leap from the cliff edge and soar out over the Pacific. Of course, it might give them ideas for a new hobby…

As one of several artillery sites developed to defend San Francisco Bay in World War II, Fort Funston is not exactly a pristine parcel of coastal wildland. It's also one of the city's more popular dog walk areas. Now that it's part of the Golden Gate National Recreation Area, however, preservation and restoration are a high priority. Beach access is available via a designated path down from the cliff tops to the water. You can head north or south for quite a distance along the ocean's edge.

San Francisco Zoo
Sloat Boulevard at 45th Avenue, San Francisco
415/753-7083 • www.sfzoo.org

Hours: Open every day of the year. Main zoo open 10:00 a.m. to 5:00 p.m. Children's Zoo open 11:00 a.m. to 4:00 p.m.; 10:30 a.m. to 4:30 p.m. through the summer.

Admission: $10; over 64 and ages 12 – 17 $7; ages 3 – 11 $4; under 3 free. San Francisco residents pay $2 to $3.50 less.

Directions: Use Western San Francisco directions in Chapter 1. From Marin, follow CA-1/19th Avenue, right on Sloat. From the East Bay and Peninsula, take John Daly Boulevard exit from I-280, west on John Daly, right on Skyline, left on Sloat.

This zoo is ready for kids of all ages! The place to head with younger ones is the Children's Zoo, a zoo-within-a-zoo offering a close-up look at nature's milder members. The Barnyard hosts a variety of domesticated animals the kids can pet and feed, including goats, donkeys, and sheep. The wonderfully conceived Nature Trail (open summer only) leads visitors along a wooded path past a selection of small mammals, reptiles, amphibians, and birds. My favorite is The Insect Zoo where kids can get close to tarantulas, scorpions, giant millipedes, and other creepy crawlies.

A Parent's Guide to San Francisco

Chapter Two

San Francisco

The larger zoo features all the classic animals and a few famous guests. Gorilla World hosts seven rare lowland gorillas, including a young female named Nneka (Ne-NE-ka). The Australian Walkabout offers kangaroos, emus, wallabies, and other species from Down Under. There's a little steam train and a carousel to ride. You can get a bird's eye view of many critters from the Safari Tram. Kids love feeding time at Penguin Island, scheduled at 3:00 p.m. daily, except for Thursday when it's at 2:30 p.m. (don't ask me why). All the rest are there—lions, tigers, bears, oh my!

Mission District

Mural Walk

2981 24th Street, Mission District, San Francisco
415/285-2287 • www.precitaeyes.org

Hours: Precita Eyes Center hours are Monday - Friday 10:00 a.m. to 5:00 p.m.; Saturday 10:00 a.m. to 4:00 p.m.; and Sunday 11:00 a.m. to 4:00 p.m. The Mission Trail Walk meets at 24th Street on Saturday and Sunday, 11:00 a.m. and 1:30 p.m. Call ahead.

Admission: Center admission free. Mission Trail Walk is $10, college students with ID $8, seniors $5, under 18 $2. The Saturday morning walk is $8, seniors $5, under 18 $2.

Directions: Follow Mission District directions in Chapter 1. From Marin, follow US-101 onto Van Ness, stay on Van Ness all the way to 24th Street, turn left for the Precita Eyes center, turn right for Café Valencia. East Bay and Peninsula visitors, exit US-101 at Cesar Chavez (US-101 South from East Bay), west on Cesar Chavez, right on Harrison, left on 24th.

There's no place in the city where public art and contemporary culture are as closely related as they are in the Mission District. Of San Francisco's nearly 600 murals, most are concentrated on once barren Mission walls. A student of the murals could trace the recent history of the largely Latino Mission District, seeing issues of identity, diversity, community, and politics vividly represented. Consider opening your older child's eyes to local arts and culture on a mural walk.

Local arts group, Precita Eyes, offers walking tours. Their Mission Trail Tour focuses on the Mission Street and 24th Street corridors. Walks depart from the Precita Eyes visitor center at the address above, except the Saturday morning walk which departs from Café Venice at 24th and Mission, near the BART station. Tours are led or accompanied by a mural artist. Call ahead to confirm tours and times.

You can also explore area murals on your own, on foot or by car. Have your young one be on the lookout for mural art on a well-planned walk or casual drive. Good concentrations of artwork can be found in Precita Park (one block south of Cesar Chavez on Harrison), along 24th from Mission to Florida, in Balmy Alley (see below), and elsewhere.

A Parent's Guide to San Francisco

Chapter Two — San Francisco

Balmy Alley

Balmy Alley, San Francisco
415/285-2287 • www.precitaeyes.org

Hours: Public access at all times.

Admission: Free.

Directions: Use the directions for Mural Walks above. Balmy Alley runs south for one block from 24th Street, 3 1/2 blocks east of South Van Ness.

The heart of the Mission District's mural movement is little Balmy Alley that links 24th and 25th Streets between Harrison and Treat. The first Balmy Alley works were painted in 1971 by neighborhood artists and members of groups such as Mujeres Muralistas, a women's mural collective. Other works are by some of the 40 PLACA artists who created 24 murals in 1984 to speak out against U.S. intervention in Central America ("placa" means to make a mark or image in call for a response). Consider the Mission Trail Walk described above or just turn down this alley on your own, older kids in tow.

South of Market

Seymour Pioneer Museum

300 4th Street, San Francisco
415/957-1849 • www.californiapioneers.org/museum.html

Hours: Open Tuesday – Friday and the first Saturday of every month, 10:00 a.m. to 4:00 p.m.

Admission: Adults $3, students and seniors $1.

Directions: From the Powell Street BART station, walk 3 blocks southeast on 4th Street. Drivers use South of Market directions. From Marin, follow US-101, taking Van Ness across Market, bearing left on 12th Street, then left on Folsom to 4th. From the south, take US-101 onto I-80 to the 7th Street exit, turn left on 7th, right on Folsom to 4th. From the East Bay and 5th Street exit, bear right onto 5th Street, then right on Folsom to 4th.

The collection of the Seymour Museum includes 2,000 paintings and prints, and over 6,000 artifacts, all from California's early days. The Gold Rush period and the Panama International Exposition of 1915 are particularly well represented.

Gold Rush goodies often appeal to the kids, particularly if their use can be vividly described by parent or guide. On the other hand, with little to do but look at displays, the Seymour may not make it to the top of your list.

A Parent's Guide to San Francisco

Chapter Two
San Francisco

Basic Brown Bear Factory

444 De Haro Street (at Mariposa), San Francisco
800/554-1910 • www.basicbrownbear.com/mainfactory.htm

Hours: Open Monday – Saturday, 10:00 a.m. to 5:00 p.m.; Sundays noon to 5:00 p.m. Drop-in tours are at 1:00 p.m., with an additional Saturday tour at 11:00 a.m.

Admission: The $12 fee includes the 12" Baby Bear model bear that your child helps to make. Different bears and bear clothes cost extra.

Directions: From US-101 North, take the Vermont Street exit, continuing across Vermont onto Mariposa, 3 blocks to De Haro. From the Bay Bridge, take the 9th Street/Civic Center exit, left onto 8th Street, bear right onto Henry Adams Street from the traffic circle, left onto Mariposa, two blocks to De Haro. From Marin, take Van Ness Avenue, cross Market, left on 16th Street, right on De Haro.

What could be more kid-friendly than a tour of the local teddy bear factory? The 30-minute tour includes a walk-through of the factory along a yellow bear paw marked path, a demonstration of how the bears are made, and a little history of teddy bears. At the end, kids get to stuff, sew, groom and "bathe" their own bear that they then take home to love.

Metreon

Corner of Mission and 4th Street, San Francisco
415/369-6000 • www.metreon.com

Hours: Main facility open every day from 10:00 a.m. to 10:00 p.m., theaters open later. Airtight Garage open 10:00 a.m. to 11:00 a.m., sometimes later. Wild things open Sunday – Thursday, 10:00 a.m. to 6:00 p.m.; Friday and Saturday 10:00 a.m. to 8:00 p.m.

Admission: Airtight Garage admission free with games ranging from $1.50 to $6. Wild Things $6. IMAX shows are $9.75, seniors $7.75, children $6.75. Movies are $9.25, seniors $6, kids $5.50.

Directions: Walk two blocks down 4th from the Powell Street BART station. Drivers use South of Market directions in Chapter 1. From Marin, follow US-101 onto Van Ness, across Market, then left on Mission. From the East Bay, bear right on 5th from the left-hand 5th Street I-80 exit, right on Mission. From the Peninsula, bear left on Bryant from the 4th Street exit, left on 3rd, left on Mission.

How would your gang like to spend time inside a combination jukebox, video game, and vending machine? Well, pry open your purse and take them to Sony Corporation's Metreon. Oh, it's free to walk in the door—and there are some free activities that qualify as 'bait'—but the rest is for sale.

Metreon attractions include the following:

Airtight Garage – A digital gaming experience featuring "Hyperbowl" where you can bowl on San Francisco streets, through Yosemite, or on board a pirate ship.

Where the Wild Things Are – Based on Maurice Sendak's marvelous book, you'll find the Goblin Kitchen, Mirror maze, tree slide, and Sendak's wild thing creatures themselves. Next door is "The Night Kitchen," also based on a creation of Sendak's and fittingly arrayed.

A Parent's Guide to San Francisco

Chapter Two
San Francisco

IMAX Theater – Perhaps the Metreon's best offering and the venue for some amazing Imax movies.

Movie Theaters – A multi-screen cinema with all the first-run movies.

Look for the neon-enhanced building across from the giant parking garage on Mission at 4th Street.

Museum of Modern Art

151 3rd Street, San Francisco
415/357-4000 • www.sfmoma.org

Hours: Open Friday – Tuesday, 10:00 a.m. to 6:00 p.m., and Thursdays 10:00 a.m. to 9:00 p.m.

Admission: Adults get in for $9, seniors 62 and up for $6, and students with ID for $5. Children 12 and under are admitted free.

Directions: Use the South of Market directions in Chapter 1. From the East Bay, bear right onto 5th from the left-hand I-80 5th Street exit, right on Folsom, left on 3rd. From Marin, follow US-101 onto Van Ness, left on Golden Gate, bear right across Market onto 6th, left on Folsom, left on 3rd. From the Peninsula, bear left on Bryant from the 4th Street exit, left on 3rd.

…or MOMA as it's known by most. While I would hesitate to take most kids to stuffy art museums with dim portraits in ornate gilt frames, a visit to MOMA is a different story. As you struggle to find deep meaning in abstraction, the kids will simply enjoy a wacky art circus and get a decent education along the way. The museum offers some excellent programs for teens through local schools—call or visit the web site for details.

Cartoon Art Museum

1017 Market Street, San Francisco
415/227-8666 • www.cartoonart.org

Hours: Open Tuesday – Friday 11:00 a.m. to 5:00 p.m.; Saturday 10:00 a.m. to 5:00 p.m.; Sunday 1:00 p.m. to 5:00 p.m. Call to confirm current hours.

Admission: Should be about $5 for adults, $3 for kids.

Directions: Take BART to the Civic Center station and walk 2 blocks east on Market. Drivers use Civic Center directions from Chapter 1. From Marin, follow US-101 onto Van Ness, left on Golden Gate, right on Market. From the East Bay and Peninsula, follow US-101 North onto Van Ness from I-80, right on Mission, left on 7th, right on Market.

At press time, the museum was scheduled to re-open at their new location, 1017 Market Street, in the fall of 2001. To know what to expect, just look at some of the museum's past exhibitions which included, "Trick or Treat: 50 Years of Wacky Cartoon Costumes," "A Tribute to Charles Schulz," and "Comic Book Superheroes: Muscles, Tights and Good Intentions." Their phone and website should remain the same, so make sure you get the latest information before you knock on their door.

A Parent's Guide to San Francisco

Chapter Two
San Francisco

Jewish Museum of San Francisco

121 Steuart Street, San Francisco
415/591-8800 • www.jewishmuseumsf.org

Hours: Sunday – Thursday, noon to 5:00 p.m.

Admission: The entry cost can vary depending on the exhibit, but one recent show featured prices of $4 for adults, $3 for students and seniors. Admission is always free the first Monday of the month.

Directions: Walk toward the water on Market from the Embarcadero BART station, right on Steuart. Drivers use South of Market or Financial District directions in Chapter 1. From Marin, follow Van Ness across Market, left on Mission, right on Steuart. From the East Bay, turn left on Fremont from the I-80 Howard exit, right on Mission, right on Steuart. From the Peninsula, bear left on Bryant from 4th Street I-80 exit, left on 2nd, right on Mission, right on Steuart.

Exhibits include the work of contemporary Jewish artists, and feature Jewish historic, cultural, and political themes. While Judaism is an anchoring theme for the works on display, the museum is accessible and inviting to people of all kinds. The works are always intriguing, and sometimes intense or provocative. It's a great place to bring your thoughtful teens.

In 2004, the Jewish Museum is scheduled to relocate to the renovated and expanded historic Jessie Street Power Substation, across Mission Street from Yerba Buena Gardens. Call for current information.

Yerba Buena Gardens/Moscone Center

Bounded by Mission, Folsom, 3rd and 4th Streets, San Francisco

Hours: Grounds open to public access at all times. Facilities hours vary.

Admission: Free to walk about.

Directions: Use the South of Market directions in Chapter 1. From Marin, follow Van Ness across Market, left on Mission. From the East Bay, bear right on 5th from the left-hand 5th Street I-80 exit, right on Mission. From the Peninsula, bear left on Bryant from the I-80 4th Street exit, left on 3rd.

This complex of facilities centers the revitalization of the South of Market area of downtown San Francisco. A variety of arts, culture, and recreation options are available around the "gardens" above while conventions and trade shows fill the hall space of the Moscone Center below. There are wonderful areas to walk around and enjoy, including a landscaped lawn, a waterfall and pools, public art displays, a play area, plazas, walks, and bridges. A café sells refreshments. For all area choices, the huge parking garage along Mission between 4th and 5th may be your best choice. The BART Montgomery Street and Powell Street stations are both about 2 blocks away.

A Parent's Guide to San Francisco

Chapter Two
San Francisco

Yerba Buena Ice Skating and Bowling Center

750 Folsom Street, San Francisco
415/777-3727 • www.skatebowl.com

Hours: Open skates are generally from noon or 1:00 p.m. to 4:00 p.m. or 5:00 p.m., plus some evenings. Call ahead. Open bowling starts at 10:00 a.m. daily, until 10:00 p.m. Sunday – Thursday, midnight Friday and Saturday.

Admission: Skating is $6.50, under 13 $5, over 64 $4.50, skate rental $2.50, lessons $5 and up. Bowling is $4 a game, under 13 and over 64 $2.50; hourly play is $20 for adults, $14 for under 13 and over 64; shoe rental is $2.50.

Directions: See Yerba Buena Gardens above.

Need something physical and fun to get the young 'uns away from their iMacs? Tie skates to their feet or put a ball in their hands and let them go.

At the Ice Center, light streams in the wall of windows as the sounds of scraping blades and shouted glee echo all around. Budding stars practice graceful spins in the middle of the rink while regular folks circle more placidly and novices cling to the rails. Experts teach private and group lessons at various times. A full line of skates is available for rent.

Next door, balls thunder down lanes, crashing into the pins or clattering noisily into the gutters. Once the kids get past the idea of wearing a pair of weird shoes that have been worn by countless others, they can join the fun. Lots of lightweight balls are available for younger arms. A snack bar sells refreshments. You should be able to drop in, but the lanes may be filled with league play so it pays to call ahead.

Zeum

Near corner of 4th and Howard, San Francisco
415/777-2800 • www.zeum.com

Hours: Open Wednesday – Sunday, 11:00 a.m. to 5:00 p.m. during the summer, weekends only during the school year.

Admission: Adults $7, seniors and students $6, ages 5 – 18 $5, members free.

Directions: See Yerba Buena Gardens above.

One of several interesting options in and around Yerba Buena Gardens, Zeum is a hands-on museum dedicated to media and the arts. The exhibits come and go, but you can count on them to be participatory. One featured digital video cameras that could be used to make movies. Another let kids build soundscapes using audio and synthesizer equipment. "Build It!" featured the construction of card towers, flying planes, futuristic buildings, and more. "Jam-O-World" involved two digital games designed by Entertainment Technology students.

Call ahead to see what's on, and what they recommend for the ages of participants.

A Parent's Guide to San Francisco

Chapter Two

San Francisco

Looff Carousel

Near corner of 4th and Howard, San Francisco
415/777-2800 • www.zeum.org

Hours: Open Sunday – Friday, 10:00 a.m. to 6:00 p.m.; Saturday 10:00 a.m. to 8:00 p.m.; holiday hours vary.

Admission: $2, two rides per ticket.

Directions: See Yerba Buena Gardens above.

Constructed in 1906, the historic Charles Looff Carousel was once an attraction at Playland-at-the-Beach—the long gone amusement park near the Cliff House and Ocean Beach. The city bought it, restored it, and housed it in a special pavilion near the main entrance of the Moscone Center. Little ones will love a ride on the beautiful, hand-crafted carousel creatures.

Children's Play Area

Near corner of 4th and Howard, San Francisco

Hours: Public access at all times.

Admission: Free.

Directions: See Yerba Buena Gardens above.

Nestled between the Zeum and Carousel atop the Moscone Center, the play structures in this small area were designed with child development in mind. As you work your way around the gardens, take a load off your feet and watch the kids play for awhile. There are bound to be several parents here doing the same thing.

A Parent's Guide to San Francisco

Chapter Two
San Francisco

Pacific Bell Park

2nd Street and King Street, San Francisco
415/972-2000, www.pacbellpark.com, giants.mlb.com, www.sfgiants.com

Hours: The 60-plus home games are played in multi-day stretches from April – September (hopefully into October). Tours run daily except on dates with home day games, departing on the hour from 10:00 a.m. to 2:00 p.m. No tours on certain, varying days due to conflicts and maintenance—call ahead.

Admission: If you can get them, seats for games range from about $10 to $40, depending on section. Tours are $10 for adults, over 54 $8, under 13 $5, discounts for groups and AAA.

Directions: Drivers use the South of Market directions in Chapter 1. From the East Bay, take a sharp left on 5th from the left-hand I-80 5th Street exit, left on Brannan, right on 4th, left on King. From the Peninsula, bear right on 4th from the I-80 4th Street exit, left on King. From Marin, follow Van Ness across Market, bear left on 12th, left on Folsom, right on 4th, left on King.

San Francisco's new downtown baseball park is one of the best in the nation, and it's right in the heart of town where train, trolley, and freeway meet. Once inside, fans can enjoy a number of diversions if the game is slow, including a terrific children's play area in left field. Kids can climb, slide, and play games beneath the giant Coca-Cola bottle honoring a major sponsor (I'll let you guess who that sponsor is.)

When the team is off or out of town, visitors can tour the facility. Make your baseball-loving progeny feel special with an inside look at a big league park. They'll visit the Press Box, Dugout, Visitors' Clubhouse, a luxury suite, and other key spots. Remember that it's a big place—the tour covers about two miles, all on foot.

Public transit connections to the ballpark are excellent. It's only an 8-block walk down 2nd Street from BART's Montgomery Street station. You can also get off at the Embarcadero station, walk two blocks down market and ride the waterfront trolley to the park. Peninsula visitors can take CalTrain to the end-of-the-line and walk 2 blocks to the Willie Mays entrance. Make it a no-car adventure!

Marin & the North Bay

In Marin County, many of the best options for your family involve getting outside and experiencing nature. That's no surprise, considering Marin's extensive network of parks, recreation areas, monuments, watershed lands, and other public open space preserves. Add the fact that Marin probably has the cleanest air in the Bay Area and outdoor activity makes sense. Visit often enough and you'll soon learn to keep hats and sunscreen in the car so you are never caught without.

Another point is that the wild lands of Marin County are just plain gorgeous. While children may not say so, the natural beauty fills their sails like wind, charging them up for exploration and discovery. Besides, your sails may need a little wind too. When you take your kids to play in Marin County, you're not in Kansas anymore, and that's a good thing.

The Sonoma and Napa valleys (located in counties with the same names) also offer plenty for parents and kids, as does the rest of the North Bay. While primarily famous for wine and wineries, you'll also find interesting history, natural wonders, amusement parks, and airborne adventures. Many options may call for more of a drive then you had in mind, but if you break up the trip with several stops, you can keep your little travelers from reaching the are-we-*there*-yet phase.

The first set of listings ahead begin by tracing the coast northward from the Golden Gate Bridge to the tip of Point Reyes. The second set starts again from the bridge, but this time follows the bay north from Fort Baker and Sausalito, then on to Petaluma, Sonoma, and the Napa Valley.

A Parent's Guide to San Francisco

Chapter Three
Marin & the North Bay

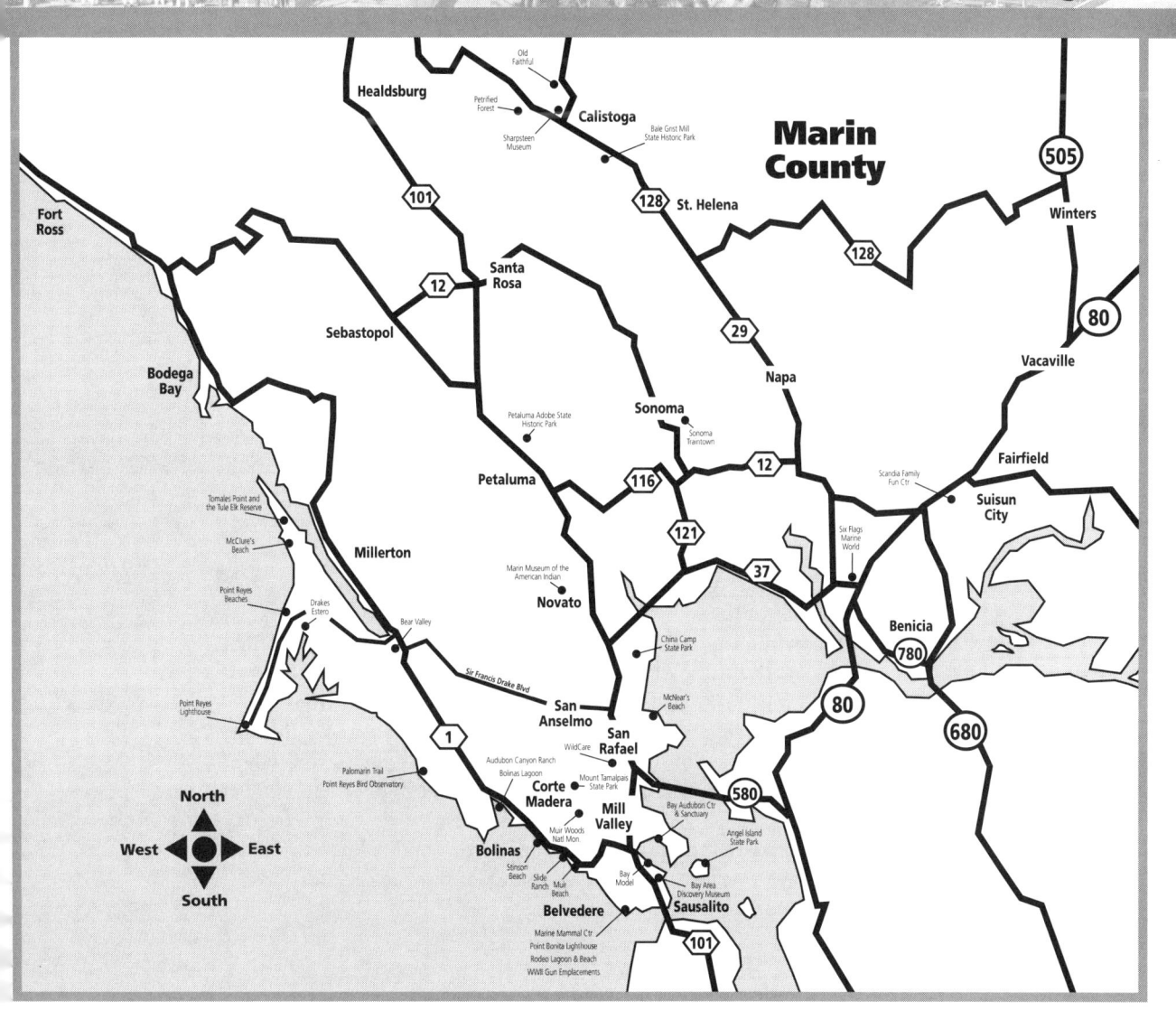

A Parent's Guide to San Francisco

Chapter Three
Marin & the North Bay

Marin Headlands

WWII Gun Emplacements

Conzelman Road, Marin Headlands, Marin County
415/331-1540 • www.nps.gov/goga

Hours: Always open to public access.

Admission: Free.

Directions: Take the Alexander Avenue exit from US-101, just north of the Golden Gate Bridge. From the south, turn left after exiting, passing under the freeway, then left again. From the north, bear right and up onto the headlands on the Conzelman Road.

During World War II, San Francisco Bay was a major hub of naval operations, and thus a tempting target for the Japanese. Liberty ships were built by the hundreds in Richmond while aircraft, men and materiel were prepared and dispatched from several area bases. To protect this massive operation, the high headlands of southern Marin County bristled with big guns, anti-aircraft units, radar stations, ammunition bunkers, and observation posts.

Today, the guns and hardware are gone, but the roads, bunkers, and other concrete works remain. Parents can soak in the stunning views of San Francisco, the Golden Gate Bridge, and the Pacific, while the young ones discover the ruins, climbing to high perches and shouting as they race through bunker tunnels.

The two best options are right on the Conzelman Road that climbs west from the north end of the Golden Gate Bridge. Spencer Battery is well marked about a half mile up the road, but the best views are had at the road's summit where it passes through a gate to descend to Point Bonita Lighthouse. Park when you can't go higher and you see the tunneled bunker.

Watch for the migrating hawks that frequent the hilltops from mid-August through mid-December. Also keep an eye out for poison oak—source of pure misery for kids and the parents who have to comfort them.

A Parent's Guide to San Francisco

Chapter Three
Marin & the North Bay

Point Bonita Lighthouse

Marin Headlands, Marin County
415/331-1540 • www.nps.gov/goga

Hours: Open Saturday – Monday from 12:30 p.m. to 3:30 p.m., though it is sometimes closed when weather conditions are bad, or for maintenance.

Admission: Free.

Directions: Take the Alexander Avenue exit from US-101, just north of the Golden Gate Bridge. From the south, turn left on Alexander, passing under the freeway. From the north, bear right and up onto the headlands via Conzelman Road, continue to summit and onto a one-way lane that descends to the point.

Clinging precariously to a virtual island of rock at the southwestern tip of Marin County, Point Bolinas Light marks the entrance to the Golden Gate. It's still an active lighthouse, serving to keep large and small craft alike from missing the entrance to the bay. The sea can be wild at the point where coastal currents meet bay tide flows and ragged headlands. It's an inhospitable place to spend a lot of time.

There's about a half-mile hike from a parking area to the light, including a final stretch across a suspension footbridge that's worth the trip on its own. Visiting hours are very limited so plan carefully. Expect wind, mist, and cool when you pack the car, though you may find none of those conditions.

Marine Mammal Center

1065 Fort Cronkite, Sausalito
415/289-7325 • www.tmmc.org

Hours: Open daily except major holidays, 10 a.m. to 4 p.m.

Admission: Donations accepted.

Directions: Take the Alexander Avenue exit from US-101 just north of the Golden Gate Bridge, head toward Sausalito, take the first left on Bunker Road. The Rodeo Valley is reached via a long, one-lane tunnel. A traffic light controls the open direction, alternating every 10 minutes or so. Continue on Bunker Road to near road's end, follow signs to center, lagoon access, and beach.

Throughout the year, marine mammals of various types are injured when they run afoul of human activities or natural phenomena. When injured animals are discovered, the Marine Mammal Center is often called upon to nurse savable creatures to health with the hope of returning them to their native habitat. To date, the center has rescued over 8,000 animals representing 18 species.

The easiest place to see the work of the center is at Pier 39 in the Fisherman's Wharf area of San Francisco. It's hard to miss the boisterous California sea lions that congregate on the "K" Dock of the small marina adjoining the pier. Center staff and volunteers monitor the small colony and operate the Marine Mammal Store and Interpretive Center on the second level of the pier, close to where the sea lions congregate.

In Marin, you can visit the Center hospital and observe animals on site for rehabilitation. It's good to call ahead since there's not always much to see—animals may be away from public view, or there may not be many animals in need at the time. You can also visit the "Current Patients" web page at **www.tmmc.org/patients.html**.

A Parent's Guide to San Francisco

Chapter Three
Marin & the North Bay

Rodeo Lagoon & Beach

Rodeo Valley, Marin Headlands, Marin County
415/331-1540 • www.nps.gov/goga

Hours: Public access at all times.

Admission: Free.

Directions: Take the Alexander Avenue exit from US-101 just north of the Golden Gate Bridge, head toward Sausalito, take the first left on Bunker Road. The Rodeo Valley is reached via a long, one-lane tunnel. A traffic light controls the open direction, alternating every 10 minutes or so. Continue on Bunker Road to near road's end, follow signs to center, lagoon access, and beach.

Fronted by the long, sandy swath of Rodeo Beach, tidal flows mix with fresh water runoff in the shallow basin of Rodeo Lagoon. The lagoon is rich with wildlife. Brown pelicans are common during the summer months, ducks in the winter, and gulls year round. The lagoon serves to limit beach access to either end of the quarter-mile stretch, and only the north end of the beach is reached by the road. Stop where the road forks at the head of the lagoon to hike the southside lagoon trail. Continue to the end of Bunker Road to reach the beach for some sandy fun.

Marin Coast

Mount Tamalpais State Park

Panoramic Highway, Marin County
415/388-2070 • www.cal-parks.ca.gov

Hours: Open daily, 7 a.m. to sunset, until 10 p.m. in mid-summer.

Admission: Parking at some spots $2, summit parking free.

Directions: Take CA-1 North from US-101 in Mill Valley. Turn right at the ridgecrest on the Panoramic Highway, then right on Pantoll Road to the summit.

At 2,571 feet, Mount "Tam" dominates the skyline of southern Marin County. The park that preserves its summit and much of the surrounding region is one of the most popular in the Bay Area. About 50 miles of trails climb, descend, and contour around the heights, part of the 200-mile trail system that connects the wild lands around Mount Tam with those of the Marin Headlands, Marin County Water District, Muir Woods, Point Reyes and other designated preserves.

If the kids can stand a half hour on a winding road, drive them up to the top for the fairly short hike to the observation tower on the summit. If the weather cooperates—as it often does around the bay—they will be able to see for miles, picking out landmarks like the Transamerica Pyramid, Golden Gate Bridge, Sather Tower at UC Berkeley, and the Point Reyes peninsula. Find a spot, pull the snacks out of your knapsack, and pass around the treats.

A Parent's Guide to San Francisco

Chapter Three
Marin & the North Bay

Muir Woods National Monument

Muir Woods Road, Mill Valley
415/388-2595 • www.nps.gov/muwo

Hours: Open daily from 8 a.m. to sunset.

Admission: Admission is $2, under 17 free, parking free.

Directions: Take CA-1 North from US-101 in Mill Valley. Turn right on Panoramic Highway at the crest of the ridge, then follow the Muir Woods signs left on Sequoia Valley/Muir Woods Road to the monument.

While not the best place to find solitude, the giant redwoods of Muir Woods are very impressive and easily accessible. The tiny monument receives more visitors than all the other redwood parks combined, so be prepared for the crowd. It's best to go on a weekday, and to go early in the morning any day. Don't let fog discourage you—cool, moist, and misty is natural for redwoods, adding to their mystery and majesty.

From the monument entrance, well-used paths parallel both sides of a creek, sticking to the gentle valley floor as they pass through the best groves. The creek flows year round and even hosts a very small salmon run. Other trails head up the steep slopes and into the hills—parts of the wonderful network of trails that lace the wildlands of western Marin.

If your kids are strong and willing walkers, use a good map to devise an interesting hike. If they're good for a couple hundred yards on level ground, just do a short loop in the valley where the best features of tree and water are concentrated.

Muir Beach

CA-1, Muir Beach, Marin County
415/331-1540 • www.nps.gov/goga

Hours: Public access from dawn to dusk.

Admission: Free.

Directions: Take the CA-1 exit from US-101 in Mill Valley. Follow it 6 miles, over the ridgecrest to Muir Beach. Slide Ranch is 2.2 miles further north on CA-1 (watch for the sign), with Stinson Beach another 4 miles beyond that.

The combination of rugged headlands and wildland preservation isolate all but a few ocean beaches in southern Marin County from easy access. One of the most popular choices you can reach by road is Muir Beach, located where CA-1 comes across the hills from Mill Valley and meets the sea. The homes of the small Muir Beach Community climb the cliffs nearby.

For traditional family pleasures, stay on the main beach or hike up onto the headlands to the south. The north end of the beach attracts naturists who often bare all to the elements. If you wish to participate, or just to give your kids some perspective, head through the rocky area to the right as you reach the beach. This area is not like a similar zone beyond Baker Beach in San Francisco where adults sometimes engage in activities not meant for young eyes.

A Parent's Guide to San Francisco

Chapter Three
Marin & the North Bay

Slide Ranch

2025 Shoreline Highway (CA-1), Muir Beach
415/381-6155 • www.slideranch.org

Hours: Family activities run from 10 a.m. to 2 p.m., Saturday and Sunday. Call ahead to reserve a spot. Bring a lunch.

Admission: $10 per person in advance, $12 at the gate, $45 for families of 5 or more at the gate, no one turned away for lack of funds.

Directions: Take the CA-1 exit from US-101 in Mill Valley. Follow it 6 miles, over the ridgecrest to Muir Beach. Slide Ranch is 2.2 miles further north on CA-1 (watch for the sign), with Stinson Beach another 4 miles beyond that.

Located near Muir Beach, Slide Ranch dates back to the 1800's and was once a dairy farm. Rescued from development in 1970, the ranch now hosts an outstanding environmental education center that's a favorite of parents throughout the Bay Area. As the mission statement puts it: "Every bite of food connects us to the soil, sun, water, and air, and to the people who work to feed us. Slide Ranch teaches respect and responsibility for sustaining these connections."

Slide Ranch primarily serves school and other youth groups, but there are some great weekend options for families. On Saturdays, the ranch hosts "Family Farm Days." On Sundays, it's, "Parent-Child Workshops." Slide's activity leaders show children where their food comes from, teaching how farming can be balanced with the natural ecosystem. Your kids might find themselves milking a goat, collecting eggs from a chicken coop, snacking on the goodies in an organic garden, watching bees at work in a hive, or enjoying farm-related craft-making. They'll participate in farm chores and explore tide pools. In all, they'll get an unbeatable taste of how it is to live with the land and not just on it.

The 20-acre farm is part of a larger parcel of 134 wild acres that are surrounded, in turn, by the extensive wildlands of the Golden Gate National Recreation area and Mount Tamalpais State Park. It's easy to add a wonderful hike to round out your day on the coast. If something more relaxing suits you, Muir Beach is just down the road.

A Parent's Guide to San Francisco

Chapter Three
Marin & the North Bay

Stinson Beach

CA-1, Marin County

Hours: Public access at all times.

Admission: Free.

Directions: Take the CA-1 exit from US-101 in Mill Valley. Follow it 6 miles, over the ridgecrest to Muir Beach. Slide Ranch is 2.2 miles further north on CA-1 (watch for the sign), with Stinson Beach another 4 miles beyond that.

Just up the coast from Muir Beach, broad Stinson Beach extends invitingly for about 3 miles. There is public access at several points, though much of the northern stretch fronts vacation cottages. Pick a parking area, grab the beach toys, slather on the sunscreen, and let 'em go. The town of Stinson Beach offers food, lodging, gas, and a handful of shops. Behind the arcing stretch of sand that hosts homes, road, and beach, you'll find the wildlife-rich, 1,500-acre Bolinas Lagoon (see below).

Bolinas Lagoon

CA-1, Stinson Beach
www.bolinaslagoon.org

Hours: Public access at all times.

Admission: Free.

Directions: Follow CA-1 north from US-101 in Mill Valley. Just past Stinson Beach, the lagoon spreads to your left. Look for parking areas.

The famous San Andreas fault runs under the coast of California for hundreds of miles before heading out to sea. Nowhere is it as vividly evident as along the deep, straight valley that divides the hills and headlands of Point Reyes National Seashore from the rest of the state. CA-1 follows the valley for it's full length, from the town of Stinson Beach at the south end, along Olema Creek, through the towns of Olema and Point Reyes Station, and on along narrow Tomales Bay.

Bolinas Lagoon is a small, shallow estuary at the southern mouth of the valley. Ocean currents created the estuary, smoothing the ragged coastline by spreading sand across the gap in the gentle arc of Stinson Beach. The resulting tidal lagoon behind the beach covers about 1,500 acres. CA-1 traces its shoreline for 3 1/2 miles. The lagoon is maintained by the continuing subsiding of the lands along the fault.

As you zip along CA-1 on your way to park, beach, or home, pull off into one of the parking turnouts, get out your binoculars and bird book, and teach your kids some science. The lagoon is a vital resting, feeding, and breeding area for numerous species. You might see harbor seals basking on a beach. Waterbirds include great blue herons, willets, brown pelicans, night herons, gulls, and sandpipers. Hawks, owls, falcons, and osprey seek prey from the air, while the fox prowls below.

A Parent's Guide to San Francisco

Chapter Three
Marin & the North Bay

Audubon Canyon Ranch

4900 CA-1, Stinson Beach
415/868-9244 • www.egret.org

Hours: Open to the public Saturdays, Sundays, and holidays from mid-March through mid-July, 10 a.m. to 4 p.m. Call for details.

Admission: Free, but donations are suggested and welcomed.

Directions: Take CA-1 north from US-101 in Mill Valley. Watch for entrance on right, 3 miles north of the town of Stinson Beach.

Courtesy: Audubon Canyon Ranch

Just above Bolinas Lagoon in Picher Canyon, as many as 100 pairs of great blue herons, great egrets, and snowy egrets court and nest in the tops of the redwood trees. From the time of the first arrival of herons in January to the departure of the last fledglings in mid-summer, the birds enjoy a carefully monitored refuge in the 1,000-acre Audubon Canyon Ranch preserve. The public is only admitted at certain times and viewing access is limited to a couple of overlooks where spotting telescopes are available to supplement the binoculars you bring. Even so, the kids will never forget the look they get at these large, long-legged birds courting and nesting so high above their wetland feeding habitat.

Town of Bolinas

Bolinas

www.visitmarin.org/south.html

Hours: Public access to the town.

Admission: They aren't charging visitors yet.

Directions: Take CA-1 north from US-101 in Mill Valley. Continue past Stinson Beach and Bolinas Lagoon. Turn left on Bolinas Road, which may be unmarked (the first left after the lagoon).

Known for a long time as a town that time forgot, Bolinas has mellowed in its pursuit of isolation—not the least because of a meteoric rise in real estate values that is changing the character of the residents. It maintains, however, a unique spirit of community rooted in social ideals of the 60's. You'll find smiling, laid-back people, wonderful vegetable gardens, and some intriguing shops. At the least, stop in at the Shop Café for refreshment as you pass through town on your way to Point Reyes' southern trailheads. The kids might acquire a touch of civility and communal spirit as they sip their Cokes.

A Parent's Guide to
San Francisco

Chapter Three
Marin & the North Bay

Point Reyes National Seashore

Point Reyes Bird Observatory

Mesa Road, Bolinas
415/868-1221 • www.prbo.org

Courtesy: Point Reyes Bird Conservatory

Hours: Self-guiding nature trail and visitor center open dawn to dusk, 365 days a year. Netting and banding occur Tuesday – Sunday from May through Thanksgiving, Wednesdays, Saturdays, and Sundays the rest of the year.

Admission: Free.

Directions: Take CA-1 North from US-101 in Mill Valley, continue north past Stinson Beach, first left after Bolinas Lagoon on Olema-Bolinas Road (sometimes unmarked), right on Mesa Road.

Biologists work year round at the Palomarin Field Station of the Point Reyes Bird Observatory, spreading nearly invisible mist nets to catch coastal birds. During the period that the nets are open, the scientists inspect them every 40 minutes. They gently extract trapped birds from the nets, take them back to the lab for measuring and banding, then release them, none the worse for wear.

While you can visit the station for a self-guided nature walk at any time, the thing to do with your young scientists is to be there when the nets are open. Groups of five or less can drop in any time to join a biologist on the walk to recover birds and watch the banding and measuring process. The nets are opened 15 minutes after sunrise and left open for 6 hours. To pick a morning, check the schedule above, but you should also call ahead to check conditions. Netting is sometimes suspended on short notice due to rain, heavy fog, or strong winds.

Palomarin Trail

Road's End, Mesa Road, Bolinas
415/663-1092 • www.nps.gov/pore

Hours: Public access dawn to dusk.

Admission: Free.

Directions: Same as Point Reyes Bird Observatory.

At the southern end of Point Reyes National Seashore, several small lakes offer wonderful destinations for day hikers with children who enjoy a walk. It's roughly 2.5 miles to Bass Lake from the Palomarin trailhead, the first half along the coast, the second up into the hills a bit. Two other lakes are about 3/4-mile further along by different routes. Watch for poison oak!

Children often like having a target for their walks and a lake is perfect. After being cooped up in the car, they will enjoy the first mile on fresh legs. They may have their doubts as the second mile involves some uphill effort, but then they'll see the lake and their spirits will rise. At the shore at last, they can enjoy a snack and some fishing or water play. The return hike is more downhill than up, and they're ready for a quiet ride to the pizza joint.

A Parent's Guide to San Francisco

Chapter Three
Marin & the North Bay

Bear Valley

Bear Valley Road from CA-1, Olema
415/464-5100 • www.nps.gov/pore

Hours: Park open dawn to dusk. Visitor center open Monday – Friday, 9 a.m. to 5 p.m., weekends and holidays 8 a.m. to 5 p.m. Closed Christmas Day. Restrooms accessible 24 hours (great for late finishes to hikes!)

Admission: Free.

Directions: Take the Sir Francis Drake Road exit from US-101 in Larkspur, just south of San Rafael. Follow Sir Francis Drake west to CA-1, turn right, then left on Bear Valley Road to the visitor center.

The Bear Valley Visitor Center is the main visitor facility at Point Reyes National Seashore and is particularly well suited to families. The center building itself features natural history and other exhibits that introduce you to the wild land and life of the park, including a weather station, touch table, and seismograph. The standard park visitor center slide program is a good one, and is available to see upon request. Outside, there are picnic spots.

Virtually all of Point Reyes is actually sliding northward along the California coast at a rate of about two inches per year. Geologically speaking, the park rides on the Pacific Plate, which is divided from the North American Plate by the quake-prone San Andreas Fault. As you drive CA-1 north from Bolinas, you follow the faultline as it runs beneath the Olema Valley and Tomales Bay. In the great quake of 1906, Point Reyes moved 20 feet north in one shot.

All but those in the first year or two of toddling can handle the Earthquake Trail near the visitor center. Evidence of earthquakes and faultline movement are pointed out along the easy, half-mile path. You are also likely to see the deer that browse in and around Bear Valley meadows.

If you're feeling ambitious, make sure your older kids have good walking shoes, pop the baby in a backpack or jog stroller, and head west on the Bear Valley Trail. It's a 4.1-mile moderate hike to the waters edge and junction with the coast path, but ocean views begin to open out sooner. If you have reserved a spot ahead of time, you can tote gear in to one of four hike-in camping areas for an overnight in the wild.

A Parent's Guide to San Francisco

Chapter Three
Marin & the North Bay

Point Reyes Beaches

Sir Francis Drake Boulevard, Point Reyes
415/663-1092 • www.nps.gov/pore

Hours: Public access from dawn to dusk.

Admission: Free.

Directions: Take the Sir Francis Drake Road exit from US-101 in Larkspur, just south of San Rafael. Stay on Sir Francis Drake all the way, west to CA-1, right nearly to Point Reyes Station, left through Inverness. The Drakes Estero trailhead access road is about 3 1/2 miles beyond Inverness. Beach access roads are another 1 to 3 miles further on. The lighthouse is at roads end.

Your child-centered Point Reyes tour won't be complete without a stop at a beach for some basking and play. One of my favorite beach areas in the region is found along Point Reyes' northwest shore. You'll enjoy clean, abundant sand, comparatively few people, and long open stretches for beachcombing. Look for the right turns to North Beach and South Beach along Sir Francis Drake Boulevard within a few miles of the lighthouse.

For calmer waters and a more developed area, take the left turn from Sir Francisco Drake down to Drakes Beach. The long, wide, south-facing beach is sheltered by the promontory of Chimney Rock, and comes complete with a visitor center and the Drakes Beach Café.

On North and South Beach, do not plan on letting the little ones do any more than dip their toes into the surf—the rip tides here are notoriously strong. Heed all warning signs about currents and undertow no matter where you go.

Drakes Estero

Sir Francis Drake Boulevard, Point Reyes
415/663-1092 • www.nps.gov/pore

Hours: Public access from dawn to dusk.

Admission: Free.

Directions: See Point Reyes Beaches above.

Behind the sandy arcs of Drakes Beach and the Limantour Spit, the brackish waters of Drakes Estero stretch in four, finger-like bays into the surrounding low hills. Like all true estuaries, the fresh water from runoff mixes with the incoming tidal waters, rising, falling, and mixing in a process essential to many to the life cycles of many species. A hike on the easy Estero Trail will put you close to the abundant bird life of the estuarine ecosystem.

A Parent's Guide to San Francisco

Chapter Three
Marin & the North Bay

Point Reyes Lighthouse

Road's End, Sir Francis Drake Boulevard, Point Reyes
415/669-1534 • www.nps.gov/pore

Hours: Open all year, Thursday – Monday, 10 a.m. to 4:30 p.m., weather permitting. Evening programs that include illumination of the historic light are on first and third Saturdays, April – December.

Admission: Free.

Directions: Take the Sir Francis Drake Road exit from US-101 in Larkspur, just south of San Rafael. Stay on Sir Francis Drake all the way to Point Reyes, first west to CA-1, right nearly to Point Reyes Station, left through Inverness and into the park. Turn right on Pierce Point Road.

No point of land in the Bay Area shows more disdain for the erosive forces of Pacific currents than Point Reyes. Enjoy it now; it's likely to be gone if you return in a few thousand years. Perched oh-so-precariously on the westernmost tip of the peninsula is the Point Reyes Historic Lighthouse. It's a stubby little thing—unlike the glorious Pigeon Point and Point Arena lights to the north and south—but it has helped thousands of passing ships from joining dozens of others that dashed themselves to pieces on the rocks.

There is plenty to explore all about the point, including a visitor center with maritime exhibits. Sea lions can be seen basking on the rocks and shorebirds are all about. During whale migration season from December – April, this is the best place to get a view of the passing behemoths. Because whale watching is so popular, the road is closed about 4 miles from the point on peak weekends and you have to ride a shuttle bus to the light. Call or check the web site for current details.

Plan on a moderately strenuous, exciting, half-mile walk after you park, including a descent of 300 steps (the equivalent of 30 stories!). There are plenty of chances along the way to stop and enjoy the incomparable views. All bets are off, however, when fog rolls over the point, which occurs on most summer afternoons and may persist well into the following mornings. Check the weather and call ahead.

Chapter Three
Marin & the North Bay

Tomales Point and the Tule Elk Reserve

Pierce Point Road, Point Reyes
415/663-1092 • www.nps.gov/pore

Hours: Public access from dawn to dusk.

Admission: Free.

Directions: Take the Sir Francis Drake Road exit from US-101 in Larkspur, just south of San Rafael. Stay on Sir Francis Drake all the way to Point Reyes, first west to CA-1, right nearly to Point Reyes Station, left through Inverness and into the park. Turn right on Pierce Point Road.

My favorite of all Point Reyes hikes follows an old ranch road out to Tomales Point. This long, narrow, gently crested peninsula separates the similarly long and narrow Tomales Bay from the wide Pacific. Though the terrain is easy, it's 4+ miles to the point itself—the 8 or 9-mile there-and-back hike on the treeless, windy trail is a bit much for most under-10's.

While the views are unmatched, the real draw is the presence of a large herd of Tule Elk, roaming freely across the broad crest of the ridge. This is another one of those places I'd be tempted to surprise your kids. It's almost impossible to miss seeing the elk on a round trip hike of at least 2 miles. While there may be elk around the gate and parking area, most congregate in fields a bit further out the peninsula. They are used to people so you can pass nearby without spooking them—though, as with all wildlife, they should be left completely alone. When the antlers of the bull elk are full grown in autumn, it won't take much of a suggestion to discourage your children from approaching. They are harmless when not disturbed.

The heights also attract a number of raptors, including hawks and owls that may be seen perching on rocky outcrops. If it starts to get dark on your return hike, the owls seem like shadowy fingers on the rock tops until the silently take wing in search of small game.

The parking area for Tomales Point is at the historic Pierce Point Ranch that features wonderful old ranch buildings and fences. There are no regular public activities at the ranch.

A Parent's Guide to San Francisco

Chapter Three
Marin & the North Bay

McClure's Beach

Pierce Point Road, Point Reyes
415/663-1092 • www.nps.gov/pore

Hours: Public access from dawn to dusk.
Admission: Free.
Directions: See Tomales Point and the Elk Reserve above.

As you near Pierce Point Ranch on Pierce Point Road, you'll come to the signed access road to pleasant McClure's Beach heading off to the left. This fairly isolated beach can be moderately busy on peak summer weekends, but is often nearly deserted. It's a great place to beach comb and bask, and you can explore the rocky areas that frame the sand. As with all California beaches—and particularly those on Point Reyes' north shore—beware the undertow and rip tides! It is not a beach for very young swimmers—up to the ankles is plenty deep enough. Heed all warning signs, but enjoy!

Fort Baker

Bay Area Discovery Museum

East Fort Baker, 557 McReynolds Road, Sausalito
415/487-4398 • www.badm.org

Hours: Open Tuesday – Thursday, 9 a.m. to 4 p.m., Fridays and Saturdays from 10 a.m. to 5 p.m. Closed Easter, Memorial Day, July 4th, Labor Day, Thanksgiving, Christmas, and New Years Day.
Admission: $7 for adults and kids, under 1 free.
Directions: Take the Alexander Avenue exit from US-101 just north of the Golden Gate Bridge, head toward Sausalito, follow signs for the museum and East Fort Baker, which is on the right near the foot of the bridge.

Wonderfully situated near the shores of the Golden Gate, this is a must-visit for parents of kids under age 10. The museum focuses on science, media, arts, and literature through exhibits, events, and performances, all presented in the several buildings of historic Fort Baker.

The excellent permanent exhibits include the Maze of Illusions, which is just what you'd expect. You will also find the ToT Spot where kids 3 and under can interact with fun stuff in the "Bat Bungalow," "Animal Atrium," and "Sleepy Hollow." Neat things can be created in the Media Center, Ceramics Studio, Art room, and Architecture & Design room.

The Changing Exhibits offer a reason to come back often. Recently, "The Science of Oz" gave kids the chance to step inside a tornado and make rainbows, as well as to see The Wizard of Oz for free. Check the web site or call for information on current exhibits and events.

Chapter Three
Marin & the North Bay

Sausalito

Bay Model

2100 Bridgeway, Sausalito
415/332-1851 • www.baymodel.org

Hours: Open Tuesday – Saturday, 9 a.m. to 4 p.m.

Admission: Free, donations welcomed.

Directions: From US-101, take the Sausalito/Marin City exit, follow Sausalito signs onto Bridgeway then follow Bay Model signs to a left on Harbor, then a quick right on Marinship Way to the model building.

It's amazing just to hear about it: a 1.5-acre scaled operational model of the San Francisco Bay and Delta! Every nook and cranny of the land beneath the waters has been carefully sculpted to allow various kinds of research on the natural and human processes that define this massive ecosystem. The model even holds water, though it's filled only for brief periods, usually on Fridays and Saturdays. It's fun to see it filled and "operating", but perhaps more revealing and educational to get a good look at the bay floor when its empty. All the human additions to the bay are modeled as well, including piers, bridges, breakwaters, and more. You can take a self-guided audio or ranger-led tour that gets you around the model in about an hour.

There are many other exhibits at the Bay Model Visitor Center—the true buff could spend half a day looking everything over.

A Parent's Guide to San Francisco

Chapter Three
Marin & the North Bay

Tiburon

Bay Audubon Center & Sanctuary

376 Greenwood Beach Road, Tiburon
415/388-2524 • www.marinaudubon.org

Hours: Open 9 p.m. to 5 p.m. daily, except for some holidays. Hours may change with season. Lyford House open Sundays, 1 p.m. to 4 p.m.

Admission: Donations welcomed.

Directions: Take the Tiburon/Blithedale exit from US-101 north of Sausalito, head east on Tiburon Boulevard, right on Greenwood Beach Road to entrance.

Preserving 900 acres of tidelands in Tiburon, the Richardson Bay Audubon Center provides a vital sanctuary for resident and migrating waterbirds. The center offers tours for school and other groups, but you can stop by for some self-guided educational fun most days of the year. Use a guide pamphlet or signs to follow the 1/3-mile nature trail. The best months to observe the birds are November – March. Call for information on guided walks and public activities.

At low tide, explore the tide pool areas along the shore, making sure to remind your kids to treat the delicate tidal life with care. Step carefully, be gentle when turning over rocks, and restore them to their original positions after a peek.

Consider a visit to the historic Lyford House—an old Victorian right on the shore. It's open on Sunday afternoons.

A Parent's Guide to San Francisco

Chapter Three
Marin & the North Bay

Angel Island State Park

San Francisco Bay
415/435-1915, 415/435-5390 (ranger station)
415/897-0715 (tram, rentals) • www.cal-parks.ca.gov

Hours: Open daily, 8 a.m. to sunset. No weekday ferry service in winter. Check your ferry company's schedule with care so you don't miss the last return boat! Tram tours run March – November at 10:30 a.m., 1 2:15 p.m., and 1:30 p.m. (weekends only November and March). A 3:15 p.m. tour is added on weekends, April – October.

Admission: Free, plus the price of the ferry (see ferry contact information in Chapter 1). Tram tours are $11.50, $10.50 for age 62 and over, $7.50 ages 6-12, under 6 free if sitting on a lap. Bike rentals are $30/day or $10/hour, child trailers are $15/day or $5/hour.

Directions: Access is by ferry from Pier 41 or 43 1/2 in San Francisco, from the harbor at the end of Tiburon Boulevard in central Tiburon, or from Vallejo.

This splendid isle draws visitors with both history and natural beauty. For hundreds of years, Miwok Indians used Angel Island as a site for hunting and fishing. It was the West's equivalent of Ellis Island from 1910 – 1940, though while Ellis Island generally offered a welcoming experience, Angel is remembered for its long detentions and deportations. During the same period, thousands of American soldiers came through the island's Fort McDowell on their way to or from overseas duties. POW's were held here in World War II, as were a number of American citizens of Japanese background. Nike missiles were based here in the '50s and '60s.

You'll arrive at the ferry pier in Ayala Cove, a common mooring site for private boats and home to a café, tram tour station, and bike rental shop. While there are nice trails for hiking, including a couple routes to the 781 foot-high Mount Caroline Livermore, this is a great place for a bike ride. You can rent them (see below) or bring your own across on the Angel Island-Tiburon Ferry for $1 extra.

The views of city and headlands are excellent. It's easy to reach an old missile platform and a couple of nice beaches. The walk to the other side of the island to see the immigration station and museum is a bit long for short legs, but bikes make it a breeze. Tram tours last an hour and circle the island, stopping at Civil War era Camp Reynolds, World War II sites, and the immigration station. There are good picnic spots.

A Parent's Guide to San Francisco

Chapter Three
Marin & the North Bay

San Rafael

McNears Beach

North San Pedro Road, San Rafael
415/446-4424 • www.co.marin.ca.us/depts/pk/main/pos/parks.html

Hours: Open spring and summer weekends, 7 a.m. to 8 p.m., weekdays 10 a.m. to 6 p.m., pool 10 a.m. to 6 p.m. Open fall and winter, 9 a.m. to 5 p.m. daily.

Admission: Parking $7 ($5 fall and winter), walk-ins $2, pool fee $4.

Directions: Take the Central San Rafael exit from US-101, turn east on 2nd Street which becomes Point San Pedro Road, continue about 4 miles to beach, or on further to China Camp.

This lovely, bayside recreation spot is a magnet for families in the know. Swimmers can choose between setting up on the sandy beach for free, or enjoying the chlorinated waters of the lifeguard-watched pool for $4. A 500' long fishing pier hosts anglers of all levels, including kids who are taking their first turns with line and tackle. There are plenty of picnic tables, including a shady spot or two at the waters edge. Sprawling lawns invite Frisbee tossing, tumbling, and tag.

China Camp State Park

North San Pedro Road, San Rafael
415/456-0766 • www.cal-www.cal-parks.ca.gov

Hours: Open 8 a.m. to sunset, except for campers.

Admission: Small parking fee.

Directions: See McNears Beach above.

In the 1880's, a bustling Chinese shrimp-fishing village occupied a spot along the south shore of San Pablo Bay—the large, round, northerly extension of San Francisco Bay. At its peak, nearly 500 people lived here, harvesting and drying shrimp for sale in China and Chinese communities throughout the US. Several structures of the village survive today, preserved in the state park.

You can walk through the village, or enjoy a longer hike through this popular, 1,640-acre park on its 15 miles of trails. Easy access to beaches offers the chance for bayside fun. There are many picnic sites, though you should call about reservations if you want to be sure of your plans. China Camp is a very popular park—expect crowds, particularly on spring and summer weekends. There is a campground.

A Parent's Guide to San Francisco

Chapter Three
Marin & the North Bay

WildCare

76 Albert Park Lane, San Rafael
415/453-1000 • www.wildcaremarin.org

Courtesy: Bob Brown/WildCare

Hours: Open 9 a.m. to 5 p.m., Monday – Friday, call for summer hours.

Admission: Donations welcomed.

Directions: Take the Central San Rafael exit from US-101, turn west on 4th Street, left on B Street, left on Albert Park Lane. WildCare is across from the park.

Tucked away among the side streets of San Rafael, WildCare (a.k.a. Terwilliger Nature Education & Wildlife Rehabilitation) rescues and rehabilitates orphaned or injured animals in the hopes of returning them to the wild. Over 300 volunteers care for whatever comes through the door, no matter what the species. Other volunteers lead classes and nature hikes for kids throughout the region.

Visitors can check out the exhibit hall and courtyard for a good look at many of the animals that are being nursed back to health, as well as a select few that have recovered but cannot be returned to the wild for various reasons. It's a great way to give kids a close-up look at the creatures that live right outside the door in the Bay Area. Call or visit the web site for information on classes and hikes.

Novato

Marin Museum of the American Indian

2200 Novato Boulevard in Miwok Park, Novato
415/897-4064 • www.marinindian.com

Hours: Gallery and store open Tuesday – Saturday, call for current hours.

Admission: Donations welcome.

Directions: From US-101, take the San Marin/Atherton exit. Follow San Marin west for about 3 miles. Turn left on Novato Boulevard and drive 1/3 mile to the park and museum.

Although hopes are high for a move to a larger facility, the Marin Museum of the American Indian has been in the same modest location for over 25 years. The museum receives about 30,000 visitors annually, nearly half of whom are students participating in the excellent hands-on learning programs. Exhibits focus on the culture and history of the Miwok and Pomo Indians who were native to the area.

One must-see event for kids in my book is the annual "Trade Feast" which typically occurs in early September. This two-day Native American cultural gathering features dancers, traditional music, storytellers, games, demonstrations, and more. Food, arts, and crafts are sold. In 2000, tickets were $5, kids under 12 free.

You might also want to inquire about the museum's "Coyote Camp" summer programs. Participants study a different Native American culture each day of the camp and do related art projects.

A Parent's Guide to San Francisco

Chapter Three
Marin & the North Bay

Vallejo

Six Flags Marine World

2001 Marine World Parkway, Vallejo
707/643-6722 • www.sixflags.com/marineworld

Courtesy: Six Flags Marine World

Hours: Schedule varies; call or check website. Generally open weekends, mid-March – October, weekdays during spring and summer school break periods. Opens at 10 a.m., closes at 7 p.m., 8 p.m., 9 p.m. or 10 p.m. with longest hours on summer weekends.

Admission: $40, seniors $30, kids 48" and under $20, under 4 free. Watch the media for special deals and coupons.

Directions: From I-80 in Vallejo, take the Marine World Parkway exit, head west to the amusement park.

Once known as "Marine World Africa USA," this busy amusement park still features animals, both on display and in performance. Now, however, your clan can enjoy stomach churning rides while they wait for the next show at Tiger Island Splash Attack. How about trying Vertical Velocity, "…the only suspended, spiraling impulse coaster on the West Coast…and the tallest, fastest supercoaster in Northern California." And how could you go wrong with rides named Kong, Roar, Cobra, Medusa, Voodoo, Thrilla Gorilla, and Wave Swinger?

Don't worry about the little ones; they can enjoy the interactive play area, meet the Looney Tunes characters, and try several gentle rides like the Seaport Merry-Go-Round. Animal exhibits and acts include Butterfly Habitat, Elephant Encounter, Dolphin Harbor, Reptile Discovery, and many more. The park hosts special events and festivals throughout the summer.

Fairfield

Scandia Family Fun Center

Suisun Valley Road at I-80, Fairfield (Cordelia)
707/864-8558 • www.scandiafamilycenter.com

Hours: Open every day of the year, 10 a.m. until "late" (opens at noon Christmas and New Years Day).

Admission: Various prices and passes available. Golf is $7, ages 6 – 10 and over 64 $5, under 5 free with paying partner, $4 on rainy days. A train trip around the park is $2. Batting cages are 20 pitches for $1.50, $10 for 15 minutes, $20 for 30 minutes, $30 for 60 minutes. Indy prices range from $3.50 to $5.50 for 5 minute race.

Directions: From I-80, take the Suisun Valley Road exit, head south, left at Central (the first intersection south of the freeway).

Pick your pleasure at this family funland that falls short of being an amusement park. Let your young Sammy Sosa or Barry Bonds take some swings at the batting cages. Strap them into GoKarts for a few circuits of the track at Lil' Indy and Lil' Indy Junior. Ride the Copenhagen Express Train, try the Waterbug Bumper Boats, or just let them loose in the Grand Arcade.

Best of all, perhaps, is the rather impressive miniature golf course. If you're looking to spend some quality family time—rich with laughs and conversation where skills are taught and learned and patience nurtured—miniature golf can't be beat.

81

A Parent's Guide to San Francisco

Chapter Three
Marin & the North Bay

Petaluma

Petaluma Adobe State Historic Park

3325 Adobe Road, Petaluma
707/762-4871 • www.cal-www.cal-parks.ca.gov

Hours: Open 10 a.m. to 5 p.m. daily with extended hours for some events.

Admission: Free, except for small fees for certain events.

Directions: Take the Lakeville Street exit from US-101 in Petaluma, east on Lakeville, left on Casa Grande, 2 1/2 miles to park.

Visit the Petaluma Adobe and you'll see one of the oldest preserved buildings in Northern California, as well as one of the most important estates of the Mexican Land Grant period. M.G. Vallejo, then the commandant of the Presidio in San Francisco, first owned it. Vallejo is a famous figure in California history, which explains why many streets, a city, and even a winery are named after him.

With the spacious, open grounds, great view, neat balcony, and cool old stuff all over the place, kids will like this place even on a slow day. The best time to visit, however, is when volunteers dress and act the parts of people of yesteryear during living history events that often include hands-on opportunities for visitors. Check the web site or call for info on "Sheep Shearing Day" and "Living History Day" in the spring, "All Nations Big Time" and "Adobe Fiesta" during the summer, "Fandango" time in autumn, and whatever winter event they come up with.

Sonoma

Sonoma Traintown

20264 Broadway (CA-12), Sonoma
707/938-3912 • www.sonomatraintown.com

Hours: Open 10 a.m. to 5 p.m., daily from June through Labor Day, Friday, Saturday, and Sunday the rest of the year. Trains depart every 20 minutes.

Admission: Adults tickets are $3.75, kids $3.25.

Directions: Traintown is located 1 mile south of the Sonoma Town Plaza on CA-12. Take CA-37 east from US-101 in Novato, left on CA-121, left on CA-12.

Of all the mini-train rides kids can take around the Bay Area, this gets my vote as #1 by far. Traintown features 1 1/4 miles of track, 5 bridges and trestles, and two tunnels—one 140' long. When you board the train in the quarter-scale town of Lakeview, one of four engines will be leading the way. You'll also find a petting zoo, carousel, Ferris wheel, other rides, a nice lake with a fountain, and a refreshment stand. While Sonoma summer days can be hot, there are plenty of spots to stay cool in the shade. The price is a bargain, too!

A Parent's Guide to San Francisco

Chapter Three
Marin & the North Bay

St. Helena

Bale Grist Mill State Historic Park

CA-29, 3 miles north of St. Helena
707/942-4575 • www.cal-parks.ca.gov

Hours: Open 10 a.m. to 5 p.m., closed on Thanksgiving, Christmas, and New Years Days.

Admission: $2 per person.

Directions: The mill is on the west side of CA 29, 5 miles north of St. Helena. From I-80, take CA-12 north to CA-29.

Built in 1846 and now fully restored, the Old Bale Mill makes a quick and fun stop-off on your Napa Valley excursion. The young ones will love the giant, working water-wheel and old milling gear. Inside, the large grinding stone still turns out flour while docents in period garb answer questions and offer tours of the facility. You can buy a small bag of ground grain for $2.

Consider tying the visit into a larger history lesson. After showing the kids how it was done around the time of the gold rush, take your stone ground cornmeal home and teach them how to make a batch of muffins. The dinner table will host a special enthusiasm that evening.

Bothe-Napa State Park surrounds Bale Grist Mill, extending up into the hills. The park offers camping, a stream that flows year-round, picnic areas, and hiking trails.

Napa & Sonoma Valleys

Winery Visit

From CA-29 or CA-12, Napa, Sonoma, and Beyond

Hours: Buena Vista open daily, 10:30 a.m. to 5 p.m. Hop Kiln open daily, 10 a.m. to 5 p.m. Gundlach-Bundschu open daily, 11 a.m. to 4:30 p.m. Robert Mondavi open daily, 9 a.m. to 5 p.m. May – October, 9:30 a.m. to 4:30 p.m. November – April.

Admission: Free, except for Mondavi which charges for a tour with tasting (call for details and to reserve).

Directions: See individual wineries below. Many wineries are accessible for drop-in visits along CA-29 north of the town of Napa, and on many surrounding roads and byways in Napa and Sonoma Counties.

The production of alcoholic beverages may not strike everyone as an appropriate subject area for kids, but I think there is value in introducing the topic gradually to young minds who will be deciding the issue for themselves all too soon. A winery visit supports your own habits at the dining table to instill notions of civility, artfulness, and moderation.

Besides, wineries are cool! Many have amazing buildings and grounds that cry out to be explored. What kid won't go wide-eyed at a collection of working machines, pipes, vats, barrels, and tractors? There may be caves to enter and vineyards to run through. As you drive through the Napa and Sonoma valleys, the upper Russian River, or other Coast Range valleys, follow inspiration and check one out.

A Parent's Guide to San Francisco

Chapter Three
Marin & the North Bay

For some likely winners, try one of these:

Buena Vista Winery
18000 Old Winery Road, Sonoma, 800/926-1266

Billed as California's oldest premium winery, Buena Vista dates back to 1857. The beautiful grounds are perfect for picnics and exploration. Call to reserve a picnic spot. Take CA-12 into the central Sonoma Plaza, head or continue east on East Napa Street, left on Old Winery 3/4 miles to winery.

Hop Kiln Winery
6050 Westside Road, from Healdsburg, 707/433-6491

This National Historic Landmark is housed in a restored "hop kiln," once used to dry hops for beer. Have the kids watch out for the three large chimney's as you approach. Take the Healdsburg Avenue exit from US-101 in Healdsburg, take the left fork into town, turn left on Mill, which becomes Westside, continue 6 miles to winery.

Gundlach-Bundschu Winery
2000 Denmark Street, from 8th Street East, Sonoma, 707/938-5277

A quiet winery, set in the hills, with picnic spots and a pleasant little lake. On weekends in summer, you can take a cave tour for a little intrigue, and to escape the heat. From CA-12 about 1 mile south of the central Sonoma Plaza, turn east on Napa Road, go about 2 miles, turn left on Denmark to winery.

Robert Mondavi Winery
7801 St. Helena Highway (CA-29), Oakville, 800/MONDAVI

This big winery is probably Napa's most famous. Join the tourists here for an interesting tour of the large wine-making plant. Take CA-29 north of Napa to Oakville.

A Parent's Guide to San Francisco

Chapter Three
Marin & the North Bay

Napa Valley

Balloon, Glider & Vintage Plane Rides

Napa and Sonoma Valleys

Hours: Call ahead and reserve for all.

Admission: Costs vary and change frequently. One-hour balloon flights are about $200, glider flights range from about $130 to $230, and vintage plane rides range from $100 to $200.

Directions: From US-101, take CA-37 East, left on CA-121, 7 miles, right on CA-121 (Sonoma Valley Airport on this stretch), continue on CA-121/CA-12, left on CA-29 to Yountville and Middletown.

Talk about excitement! If you're prepared to shelve your doubts and spend some money, consider amazing your kids with an airborne adventure. Several options are available in the Napa Valley:

Napa Valley Balloons, Inc.
707/944-0228, 800/253-2224

Offering daily balloon flights departing at sunrise from Yountville, 10 miles north of Napa on CA-29. Plan on 3 to 5 hours total including shuttling and pick-up time. Dress the young ones in layers they can shed as the morning chill gives way to the heat of the day. Don't forget sunscreen, glasses, and hats.

Crazy Creek Soaring
707/996-8566

Glider flights of 20 to 40 minutes depart from the airstrip in Middletown, 17 miles north of Calistoga on CA-29. Only one or two people can be accommodated at a time.

Vintage Aircraft
23982 Arnold Drive (CA-121), Sonoma, 707/938-2444

How about a roaring trip in a World War II fighter plane? If you're game for some loops and dives, try the "Kamikaze" flight. The 20 to 40-minute flights depart from the Sonoma Valley Airport.

A Parent's Guide to San Francisco

Chapter Three
Marin & the North Bay

Calistoga

Old Faithful

1299 Tubbs Lane, Calistoga
707/942-6463 • www.oldfaithfulgeyser.com

Hours: Open 9 a.m. to 6 p.m. daily, 9 a.m. to 5 p.m. in winter.

Admission: $6.

Directions: The entrance is on Tubbs Lane which links CA 29 and CA 128 about 2 miles north of Calistoga. Turn right on Tubbs from CA-128 or left from CA-29

Yes, California has its version of Yellowstone's centerpiece! In the shadow of volcanic Mount St. Helena, molten rock lies close to the surface beneath the town and environs of Calistoga. Hot springs abound in the region. Indeed, the town of Calistoga was created in 1859 as a resort where weary San Franciscans could soak away their troubles. Unfortunately for founder Sam Brannan, the city folk didn't come and he lost his shirt.

Today, several springs resorts flourish, as does the local Old Faithful geyser that shoots a fountain of steaming waters to a height of 60 to 100 feet. Depending on the water table, it erupts as frequently as every 15 minutes. The average time between eruptions across the year is about every 30 minutes, making the longest wait time bearable for most little ones (call ahead to check on the current frequency). Eruptions last from 3 to 4 minutes.

A Parent's Guide to San Francisco

Chapter Three
Marin & the North Bay

Petrified Forest

4100 Petrified Forest Road, Calistoga
707/942-6667 • www.petrifiedforest.org

Hours: Open daily, 10 a.m. to 6 p.m., winter 10 a.m. to 5 p.m.

Admission: $5, over 60 and ages 12 – 17 $4, ages 4 – 11 $2, under 4 free.

Directions: From CA-128 about a mile north of downtown Calistoga, turn west on Petrified Forest Road and go 4 miles.

This could be a hokey place but isn't, thanks to the genuinely exceptional examples of petrified trees you'll see along the path. Dead trees petrify when they are protected in some way from the elements, and when the chemistry of the surrounding ground is right to allow mineral deposition to be guided by the patterns of the original organic material. In this case, giant redwood trees were covered by ash from the erupting of Mount St. Helena—the biggest peak in the region, clearly visible from many points.

The self-guiding nature trail leads you past several minor items and eight major sites, including the Robert Louis Stevenson Tree with its clearly visible growth rings, the Queen Tree, which sports an oak tree growing in its middle, and the Mammoth Tree—the largest intact petrified tree in the world.

A guided walk goes out at 2 p.m. on Sundays. Call for details.

A Parent's Guide to San Francisco

Chapter Three
Marin & the North Bay

Sharpsteen Museum

1311 Washington Street, Calistoga
707-942-5911 • www.sharpsteen-museum.org

Hours: Open 10 a.m. to 4 p.m. daily in summer, noon to 4 p.m. daily from November through March.

Admission: The suggested donation is $3, under 12 free.

Directions: Take CA-29 through the Napa Valley to Calistoga, right on Lincoln to Washington.

Located in the heart of Calistoga, the museum features regional history exhibits, including some neat dioramas of Calistoga's origins as a retreat for the weary wealthy of San Francisco. You can also visit Brannan Cottage, the home of failed entrepreneur Sam Brannan who built the first Calistoga resort in 1859. The cottage was restored and relocated, and is now joined to the Sharpsteen Museum.

If your children aren't usually interested in museums of local heritage, 15 minutes here may do it for you. What might make a difference, however, are the displays relating to Ben Sharpsteen, one of the museum's founders. Sharpsteen was an Academy Award winning animator for Walt Disney Studios, where he also produced and directed. You'll find Disney memorabilia that includes some original animation plates, as well as family items and Ben's Oscar.

The East Bay

As a long-time resident of Berkeley, I'm a great fan of the East Bay. Just as the name indicates, the area consists of communities east of San Francisco Bay. From the bay shore, a swath of land packed with homes and businesses sweeps upward to the crest of the Oakland Hills. Here, the landscape abruptly changes to undeveloped land, preserved in a series of regional parks, watershed lands, and open space preserves. A family that loves the outdoors could enjoy weekend adventures for years in these backyard public lands.

About half a million people live in Berkeley and Oakland, the chief cities of the region. Berkeley's importance and character come from the University of California, seasonal home to over 30,000 students. Oakland offers a vibrant urban center—largest in the East Bay—and hosts the bustling Port of Oakland, major arts organizations, and three major professional sports teams.

A Parent's Guide to San Francisco

Chapter Four
The East Bay

Several other cities are found along the East Bay shores. Richmond played host to construction of scores of Liberty Ships in World War II. Tiny Emeryville has added a small but tall skyline to the waterfront. Island town Alameda offers beach parks, golfing, and the *U.S.S. Hornet* Museum. Hayward is the site of a California State University campus. Other communities are home to tens of thousands of Bay dwellers, most glad to be part of the California experience.

Beyond the hills are more hills, but the valleys between are filling rapidly with the houses of San Francisco's sprawling suburbs. The main area of development is a band of towns along I-80 and I-680, which loop around the northern tip of the Oakland Hills, then back south along the western flank of Mount Diablo, tallest peak in the region. Walnut Creek and Concord are the largest of several communities in this area. Another concentrated region is found along the I-580 corridor where it runs east-west through the Livermore Valley, including the towns of Pleasanton and Livermore.

The following attractions roughly trace a counterclockwise loop, starting with Berkeley and proceeding south through the hills and flats along the Bay to Fremont. Crossing east of the Oakland Hills to Pleasanton, the path returns northward along the I-680 corridor to I-80 and the Sacramento River delta.

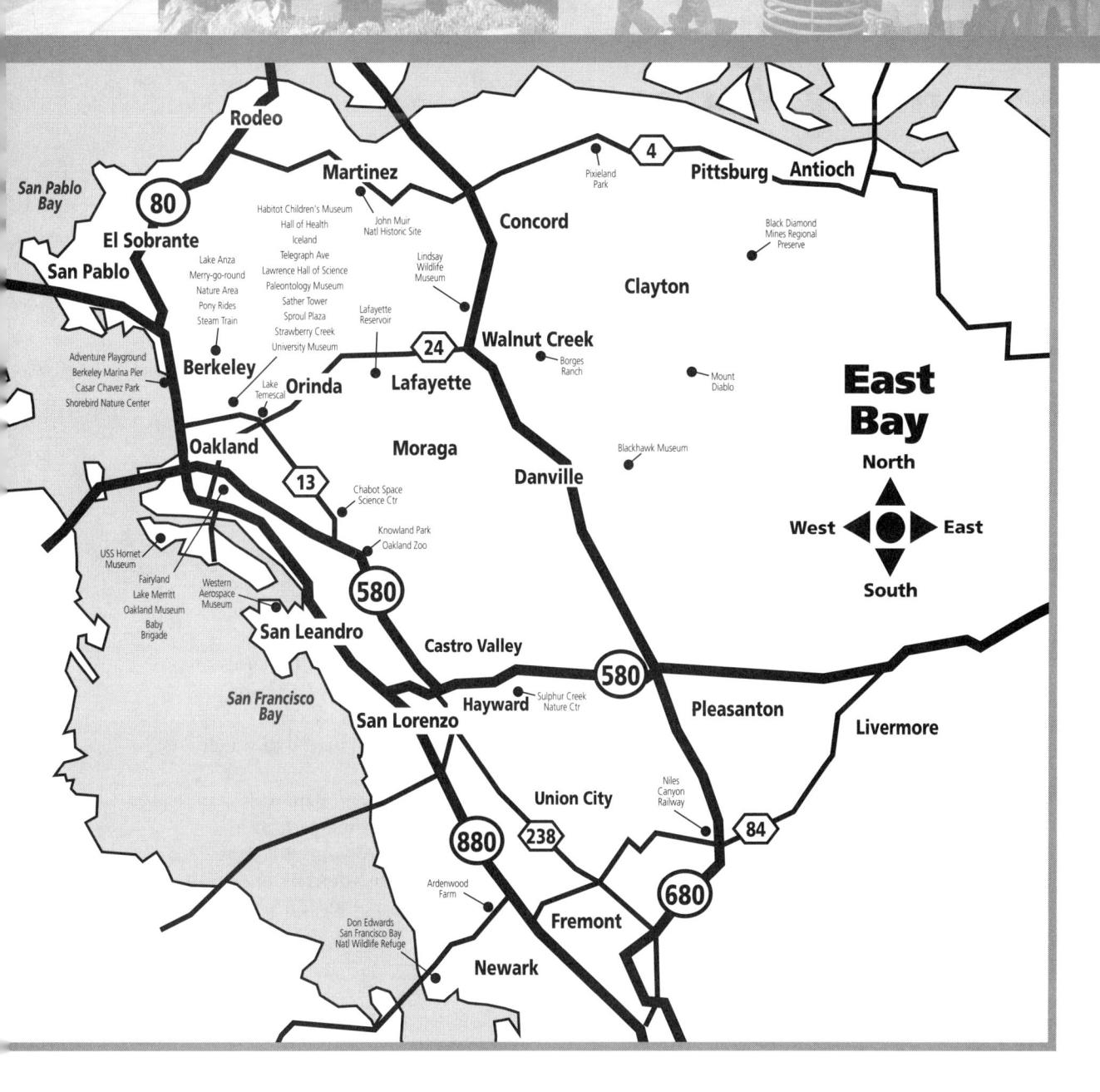

A Parent's Guide to San Francisco

Chapter Four
The East Bay

East Bay

North / West / East / South

- Rodeo
- Martinez
  - Pixieland Park
- Pittsburg
- Antioch
- San Pablo Bay
- El Sobrante
- San Pablo
- Concord
- Habitot Children's Museum
- Hall of Health
- Iceland
- John Muir Natl Historic Site
- Black Diamond Mines Regional Preserve
- Telegraph Ave
- Lake Anza
- Merry-go-round
- Lawrence Hall of Science
- Nature Area
- Paleontology Museum
- Pony Rides
- Sather Tower
- Steam Train
- Sproul Plaza
- Strawberry Creek
- University Museum
- Lindsay Wildlife Museum
- Clayton
- Lafayette Reservoir
- Adventure Playground
- Berkeley Marina Pier
- Cesar Chavez Park
- Shorebird Nature Center
- Berkeley
- Walnut Creek
  - Borges Ranch
- Lake Temescal
- Orinda
- Lafayette
- Mount Diablo
- Oakland
- Moraga
- Blackhawk Museum
- Danville
- Chabot Space Science Ctr
- Knowland Park
- Oakland Zoo
- USS Hornet Museum
- Fairyland
- Lake Merritt
- Western Aerospace Museum
- Oakland Museum
- Baby Brigade
- San Leandro
- Castro Valley
- San Francisco Bay
- San Lorenzo
- Hayward
- Sulphur Creek Nature Ctr
- Pleasanton
- Livermore
- Union City
- Niles Canyon Railway
- Ardenwood Farm
- Fremont
- Don Edwards San Francisco Bay Natl Wildlife Refuge
- Newark

91

A Parent's Guide to
San Francisco

Chapter Four
The East Bay

Berkeley Marina
Adventure Playground

University Avenue, Berkeley Marina, Berkeley
510/644-6376 • www.ci.berkeley.ca.us/parks/marina

Hours: Open Saturdays, Sundays, and holidays from 11:00 a.m. to 5:00 p.m. during school year (closes at 4:00 p.m. November – March). Open daily during summer vacation, weekdays 11:00 a.m. to 5:00 p.m., weekends 9:00 a.m. to 5:00 p.m.

Admission: Free for kids with adults, $5 for child to stay up to 3 hours without an adult, group discounts with reservation.

Directions: In Berkeley, follow University Avenue westward into the Marina, bearing left where the road forks. The playground is at the west end of the large parking lot to the left, the Nature Center just beyond.

Of all the wonderful playgrounds throughout the Bay Area, there's none quite like this one. What at first glance appears to be an old scrap yard full of lumber reveals itself as a complex of play structures, all designed and built by kids. In this litigious era when sanctioned playgrounds have been made as safe (and boring) as possible, the Adventure Playground delivers what its name promises.

But don't be scared off! While the potential for scrapes and bruises may be a tad greater, everything here has been inspected and corrected by construction-savvy parents. Besides, kids quickly learn how to navigate and explore, and it's a joy to watch them enter a world that is truly their own.

The playground is locked up when closed and fully supervised when open. Kids 7 and over can sign in for up to 3 hours while you head off for a jog in the park or a stroll on the pier. You'll need to stay with your under-7s. Regardless of your children's ages, you'll want to stay—both because it's so much fun, and because you can't quite believe it's safe to let your pre-teens climb and run in an area that's not all soft plastic and rubber mats.

A Parent's Guide to San Francisco

Chapter Four
The East Bay

Shorebird Nature Center

University Avenue, Berkeley Marina, Berkeley
510/644-6376 • www.ci.berkeley.ca.us/parks/marina

Hours: Open to the public from 1:00 p.m. to 5:00 p.m., Tuesday – Saturday.

Admission: Free.

Directions: See Adventure Playground above.

Located right on the shores of the San Francisco Bay in the Berkeley Marina, the center features a 100-gallon salt water aquarium, alive with marine life from the surrounding waters. You'll also find a "Touch Table" with intriguing natural items kids can handle, as well as a variety of other wildlife exhibits. Morning hours are devoted to classes and school groups, but you can drop in any afternoon.

Berkeley Marina Pier

East end of University Avenue, Berkeley Marina, Berkeley
www.ci.berkeley.ca.us/parks

Hours: Public access at all times.

Admission: Free.

Directions: In Berkeley, follow University Avenue westward into the Marina, bearing left where the road forks. The pier starts where the road ends with free parking all around.

Nothing gets young legs going like a long, wide, straight runway leading out into the middle of the ocean. ...Well, the *bay* to be precise, but it 's a big bay. Years ago, the pier served to shorten the ferry ride to the city before the Bay Bridge was built. Only 600 yards now remain, but the pilings of the original still march on, arrow-straight far out into the bay, offering a hazard to unwary sailors. Today, it makes a great place for a family walk, day or evening. You'll find a few hardy souls fishing for dinner, couples smiling at the sunset, and families like yours exploring the world.

93

A Parent's Guide to San Francisco

Chapter Four
The East Bay

Cesar Chavez Park
Berkeley Marina, Berkeley

Hours: Open to public access at all times.
Admission: Free.
Directions: In Berkeley, follow University Avenue westward into the Marina, turning right where the road forks. The road passes the hotel entrance, then turns left to follow the park boundary. Park where the signs permit.

The area known loosely as the Berkeley Marina is a large, T-shaped projection created from landfill that extends from the more-or-less natural shoreline of San Francisco Bay. In recent years, the north end of the T's crosspiece was transformed into a wonderful park, complete with a 1-mile paved walkway around its edge. A special portion is designated as an off-leash area for dogs and their masters.

If your kids are old enough to avoid the joggers and strollers, you might opt for a family bike ride or roller blade excursion around the rim. Stop here and there for a walk on the rocks, some seabird viewing, or an easy climb to a hilltop. Save your snacks for the northwestern point where you'll find splendid views of San Francisco, Marin County, and the bridges that access them.

Model airplane hobbyists and kite flyers frequent the park as well. You'll find them concentrated in the southwestern section of the park, near the road that divides it from the harbor and hotel. You may even find a van-based business that rents kites for a modest charge, conveniently parked at the end of the road. It's hard to resist joining those who send their colors aloft to ride the breeze.

Berkeley

Habitot Children's Museum
2065 Kittredge Street, Berkeley
510/647-1112 • www.habitot.org

Hours: Open Monday and Wednesday from 9:00 a.m. to 1:00 p.m.; Tuesday and Friday from 9:30 a.m. to 5:00 p.m.; Thursday 9:00 a.m. to 7:00 p.m.; Saturday 10:00 a.m. to 5:00 p.m.; and Sunday 11:00 a.m. to 5:00 p.m. Closed Sundays from Memorial Day through Labor Day, Easter, July 4, Labor Day, Thanksgiving, and Christmas.
Admission: First child under 7 $6; additional under-7s $3; adults $4; older kids free with adult and child under 7; 10% discount for seniors and disabled; under 7 months free.
Directions: From University Avenue in Berkeley, turn south on Shattuck. From Ashby Avenue (CA-13), turn north on Shattuck. Facilities beneath Shattuck Cinema theaters downtown.

Habitot bills itself as "…the only hands-on discovery museum for young children in the East Bay." The key word here is "young." This one is for kids 7 and under—way under—and it's a must-visit on my list for parents of wee ones. Even though all materials provided are washable, activities can be messy; dress them accordingly and consider bringing a change of clothes.

A Parent's Guide to San Francisco

Chapter Four: The East Bay

The museum regularly varies its offerings, making it a great place to return to again and again. You might find Egg Crafts on the schedule one day, papier-mâché frame-making another, miniature jewelry box decorating on the next. A professional photographer may be on hand for a couple of hours one day to shoot portraits of kids and parents. Storytellers make regular appearances to teach and entertain. Family Art days encourage all to work together making recycled art sculptures, tissue paper flowers for floats, and more.

Safety, education, and outreach are also a big part of Habitot's mission. The police and fire departments cooperate on events that support tricycle and bike safety, home childproofing, car seat checks, etc. A Mother's Day pancake breakfast and similar events are staged off-site. Pick up Habitot's seasonal calendar when you visit or check out their website for upcoming activities.

Hall of Health

2230 Shattuck Avenue, Berkeley
510/549-1564 • www.hallofhealth.org

Hours: Open Tuesday – Saturday, 10:00 a.m. to 4:00 p.m.

Admission: Free.

Directions: See Habitot Children's Museum above.

Since 1974, the Hall of Health has offered interactive, educational exhibits and events on health and the human body. Stop in and let the kids play computer games to learn about genetics, ride an exercise bike to see how many calories they burn, check their blood pressure, look through microscopes, and study full-size models of the body. You can do the same! The Hall also offers scheduled puppet theater presentations and special presentations for adolescents on puberty, nutrition, drugs, and other topics. It's right across the hall from Habitot, below the Shattuck Cinemas.

A Parent's Guide to San Francisco

Chapter Four
The East Bay

Iceland

2727 Milvia Street, Berkeley
510/843-8800 • www.berkeleyiceland.com

Hours: Vary, call ahead or check the web site.
Admission: The cost for open skating session is $6, skate rental is $3.
Directions: From University Avenue in Berkeley, turn south on Shattuck, from Ashby Avenue (CA-13), turn north. Turn west on Derby, left on Milvia.

Ice time is in demand around the Bay Area—the rinks are doing well, and Iceland is no exception. It's not as easy as it once might have been to drop in, strap on your skates, and zip your way (or inch your way) around in circles for minutes on end. Now the schedule is filled with hockey practices, broomball, lessons, parties, and more, leaving the casual skater short on available hours. Iceland is open pretty much every day, but you should call about hours for public skates, or check the web site.

Telegraph Avenue

Telegraph Avenue between Dwight and Bancroft, Berkeley

Hours: Public access at all times.
Admission: Free with an open mind.
Directions: From I-80, take the University Avenue exit in Berkeley, follow University east toward the hills to the end, turn right on Oxford, then left on Durant to Telegraph. From CA-13 (Ashby Avenue), turn north on Telegraph to Dwight, park and walk.

Want to give your kids a lesson in strangeness, diversity, and free expression? Then show them the heart of Berkeley. Take them on a walk along the 4-block stretch of Telegraph Avenue from Dwight Way to the University of California, then onto Sproul Plaza—the large campus plaza surrounded by the student union, the administration building, and Sather Gate. Where else might you find a skateboard gypsy asking a Nobel laureate for spare change?

Visit some of the weird and wonderful shops along the way. Check out the wares offered by the curbside street vendors. Have lunch in one of the more than 40 eateries concentrated along this popular stretch. Grab a cone at Yogurt Park, a few doors west of Telegraph on Durant and one of my favorite stops on any walkabout.

Head east 1/4 block on Haste Street to show your old-enough kids People's Park—the green space with basketball court, lawn, gardens, and grove. This university owned parcel was taken over by activists in 1969. The university evicted them and put up a fence, only to remove it later after intense protesting. Now it exists in an awkward state, co-managed by university, city, and citizens. The museums and other attractions of the university are all a short walk from the commercial strip.

A Parent's Guide to
San Francisco

Chapter Four
The East Bay

University of California

Sproul Plaza

Bancroft at Telegraph, University of California, Berkeley
510/642-5215 • www.berkeley.edu

Hours: Open to public access at all times.

Admission: Free.

Directions: See Telegraph Avenue above.

Telegraph Avenue ends at Bancroft Way, which serves as the southern boundary of the university. Cross Bancroft and you'll enter Sproul Plaza, the primary gateway to the University of California campus. The plaza spreads between the student union to the west and the administration building to the east. Straight ahead are Sather Gate and the bridge over Strawberry Creek. Bring your kids here to catch the spirit of academia and activism.

The best time to visit the plaza is between noon and 1:00 p.m. on weekdays when the university is in session. At that time, you are likely to find sanctioned and unsanctioned speakers having their say, sometimes attracting groups of listeners, sometimes attracting no one. When university or national issues stir the students to action, full-scale rallies occur on the plaza, often at the beginning or end of marches through the streets.

The lunch hour also features free concerts by one of the U.C. Berkeley jazz ensembles and other groups. Bands typically play on the plaza in front of Zellerbach Hall, just below Sproul Plaza behind the student union. You can find out about scheduled performances by calling the U.C. Music Department Office at 501/ 642-4864, or just show up and follow your ears.

97

A Parent's Guide to San Francisco

Chapter Four
The East Bay

Paleontology Museum

Room 1101-A, Valley Life Sciences Building, U.C. Campus, Berkeley
510/642-1821 • www.ucmp.berkeley.edu

Hours: Foyer open 8:00 a.m. to 5:00 p.m. daily, evenings Monday – Thursday when school is in session.

Admission: Free viewing in foyer.

Directions: Adjacent to Strawberry Creek (see below), about one block above Oxford.

Dinosaurs! Is any other word necessary? Of all the creatures that could eat them for lunch, kids prefer dinosaurs. Berkeley's Paleontology Museum is really a research facility; there are only a handful of exhibits you can view, all displayed in the hall and foyer outside the museum itself. Included are a cast of a Tyrannosaurus skeleton, another of the flying dinosaur pteranodon, a triceratops skull, archaeopteryx, and a huge ammonite (cephalopod fossil). Stop in on your U.C. Berkeley walkabout.

Strawberry Creek

U.C. Campus, from Telegraph and Bancroft, Berkeley
510/642-5215 • www.berkeley.edu

Hours: Public access at all times.

Admission: Free.

Directions: Take the University Avenue exit from I-80 in Berkeley. Follow University east, toward the hills, until it ends at Oxford Street and the U.C. campus. Park and follow Strawberry Creek into campus from the corner of Oxford and Center.

The University of California in Berkeley is a great place for a family stroll on a weekend afternoon. The campus is loaded with diversions for imaginative kids. Long, vehicle-free walkways practically shout, "Run on me!" Young yells echo strangely in covered passages among mysterious buildings. A jungle of giant eucalyptus trees is perfect for hide-and-seek, while sun-dappled lawns invite tumbling and tag. Sculptures cry out to be climbed upon. Interesting people are everywhere.

The best options are found along gentle Strawberry Creek, which flows through the south side of campus. A big attraction itself, the creek threads through secret patches of wildland, dives under bridges, and wraps around tiny gravel beaches. Short trails lead to its banks from the larger walks. In order to save the downhill walk for tired legs, plan on starting your walk from the corner of Oxford Street and Center Street, or perhaps from Sproul Plaza where Telegraph Avenue ends. Strawberry Creek is always only a building or two north of Bancroft Way, that bounds the campus' southern edge.

A Parent's Guide to San Francisco

Chapter Four
The East Bay

Sather Tower

U.C. Campus, from Telegraph and Bancroft, Berkeley
510/642-5215 • www.berkeley.edu

Hours: Public access to campus at all times. Tower open daily, 10:00 a.m. to 4:00 p.m., weekends 10:00 a.m. to 5:00 p.m. Daily carillon concerts at 7:50 a.m., noon, and 6:00 p.m., with a 45-minute concert at 2:00 p.m. Sunday.

Admission: The elevator ride to the top costs $.50.

Directions: Take the University Avenue exit from I-80 in Berkeley. Follow University east, toward the hills, until it ends at Oxford Street and the U.C. campus. Park and continue east into campus from the corner of Oxford and Center. The tower is visible from many points.

The highlight of your campus day will be a trip to the top of Sather Tower, also known as The Campanile. Rising 307' above campus near Strawberry Creek, it certainly isn't hard to find. A 50-cent elevator ride takes you to the observation level for spectacular views all around. If you are on top on the hour, your family will be treated to an ear splitting bong or two from the massive tower bell. Still loud but far more pleasant are the carillon concerts, presented three times a day.

University Museum

2626 Bancroft Way, Berkeley
510/642-0808 • www.bamfa.berkeley.edu

Hours: Open Wednesday – Sunday, 11:00 a.m. to 5:00 p.m. (until 9:00 p.m. Thursday). After January 1, 2002, hours are Wednesday – Sunday, 11:00 a.m. to 7:00 p.m.

Admission: $6, students and seniors $4, under 10 free. Free to all on Thursdays!

Directions: From I-80 in Berkeley, take the University Avenue exit, toward the hills on University, right at the end on Oxford, left on Durant, cross Telegraph and park, walk 1 block north to Bancroft.

While it's doubtful that many of the changing exhibits will hold the attention of younger children or those who aren't artistically inclined, the museum itself can be a lot of fun. To begin with, it's a strange, modernistic building with odd angles and weird sculptures. The exhibits inside rotate, but are likely to be unusual and provocative. Duck in on a Thursday (free admission) to see what your children think of Art with a capital "A."

A Parent's Guide to San Francisco

Chapter Four
The East Bay

Lawrence Hall of Science

Centennial Drive, University of California, Berkeley
510/642-5132 • lhs.berkeley.edu

Hours: Open daily, 10:00 a.m. to 5:00 p.m., closed Labor Day. Plaza and sculptures accessible at all times. Planetarium shows presented Saturdays, Sundays, and holidays year round at 1:00 p.m., 2:15 p.m. and 3:30 p.m., daily during school vacation at the same times. Call for lab and resource room hours and usage.

Admission: $7 for ages 19 – 61, $5 ages 5 – 18 and over 61, $3 ages 3 and 4, under 3 free. Planetarium shows $2.

Directions: From I-80, take the University Avenue exit, follow University toward the hills, turn left at its end onto Oxford, first right onto Hearst, right at the end onto La Loma/Gayley, left on Stadium Rim Way to circle above the stadium, left onto Centennial, climb about a mile to the hall.

Clinging to the slopes high above the Berkeley campus, the Lawrence Hall of Science has been a top destination for parents in the know for years. Kids immediately take to the strange modern architecture, featuring an outdoor terrace with a giant model of a DNA molecule. The view from that terrace is spectacular, tempting you to send the kids into the building while you lean on the wall and soak it in.

Inside you'll find topflight interactive displays, including the computer-based ScienceView Vision exhibit, the Gravity Wall, Within the Human Brain, and Math Rules! "YEA!" stands for Young Explorers Area, and offers young kids and preschoolers books to read, blocks and other items to build with, an insect zoo, and puppet theater. Special exhibits open all the time, with names like "Scream Machines: The Science of Roller Coasters," and "Space Weather."

In addition to the exhibits, the Lawrence Hall has a planetarium, biology lab, computer lab, and resource room. It's an amazing place—plan on several visits across the growing years.

A Parent's Guide to San Francisco

Chapter Four
The East Bay

Tilden Regional Park

Lake Anza

Tilden Park, Berkeley
510/843-2137 • www.ebparks.org/parks/tilden.htm

Hours: The swimming beach is open daily during school spring break, weekends after that, then daily again during school summer break through to October. Lifeguards are on duty from 11:00 a.m. to 6:00 p.m.

Admission: $2.50 ages 16-61, $1 ages 1-15 and over 61, under 1 free.

Directions: Follow University Avenue in Berkeley east to the end, left on Oxford, first right on Hearst, right on La Loma/Gayley, first left on Stadium Rim Way to curve above stadium, left on Centennial to crest of hills, left on Grizzly Peak, right on Shasta, left on Wildcat Canyon Road, right on Central Park Drive. The Lake Anza access road will be on your right, with the merry-go-round a bit further down. Both are well signed.

A long, deep valley runs through the heart of Tilden Regional Park. Tucked in the trees on the valley floor is little Lake Anza, with its safe and sandy swimming beach. Locker rooms and lifeguards are included with the entrance fee. There's a lap lane, changing room with cold showers, and picnic tables for snacking (though no firepits or grills). Nice lawns encourage blanket basking, Frisbee tossing, or a game of tag. The lake is popular with parents and nannies throughout the summer so you can count on a kid-friendly scene.

A couple of years ago, Lake Anza was the focal point of a debate on the importance of dressing the youngest bathers in leak-proof diapers. Water testing revealed no problems with coliform or other waterborne bugs, but the park stuck by its new rules forbidding swimmers who aren't toilet trained. If you plan on dipping your toddler into some public waters, head for Roberts Pool (or another chlorinated pool) and pack some swimming diapers.

Merry-go-round

Tilden Park, Berkeley
510/524-6773 • www.ebparks.org/parks/tilden.htm

Hours: Operates from 11:00 a.m. to 5:00 p.m. weekends, holidays, and weekdays during spring and summer school vacations.

Admission: $1.

Directions: See Lake Anza above.

Round and round they go. Little kids seem to love it, and Tilden's Hershell Spillman Merry-go-round will serve nicely. All the animals are beautiful, hand-painted wood, carefully maintained. A calliope plays music. Built in 1911, the carousel was installed in Tilden in 1948 and has been pleasing the little ones ever since.

A Parent's Guide to San Francisco

Chapter Four
The East Bay

Nature Area

Tilden Park, Berkeley
510/525-2233 • www.ebparks.org/parks/tna.htm

Hours: Park open daily, dawn to dusk. Farm animals are out from 8:00 a.m. to 3:30 p.m. Call about EEC program hours.

Admission: Free.

Directions: Follow University Avenue in Berkeley east to the end, left on Oxford, first right on Hearst, left on Euclid climbing slowly to ridgecrest, first right at signed park entrance, immediate left on Canon Drive. Pony rides are on the right at fork. Turn left at fork to park for Nature Area, Little Farm, and Jewel Lake.

More than just a path with a few signs, the Tilden Nature Area is a 740-acre preserve-within-a-park. It is home to Tilden's acclaimed Environmental Education Center (EEC) where thousands of city kids have received their first real taste of the natural world. Weekday programs are for school groups only, but anyone can join in on the weekends. Call 510/525-2233 for program info.

Next door to the EEC is the Little Farm, populated with gentle animals of the cow and bunny variety. You can stop for a look anytime, whether or not you are part of a designated program activity.

As a whole, the Nature Area has several miles of paths, including a very nice self-guiding nature trail with a boardwalk along the margins of Jewel Lake.

Pony Rides

Tilden Park, Berkeley
510/527-0421 • www.ebparks.org/parks/tilden.htm

Hours: Rides are offered April 1 through Labor Day, 11:00 a.m. to 4:00 p.m., weekends only when school is in session.

Admission: $2.50.

Directions: See Nature Area above.

The word "pony" should give you a clue here; this isn't a major trail ride operation. Set the kids up on the backs of the docile beasts and let them imagine the wind in their hair. If you're piecing together a day in the north end of Tilden Park, put this in the mix with the merry-go-round and Little Farm (Nature Area).

A Parent's Guide to San Francisco

Chapter Four
The East Bay

Steam Train

Tilden Park, Berkeley
510/548-6100 • www.ebparks.org/parks/tilden.htm

Hours: Runs from 11:00 a.m. to 6:00 p.m. weekends, holidays (closed Thanksgiving and Christmas), and noon to 5:00 p.m. weekdays during spring and summer school vacations.

Admission: $1.50, $6 for 5 rides.

Directions: Take CA-13 toward Berkeley from I-80 or CA-24, turn east toward the hills on Claremont, follow to ridgecrest, left on Grizzly Peak, right at Lomas Cantada which is signed for the train, immediate left into lot.

What is it that kids like about small trains? Whatever the magic, those in the infant to primary grades range will enjoy the 12-minute ride on this lovingly maintained attraction. The setting for the train is a small valley in the pleasant heights of the Oakland Hills. The engines used are genuine steam-powered miniatures. You can ride in open or enclosed cars. There is access to a couple of good hiking trails from the overflow parking area.

Oakland

Baby Brigade Night at the Parkway

1834 Park Boulevard, Oakland
510/814-2400 • www.picturepubpizza.com

Hours: Film times vary – call or visit the web site for the schedule. Monday is generally Baby Brigade night.

Admission: $5, two for one on Wednesdays, babies free.

Directions: Take the Park Avenue exit from I-580 in Oakland. Head west on Park about a mile. The Parkway marquee is brightly visible on the left. Park on a nearby street.

This one is a dream-come-true for parents of infants up to about 1 year of age. Oakland's Parkway Theater—an independent movie house showing 2nd run films on two screens—has designated the early showing on Monday nights for parents with babies. Crying is not only permitted, it's welcomed! They just turn the sound up a bit to compensate.

There's more! Parkway tickets are only $5, and instead of just the typical, criminally overpriced popcorn and Raisinettes lineup, they offer pizza, sandwiches, salads, draft beer, and other delicious meal-makers—all at very reasonable prices. Best of all, perhaps, theater seating includes comfy sofas and armchairs with plenty of tables for food, drinks, and diaper bags. Get there early to find a good seat and compare notes with other new parents.

A Parent's Guide to San Francisco

Chapter Four: The East Bay

Children's Fairyland

Lakeside Park, Lake Merritt, Oakland
510/452-2259 • www.fairyland.org

Hours: Open October – March, Friday-Sunday and national holidays, 10:00 a.m. to 4:00 p.m.; April through mid-June and Labor Day through October, Wednesday-Sunday and national holidays, 10:00 a.m. to 4:00 p.m.; daily in summer, weekdays 10:00 a.m. to 4:00 p.m., weekends 10:00 a.m. to 5:00 p.m.

Admission: $6, includes unlimited rides. Under 1 free. Parking is $4 in the Fairyland lot, free on surrounding streets.

Directions: From I-580, take the Grand Avenue exit, turning right on Grand no matter which direction you were driving on the interstate. Turn left into Lakeside Park via Bellevue Avenue.

More than a glorified playground but less than an amusement park, Children's Fairyland is a charming throwback to quieter days. Thanks to a recent infusion of over $1,000,000 in funds, this popular facility is enjoying a much-needed rejuvenation. Like the Barney show, it's for younger kids who will love it one year and reject it the next. Ages 1 – 6 is a good target range.

Fairyland has a few options that qualify as rides, including the Jolly Trolley, Magic Web Ferris Wheel, Wonder-Go-Round, Toyland Boat Ride, and the Lakeside Train. The rest of the attractions are what they call "Story Sets." These range from climbing structures to big fiberglass figures, to a small petting zoo. All relate to a fairy tale, poem, or other children's story of some sort. It's enchanting for the wee ones.

A Parent's Guide to
San Francisco

Chapter Four
The East Bay

Lake Merritt Rotary Nature Center

600 Bellevue Avenue, Lakeside Park, Oakland
510/238-3739 • www.oaklandnet.com/parks/facilities/points.asp

Hours: Open 10 a.m. to 5 p.m. daily. Call regarding program schedules

Admission: Free.

Directions: See Children's Fairyland.

Established in 1870, Lake Merritt serves as the oldest wildlife refuge in the U.S. The Rotary Nature Center helps bring the lake's natural assets into focus for individuals and school groups from around the region. Drop by on your day in Lakeside Park for a look at the few, simple exhibits on hand, which have included displays of animal skulls and bones, a collection of live spiders, and an animal or two. Call about their summer day camp.

Lake Merritt Boating Center

568 Bellevue Avenue, Lakeside Park, Oakland
510/444-3807 • www.oaklandnet.com/parks/facilities/points.asp

Hours: From June – September, rentals are available weekdays from 9:00 a.m. to 6:00 p.m., weekends from 9:00 a.m. to 7:00 p.m. The rest of the year, the facility is open 10:30 a.m. to 5:00 p.m. daily, closed Mondays.

Admission: Pedal-boats and 1- or 2-person kayaks are $6/half-hour, $8/hour. Rowboats and canoes go for a straight $8/hour. There's a $10 deposit per boat.

Directions: See Children's Fairyland.

Right next to the Nature Center, you'll find the *Lake Merritt Boathouse*. It's a great place to take in the view across the lake, but you can also rent a small boat and head out onto the placid waters. Pedal-boats are a good choice for fun with virtually no chance of tipping. Rowboats and canoes offer greater range, while kayaks let you zip along. Bring a driver's license to leave as security while you're paddling around.

105

A Parent's Guide to San Francisco

Chapter Four
The East Bay

Chabot Space & Science Center

10000 Skyline Boulevard,
510/336-7300 • www.chabotspace.org

Hours: Open Tuesday – Sunday, 10:00 a.m. to 5:00 p.m. Planetarium and theater are also open Friday and Saturday evenings with shows from 6:45 p.m. to 10:00 p.m. Free telescope viewing offered Friday and Saturday, dusk to 11:00 p.m., weather permitting.

Admission: General Admission is $8, $5.50 for ages 4–12 and over 65. Planetarium or theater admission is $8.75, $6.50 ages 4 – 12 and over 65. General admission plus planetarium or theater admission is $14.75, $11 ages 4-12 and over 65. Admission to all three is $19.75, $15.50 ages 4-12 and over 65. Evening planetarium or theater shows are $8.75, $6.50 for ages 4 – 12 and over 65; or both for $14, $11 ages 4 – 12 and over 65. Kids under 4 get in free to all. Students with valid ID enjoy a $1 discount.

Directions: From I-80, take I-580 to CA-24, follow CA-13 south to the Juaquin Miller/Lincoln exit, east on Juaquin Miller to the crest of the ridge, left on Skyline. From CA-24, exit on CA-13 south and take the Juaquin Miller exit as described above.

Recently opened after a major upgrade, this outstanding facility is a must-visit for all parents interested in the science education of their young ones. The center is perched on the crest of the Oakland Hills, just off of aptly named Skyline Drive. To the west is the bustling Bay Area; to the east are thousands of acres of open space and parkland.

The Chabot Center is rich with options, but they're priced separately and aren't cheap. The main exhibit space features interactive sculptures that teach about planet-shaping forces, as well as a variety of exhibits on the history and scope of astronomy. Interesting temporary exhibits include a special hands-on theme that changes every three months. "Rockets" was a recent offering in which participants had the chance to build and launch small rockets as part of the learning experience (call for exact schedule).

The Ask Jeeves Planetarium seats 240 people under a 70' diameter dome for star shows. The modern Zeiss projector uses fiber optic technology to put up as many as 9,000 stars at a time, along with constellation imagery and numerous other effects. You can choose from about 4 different shows that are offered during any one period, knowing that new offerings are always in development.

Last but not least is the MegaDome Science Theater. A 70mm projector creates a huge image on a 70' domed screen that seems to swallow your vision. Again, about 4 shows are offered at a time. A recent menu included "Mysteries of Egypt," "Solarmax," "To Be an Astronaut," and "Antarctica." If the kids (or you) get queasy, just tell them to close their eyes for a few moments.

A Parent's Guide to San Francisco
Chapter Four
The East Bay

Lake Temescal

From Broadway at CA-24 and Broadway Terrace at CA-13, Oakland
510/562-PARK • www.ebparks.org/parks/temescal.htm

Hours: Grounds open from 5:00 a.m. to 10:00 p.m. daily, swimming generally an option from 10:00 a.m. to 6:00 p.m. daily, spring through fall.

Admission: $2.50 for ages 16 to 61, $1.50 ages 1-15 and over 61, under 1 free.

Directions: From I-580, take CA-13 north to the Broadway Terrace exit, CA-24 east to the Broadway exit, or CA-24 east to CA-13, then south to the Broadway Terrace exit. From the Broadway exit, turn left on Broadway then immediately right, stay right (don't re-enter CA-24) and follow Broadway along freeway to park entrance, on right. From Broadway Terrace exit, take first right from Broadway Terrace west of the freeway (CA-13).

Tucked quietly away in a corner of intersecting freeways, the clean waters of this small lake attract families throughout the year. You'll find a nice swimming beach about 500 feet from the north, Broadway entrance that's served by lifeguards at posted times (call ahead). As with all non-chlorinated swimming areas in the East Bay Regional Parks, only toilet-trained kids can officially go in. At each entrance, there are picnic areas and playgrounds. The lake is periodically stocked with rainbow trout, and you are welcome to try your luck. A snack shop sells goodies and trails circle the waters.

Oakland Museum of California

1001 Oak Street, Oakland
510/238-3401 • www.museumca.org

Hours: Open Wednesday – Saturday, 10:00 a.m. to 5:00 p.m.; Sunday noon to 5:00 p.m.; open until 9:00 p.m. the first Friday of the month.

Admission: $6; over 64 and youth $4; adult students with valid ID $4; under 6 free. Free to all the second Sunday of each month.

Directions: From I-80 or CA-24, take I-580 to I-980, follow I-980 to the Jackson Street exit, straight to Oak (3rd light), turn left, go 5 blocks to 10th Street. From I-880 north, take the Oak Street exit, right on Oak, go 4 blocks to 10th Street.

Perhaps the best of its kind in the state, the Oakland Museum is really three museums in one. The Gallery of California Art displays over 600 pieces, including paintings, sculptures, photographs, prints, and decorative arts items. Named California: A Place, A People, A Dream, the history wing features thousands of artifacts covering all aspects of the state's past, from the days before European exploration to the present. My favorite is Walk Across California where visitors follow the changing ecosystems of the state from coastline to high mountains to desert in the natural science wing of the facility.

Several traveling and special exhibitions are typically on at any time. Recent offerings included Natural Science's look at unearthing a mastodon, the History Department's coverage of the United Farm Workers story, and the Art Department's display of furniture by Gary Knox Bennett.

A Parent's Guide to San Francisco

Chapter Four
The East Bay

Oakland Zoo

9777 Golf Links Road, Oakland
510/632-9523 • www.oaklandzoo.org

Hours: Open daily, 10:00 a.m. to 4:00 p.m. Closed Thanksgiving, Christmas, and during inclement weather (call if in doubt)

Admission: $7.50; ages 2-14 and over 54 $4.50; under 2 free. Rides range from $.75 to $1.50. Parking $3 per car.

Directions: Take the 98th Avenue/Golf Links Road exit from I-580, head east on Golf Links, toward the hills. Follow the signs for the zoo.

Set in 525-acre Knowland Park, the Oakland Zoo hosts 400 animals representing over 100 different species, native and exotic. You'll find the classic favorites—elephants, zebras, lions, chimps, etc.—but there are some interesting rarities, like the sun bear. All are hosted fairly comfortably in 60 exhibits.

A rides area features a miniature train and carousel. The Sky Ride is an aerial tram that lets you get a bird's eye view of many animals and exhibits. You can buy snacks at the Safari Café, or head out into Knowland Park for a picnic and play. The zoo will host junior's birthday bash if you're interested.

Knowland Park

9777 Golf Links Road, Oakland

Hours: Open 8:00 a.m. to 5:00 p.m.

Admission: Free for people, cars $3.

Directions: See Oakland Zoo above.

I don't often hear of folks going to Knowland Park without visiting the zoo, but you can. In the lower part of the park, near the zoo, there are picnic areas and plenty of room for frolicking. A couple of trails access the higher, open space areas, though Knowland isn't known as a hiker's destination. If you are not going to the zoo, I'd pick a different park, otherwise you'll have to explain to the kids why they can't watch the flamingos strut.

Western Aerospace Museum

North Field, Oakland Airport, Oakland
510/638-7100

Hours: Open Wednesday – Sunday, 10:00 a.m. to 4:00 p.m.

Admission: $3 for all over 12, under 12 free, additional $2 for tour of Short Solent Flying Boat.

Directions: Take the Hegenberger Road exit from I-580 and turn west, towards the Bay. From Hegenberger, take the first right after Doolittle onto Earhart (at North Field sign), go about 3/4 miles, then right on Cooke (at the Alaska Airlines hangar). You'll see the museum.

Located in a hangar of Oakland's historic North Field, the Western Aerospace Museum has an excellent collection of vintage planes. Amelia Earhart flew from North Field, as did a number of the first pilots to cross the Pacific.

A Parent's Guide to San Francisco

Chapter Four
The East Bay

The museum features several military aircraft, including attack fighters, a patrol plane, a torpedo bomber, and a trainer. The best piece is the one you'll spot as you approach the facility—a 1946 Short Solent 4-engine Flying Boat. If the name means nothing to you, don't worry; the plane speaks for itself, as does the quality of the restoration work.

Indoor and outdoor exhibits should fascinate kids with big ideas.

Alameda

U.S.S. Hornet Museum

Pier 3, Alameda Point, Alameda
510/521-8448 • www.uss-hornet.org

Hours: Open Wednesday – Monday, 10:00 a.m. to 5:00 p.m., gate closes at 4:00 p.m. Open Tuesdays (gate closes at 1:30 p.m.) but with no access to superstructure and engine room due to ship maintenance.

Admission: Adults $12; over 64, military, and students with ID $10; ages 5 – 18 $5; under 5 free. Tuesday admission $5 for all, under 5 free.

Directions: From I-880 in central Oakland, take the Broadway exit. From I-880 northbound, turn right on Broadway then immediately right on 7th, right on Webster and through tunnel. From I-880 southbound, turn right on 5th after exit, merge into left lane after 3 blocks, follow Alameda signs via Webster Street tunnel. Once through tunnel, follow Webster, right on Atlantic, through gate, left on Ferry Point to ships.

Ever wanted to stand on the deck of an aircraft carrier? Well, your kids have, even if they never told you. Your family has its chance on the Alameda waterfront at the *U.S.S. Hornet* Museum.

There have been 8 ships named *Hornet* in the U.S. Navy. The first saw distinguished service in the Revolutionary War. The seventh fought in the World War II Battle of Midway and was sunk shortly thereafter in the Battle of Santa Cruz. Number 8æthe one you'll seeæwas commissioned in 1943 and saw heavy action in the Pacific. While her pilots were responsible for shooting down hundreds of enemy planes and damaging or destroying numerous ships, the *Hornet* was never hit by enemy fire.

The *Hornet* is also famous as the aircraft carrier that retrieved the Apollo 11 space capsule after the first landing on the moon. I remember, as I suspect some of you do, watching Neil Armstrong emerge onto the deck to the welcome of the servicemen and the wonder of millions of TV viewers before being closed up in a quarantine chamber. See if you can't evoke a bit of that wonder in your kids by telling the story with a bit of passion, getting them to envision life before iMacs and Donkey Kong.

A Parent's Guide to
San Francisco

Chapter Four
The East Bay

Hayward

Sulphur Creek Nature Center

1801 D Street, Hayward
510/881-6747 • hard.dst.ca.us/slphrcreek

Hours: Park, Discovery Center, and Animal Lending Library are open Tuesday – Sunday: park 10:00 a.m. to 5:00 p.m., Discovery Center 10:00 a.m. to 4:30 p.m., library 10:00 a.m. to 3:00 p.m. The Wildlife Rehabilitation Center is open every day from 10:00 a.m. to 4:30 p.m. (call before coming).

Admission: Facilities admission free, except for occasional special events. Classes range from $5 or $6 to $10 or so, more when special materials are required and for overnights. The fee to check out a pet is $8.

Directions: From I-580 east in Hayward, take the Redwood Road exit, right on Redwood, becomes "A" Street, left on 3rd, left on "D" to the center. From I-580 west in Hayward, Castro Valley/Crow Canyon exit, left on Castro Valley, left on Crow Canyon, bear left on Center, left on 7th, left on "D" to the center.

Sulphur Creek Nature Center is "…a wildlife education and rehabilitation facility whose mission is to promote the conservation of local environmental resources…" Staff and volunteers work at the *Rehabilitation Center* to nurse rescued wild critters back to health with the aim of returning them to the wild. The *Discovery Center* is a combination mini-zoo and education center with reptiles, amphibians, fish, and arthropods on display inside, birds and mammals outside. You can even check out mice, rats, hamsters, and guinea pigsæliterally! The *Animal Lending Library* will let you take one home for a week with all that you need to keep it safe, healthy, happy, and fed.

Sulphur Creek also offers a range of classes and workshops for kids and families. "Toddler Time" is for 1- to 3-year-olds, and features very tame animal encounters and nature awareness activities. There are varied courses for 3- to 12-year-olds, and even some special overnight events, complete with campfire and marshmallows. The center offers occasional special events, including a "Wildlife Fair" in June and the "Un-Haunted House" in October. Call for current information on all.

A Parent's Guide to San Francisco

Chapter Four
The East Bay

Fremont

Ardenwood Farm

34600 Ardenwood Boulevard, Fremont
510/796-0199 • www.ebparks.org/parks/arden.htm

Hours: Grounds open Tuesday – Sunday, 10:00 a.m. to 5:00 p.m. year round (gate closes at 4:00 p.m.). Also open Memorial Day, Independence Day, and Labor Day, but closed Columbus, Thanksgiving, and Christmas Days. Farm center and house open Thursday – Sunday, April through mid-November only. Heavy or extended rain may close the farm without notice.

Admission: Thursday, Friday, and Sunday: Adults $5; ages 13-17 and over 61 $4; ages 4-12 $3.50; under 4 free (house tour, train ride, and wagon ride included). Saturday admission is $1 for adults, $.50 for ages 4-12, under 4 free (house tour and rides extra). House tours are limited to adults and kids over 5. Saturday house tour tickets are sold at the park entrance on a first come, first served basis: $3 for adults; $2 kids 6-12 (call 510/791-4196 for house tour information). Tuesday and Wednesday admission to park grounds only is $1 for adults, $.50 for ages 4-12, under 4 free.

Directions: Take the Dumbarton Bridge exit from I-880, continue west on CA-84, take Ardenwood Boulevard exit, turn right at the light and watch for the Ardenwood sign.

George and Clara Patterson operated the 6,000-acre Ardenwood Farm near San Jose in the late 1800s when the East Bay was thinly populated. Today, a 205-acre remnant of their holdings offers a window on the past—an island of pastoral history set amid the bustle of 21st century Fremont.

Visitors will find staff and volunteers dressed in Victorian clothing, performing farm chores and explaining the customs of the day. Traditional crops are grown using the tools and methods of Patterson's day. Farm animals of various sorts will impress the kids, especially the big draft horses that are used to pull wagons and plows. Optional activities include a ride through the farm on a horse-drawn hay wagon, a loop on the steam train, or a tour of the Ardenwood house.

A number of family-friendly events are held at the farm throughout the year. Summer events in 2001 include an "Independence Day Celebration" and "Cajun-Zydeco Festival," both featuring live music, games, activities, food, and drink. October brings the "Harvest Festival," which includes a walk through Joe Perry's pumpkin patch. In December, the farm hosts "Christmas at Ardenwood" and other seasonal events. Head out to see the traditional Victorian holiday decorations and to enjoy caroling and refreshments. For current information, call the farm or check the web site.

Chapter Four
The East Bay

Don Edwards San Francisco Bay National Wildlife Refuge

1 Marshlands Road, Fremont
510/792-0222 • desfbay.fws.gov

Hours: Visitor Center open Tuesday – Sunday, 10:00 a.m. to 5:00 p.m., closed on national holidays.

Admission: Free.

Directions: Take CA-84 west from I-80 or east across Dumbarton Bridge from US-101, exit at Thornton Avenue, south on Thornton 0.8 miles, refuge entrance on right.

Situated in the shadow of the Dumbarton Bridge—southernmost of those that cross the bay—the Don Edwards Refuge encompasses hundreds of acres of salt marsh, tidal sloughs, mudflats, and salt ponds. But there's also an odd little set of bayside hills with wonderful trails that give you a bird's eye view. Down below, paths and boardwalks enable easy access to bird heaven, with various migratory and resident species sure to be around.

Make sure to stop at the excellent visitor center that features wildlife exhibits, a bookstore, and a human or two rich with expertise. The auditorium offers slide presentations on the life of the refuge. Outside is a pleasant observation deck—all they need are umbrella tables and an espresso bar.

Also make sure you check the trail distances before following a line on the map. A couple of routes are a bit long for short legs. Best for the youngest is the self-guiding nature trail that begins near the visitor center.

A Parent's Guide to
San Francisco

Chapter Four
The East Bay

Sunol

Niles Canyon Railway

Main Street and Kilkare Road, Sunol
925/862-9063 • www.ncry.org

Courtesy: Niles Canyon Railway

Hours: Trains run every Sunday from April through September, and the first and third Sundays of other months. Trains depart every 45 minutes, starting at 10:45 a.m. with the last departure scheduled for 3:45 p.m.

Admission: Suggested donation is $7 for those over 12, $3 ages 3-12, under 3 free.

Directions: Access from I-680 heading north from San Jose, or from I-680 heading south from I-580 in Dublin. Exit at Calavares/Sunol/Ca-84 west, west on Paloma Way to Sunol, continuing bearing left on Niles Canyon road, right onto Main, curving left into town.

An amazing group of dedicated volunteers is largely responsible for maintaining, and in some cases rescuing, the engines, cars, and station of the Niles Canyon Railway. The railway offers trips on a stretch of the original Trans-Continental Railroad, including some original telegraph poles that date to the 1860s.

Various engines pull both open and closed rail cars up into Niles Canyon along a restored 6.5-mile stretch of track. The ride takes a little more than an hour. Call to see when you'll roll along behind the 1926 M-200 "Skunk" diesel railbus, or the 44-ton diesel version built in 1943, or maybe even a 1911, wood-burning steam engine! There are specially scheduled trains to view seasonal wildflowers or the stars at night.

A Parent's Guide to San Francisco

Chapter Four
The East Bay

Pleasanton

Rapids Waterslide at Shadow Cliffs Regional Park

2500 Stanley Boulevard, Pleasanton
925/846-4900 • www.locallinks.com/pleasanton/shadow_cliffs.htm

Hours: You can enjoy Rapids Waterslide from 10:30 a.m. to 5:30 p.m., May – September, weekends only when school is in session, daily throughout the summer. General park hours are longer.

Admission: Parking is $5. An all-day pass for the waterslides is $14. Half-day passes are $9, good for either the 10:30 a.m. to 2:00 p.m. or 2:00 p.m. to 5:30 p.m. sessions. You can also pay $6 an hour—perfect for a fast splash. Boat rentals range from $10 to $15 an hour.

Directions: From I-680, take Sunol Boulevard exit, head east 3 miles, turns into Stanley Boulevard, the park is on the right. From I-580, take the Santa Rita Road exit, head south about 2 miles, left on Valley Avenue, go about 1 mile, left on Stanley Boulevard. The park is on the right.

This may be the best deal around on wild water fun. Rapids Waterslide is located in Shadow Cliffs East Bay Regional Recreation Area. Where the Arroyo Del Valle cuts through an old gravel quarry, a small lake has been created, offering opportunities for swimming, fishing, and boating. If your kids are over 42" tall, they can try Rapids' four flumes for a plungingly good time.

For more moderate and cheaper fun, enjoy the more basic offerings of the park. A nice little swimming beach is watched over by lifeguards through the summer. You can rent paddleboats, rowboats, and powerboats with small electric motors for a little cruise. The lake is stocked with catfish and trout if you're interested in catching dinner. There's a refreshment stand (open summer only) and picnic areas. The quieter half of the park features hiking and biking trails along a boat-free watercourse.

A Parent's Guide to San Francisco

Chapter Four
The East Bay

Danville

Blackhawk (Auto) Museum

3700 Blackhawk Plaza Circle, Danville
925/736-2277 • www.blackhawkmuseum.org

Hours: Open Wednesday – Sunday, 10:00 a.m. to 5:00 p.m. and on Monday holidays. Closed Thanksgiving, Christmas, and New Year's Day.

Admission: $8, $5 for students and seniors, under 6 free.

Directions: From I-680, take the Crow Canyon Road exit in San Ramon, head east about 4 miles, right on Camino Tassajara, first left to museum. I-680 can be reached from Oakland via I-580 east.

Once known as the *Behring Auto Museum*, the Blackhawk Museum doesn't allow cars that are merely old. Only those designated as "classic" by the Antique Automobile Club of America make the grade. Names like Ferrari, Pierce-Arrow, Mercedes, and Rolls Royce are at home among the 100-plus vehicles, ranging from 40 to 105 years of age. A few were owned by the rich and famous of yesteryear, including the likes of Rudolph Valentino and Fatty Arbuckle. Housed in Blackhawk's gleaming, modern facility with its huge windows, the cars seem to stand out all the more.

The museum has now expanded beyond cars, adding new Natural History wing in affiliation with the Smithsonian Institute. Check out the *Discovery Room*. When you visit, expect an excellent traveling exhibit with items for the Smithsonian's vast collection.

A Parent's Guide to San Francisco

Chapter Four
The East Bay

Walnut Creek

Lindsay Wildlife Museum

1901 1st Avenue, Larkey Park, Walnut Creek
925/935-1978 • www.wildlife-museum.org

Hours: Open Tuesday–Friday, noon to 5:00 p.m.; 10:00 a.m. to 5:00 p.m. from mid-June – August. Open Saturday and Sunday, 10:00 a.m. to 5:00 p.m. Weekday mornings during the school year are reserved for school groups.

Admission: $6, seniors $5, ages 3-17 $4, under 3 free. Summer camp is about $110/week.

Directions: From I-680 in Walnut Creek, take the exit for Treat Boulevard. Coming from Concord and north, bear left from ramp onto Main, right onto Geary. From San Jose and south, turn left from exit onto Treat, which becomes Geary. From Geary, turn left on Buena Vista, right on 1st Avenue.

More than just a great museum, the Lindsay treats over 6,000 injured and orphaned wild animals a year in one of the world's largest and oldest wildlife rehabilitation centers. On display for all to see are animals representing over 50 species. The animals living in the new 8,000 square-foot facility remain only because they could not be released into the wild. As new non-releasable animals come through the hospital, they are often added to the menagerie.

The museum features a room for kids to enjoy hands-on activities that teach them about nature and wildlife. A series of classes, trips, and tours are scheduled throughout the year. The Lindsay offers a summer day camp, divided into one-week sessions. Kids aged 12 to 15 can volunteer to be guides or counselors.

Borges Ranch

1035 Castle Rock Road, Walnut Creek
925/943-5860 • www.ci.walnut-creek.ca.us/wchs.html

Hours: Open daily, 8:00 a.m. to dusk.

Admission: Free. Living history programs are $75 per child, free to chaperones (call for details).

Directions: From I-680 north of the junction with CA-24 in Walnut Creek, take Ygnacio Valley Road east, turn right on Walnut Avenue, right on North Gate, immediate right on Castle Rock to ranch.

A hundred years ago, Walnut Creek pioneer Frank Borges and his family started a ranch on 700 acres of land near the foot of Mount Diablo. Today, the original redwood home, built in 1901, serves as the ranger station for Walnut Creek's Shell Ridge Open Space Reserve, and as the home of Open Space Ranger Ron White and family. There's a visitor center in the house with historic displays, picnic tables outside, and trails.

A variety of animals reside on the ranch. You might see cattle that belong to a rancher who leases grazing rights. The 4-H Club cares for the rest of the animals, which include goats, sheep, pigs, and chickens. Your kids can certainly view some of them from behind the fence when you get back from your hike.

Better yet, sign them up for one of the living history programs that offer a chance for a hands-on taste of the historic ranching life. The three-day programs include an overnight stay.

A Parent's Guide to San Francisco

Chapter Four
The East Bay

Mount Diablo State Park

Walnut Creek
925/837-2525 • www.mdia.org

Hours: Gates open at 8:00 a.m., closed to arriving visitors 45 minutes before sunset. Day users should leave immediately after sunset to avoid being locked in. Gates are locked for the night; campers must stay until 8:00 a.m. Visitor center open 11:00 a.m. to 5:00 p.m. in summer, 10:00 a.m. to 4:00 p.m. in winter.

Admission: $3 day use fee.

Directions: Take CA-24 east to Walnut Creek from I-580 in Oakland, take the I-680 North exit, immediately exiting onto Ygnacio Valley Road, right on Ygnacio Valley, go about 2 miles, turn right on Walnut, right on Oak Grove, quick left on North into park.

It's said that you can see more of the surface of the Earth from the summit of 3,849-foot Mount Diablo than from any other point on Earth, except the top of Mount Kilimanjaro in Africa. This is because Mt. Diablo commands a view over the length of California's vast Central Valley, the edges of which curve upwards toward the surrounding mountains even as the Earth's surface curves away downward. Even so, urban and agricultural hazes often make such a point moot.

Still, it's a fact that will impress the kids, as will the walk to the summit from the nearby parking area. Once on top, they'll be at the highest point in the North Bay (Mount Hamilton is taller; see Lick Observatory in Chapter 8). The Summit Museum is up there too, featuring a small collection of artifacts.

Consider stopping at Rock City to wander among the interesting sandstone formations. Watch for climbers on the rocks named Gibraltar and Sentinel. If you have a free night coming up, reserve a camp spot at the highest campground, located near the top of the mountain. The sunset view is incredible—enough so even to impress the young'uns.

Two roads head up the mountain, merging into one part way up. Hiking trails abound, as does wildlife. Above 2,500' or so, the mountain seems to take on a life of its own, apart from the surrounding lands. You start to feel like you're heading into the Sierra Nevada. It makes a great, if somewhat challenging, day trip.

A Parent's Guide to San Francisco

Chapter Four
The East Bay

Lafayette

Lafayette Reservoir

Lafayette
925/284-9669 • www.ebmud.com/info/recreation/recmain.html

Hours: Open from 6:00 a.m. to 9:00 p.m., shorter hours in winter.

Admission: Park entry $5 per day per vehicle. Daily fishing access fee is $2.

Directions: Follow CA-24 east from I-580 in Oakland or west from I-680 in Walnut Creek, exit at Acalanes Road, go south, take an immediate left on Mount Diablo Boulevard, go about 3/4 miles to the entrance.

This pretty little man-made lake is encircled by a modest parcel of open space and offers excellent opportunities for family recreation. For some fun on the calm waters, you can rent rowboats or paddleboats, or bring your own canoe, kayak, or other boat that fits atop your vehicle (no motorized boats or boat trailers allowed). A small bait shop offers a place to get a last item or two before trying your luck with the trout. There are picnic areas with barbecues and two nice play areas for the young ones. Trails circle the reservoir and access the surrounding hills.

Concord

Pixieland Park

2740 East Olivera Road, Concord
925/689-8841, 925/676-9612 (hours) • www.pixieland.com

Hours: 10:00 a.m. to 6:00 p.m. daily through the summer season. Call for hours at other times of year.

Admission: Each ride takes one or more tickets, which are sold individually or in books at the ticket booth. Weekday prices are $1 per ticket, $9 for a book of ten, or $10 for an all-access wristband. Saturday, Sunday, and holidays, tickets are $1.25 each, $10 for ten, or buy 5 books of ten and get one book free. Kids under 1 free with adult on Antique Cars, Train, and Merry-go-round.

Directions: From I-80, take CA-4 East near Hercules, exit at Willow Pass Road toward Concord, right on East Olivera. From the south, follow I-680, take CA-242 at the split, East Olivera Road exit, 1 mile to the park.

"Mom, can I go on the Tot-Tanic Slide?!" I always thought that was a fate-tempting name for a kiddie ride, but if your young one is over 36", under 76", and lighter than 150 pounds, he or she can try it out.

Pixieland offers old-timey amusement park fun on a local scale. You buy your tickets at a booth and dole them out for the rides. You'll need to read the rules for each attraction with care to make sure your children fit the guidelines for height, and to see whether or not a big person can (or must) ride along. The Dragon Roller Coaster, Red Baron Planes, and Castle Jumper are for the bigger kids. The sleepily mild Antique Cars, Train, and Merry-go-round are perfect for your pre-schoolers.

The park has a snack bar and will be glad to host junior's birthday party.

Chapter Four
The East Bay

Antioch

Black Diamond Mines Regional Preserve

5175 Somersville Road, Antioch
510/757-2620 • www.ebparks.org/parks/black.htm

Hours: Public access from 5:00 a.m. to 10:00 p.m. unless otherwise posted.

Admission: Parking $4 per vehicle on weekends in peak season only, free at other times.

Directions: Take CA-4 east from I-80, take Somersville Road exit to the right (east toward hills), continue into park.

Most of the historic Black Diamond Mines district is now encompassed in this 5,000-acre park in the foothills near Mt. Diablo, though little remains of the five coal-mining communities where miners and their families resided. The name "Black Diamonds" refers to coal, nearly 4,000,000 tons of which were removed from the area during the last half of the nineteenth century. Later on, sand was mined for use in making glass and casting steel. When the mines closed down, ranchers salvaged materials from the towns—buildings were used as barns, railroad ties as fence posts, old boilers as water troughs. The preserve still hosts some cattle grazing.

As large as it is, the preserve offers wonderful opportunities for hiking and mountain biking. You can also explore the Hazel-Atlas Sand Mine site on a guided tour or visit the remains of the Rose Hill Cemetery. The preserve's Greathouse Visitor Center, Rose Hill Cemetery, Underground Mining Museum, and picnic areas are all close to the parking area at the end of Somersville Road, as are a set of easy hiking loops that are perfect for young explorers.

A Parent's Guide to **San Francisco** — Chapter Four **The East Bay**

Martinez

John Muir National Historic Site

4202 Alhambra Avenue, Martinez
925/228-8860 • www.nps.gov/jomu

Hours: Open year round, 10:00 a.m. to 4:30 p.m. daily. Closed Thanksgiving, Christmas, and New Year's Day.

Admission: Free for kids, $2 ages 17 and up.

Directions: The entrance is at the corner of CA-4 and Alhambra Avenue. Take CA-4 west from I-80 to the Alhambra Avenue exit, follow the signs to the site which is just north of the freeway.

John Muir is one of my heroes; your kids could do a lot worse than adding him to their own hero lists. Instrumental in awakening Americans to the wonders of wilderness, he was also a wonderful poet and writer. He wrote:

Climb into the mountains and get their good tidings.
Nature's peace will flow into you as sunshine flows into trees.
The winds will blow their own freshness into you,
and the storms their energy,
while cares drop off like autumn leaves.

For the last 14 years of his life, Muir lived in the 14-room mansion that's preserved at this site along with a sizable portion of nearby open space. Finely built and furnished in Italianate style, his home is available for self-guided or ranger-led tours. The rangers or docents can really make things come alive for young people who might otherwise be bored to near tears. On the other hand, the self-guided approach allows you to shorten the house experience and head out for a hike. Outside the house, easy paths lead through a nice orchard.

Across CA-4 to the south, the historic site's 325-acre parcel of open space hosts Mount Wanda, a modest hill draped in grass and dotted with oaks. Pick up trail info at the visitor center, which is next to the mansion. Remember to watch for poison oak, and don't let the kids go off trail into the tall grass during tick season (basically the wet season, November through April, though it can vary). You can hike completely on fire roads that are wide enough to avoid both scourges of the hills.

Call or check the web site for information on special programs, including a John Muir birthday event in May, full-moon walks in summer, "Ranch Day" in September, and both "Las Posadas" and "Victorian Christmas" in December.

The Peninsula & South Bay

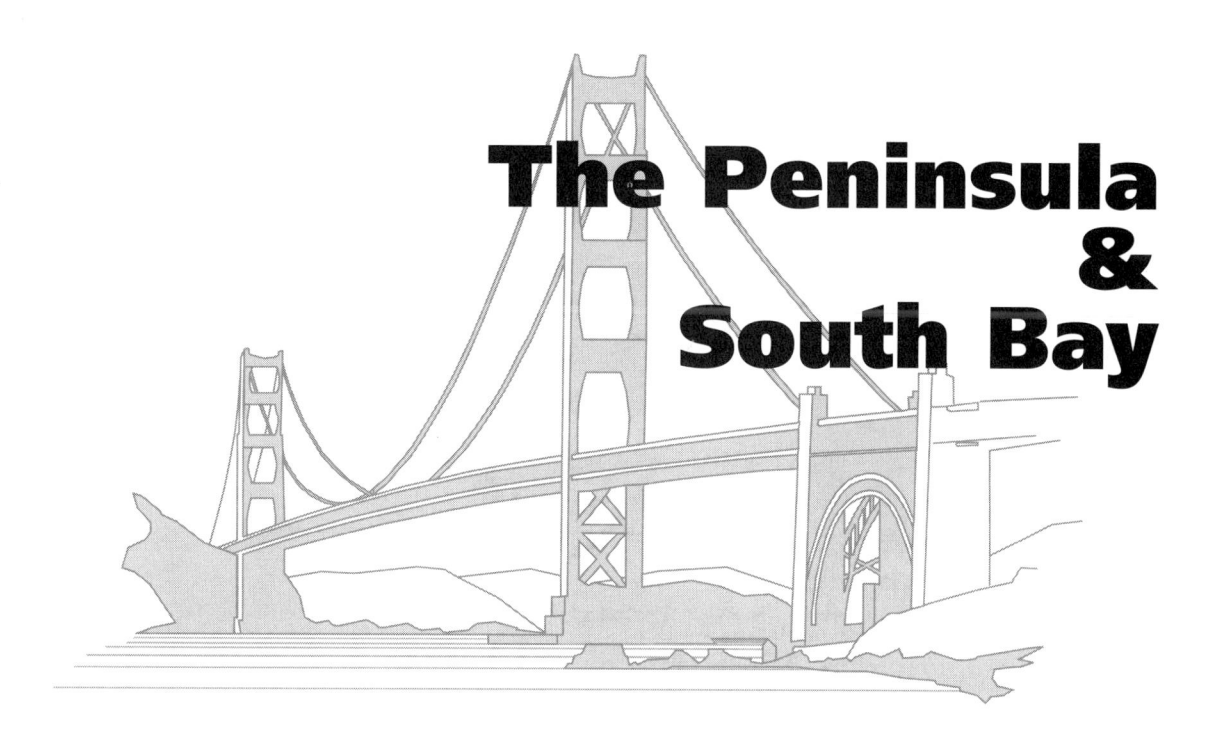

San Francisco occupies the point of "The Peninsula," the 50-mile stretch of land that divides the southern reaches of San Francisco Bay from the Pacific Ocean. The ridges of the Coast Range separate the populated Peninsula towns along the bay from the still largely rural and wild lands to the west. Most communities on the bay side are located along *El Camino Real* (The King's Road)—the chief route of travel and commerce for early Spanish missionaries, soldiers, and settlers, and now a busy, commercial artery.

The region around and beyond the southern tip of the bay is known, quite logically, as the "South Bay." Dominated by San Jose—the Bay Area's largest city—this broad basin offers a sprawling blend of housing, corporate centers, and high tech manufacturing. California's fabled Silicon Valley stretches from Palo Alto through San Jose, and even around to Fremont in the East Bay. As home to about a third of the Bay Area's more than 6,000,000 residents, the region has plenty to offer families and kids.

West of the coastal mountains, two-lane CA-1 follows the moderately rugged Peninsula Coast past wonderful parks and beaches, until it curves inward at Santa Cruz to trace the gentler shoreline of Monterey Bay. For most visitors and residents, bay side options offer easy freeway access with public transit options, while the attractions of hills and coast involve longer excursions.

The following listings are roughly in geographical order heading southward from San Francisco. The first set follow the bay and foothills to San Jose, the second traces CA-1 and the Peninsula Coast from Pacifica down to Santa Cruz.

A Parent's Guide to San Francisco

Chapter Five
The Peninsula & South Bay

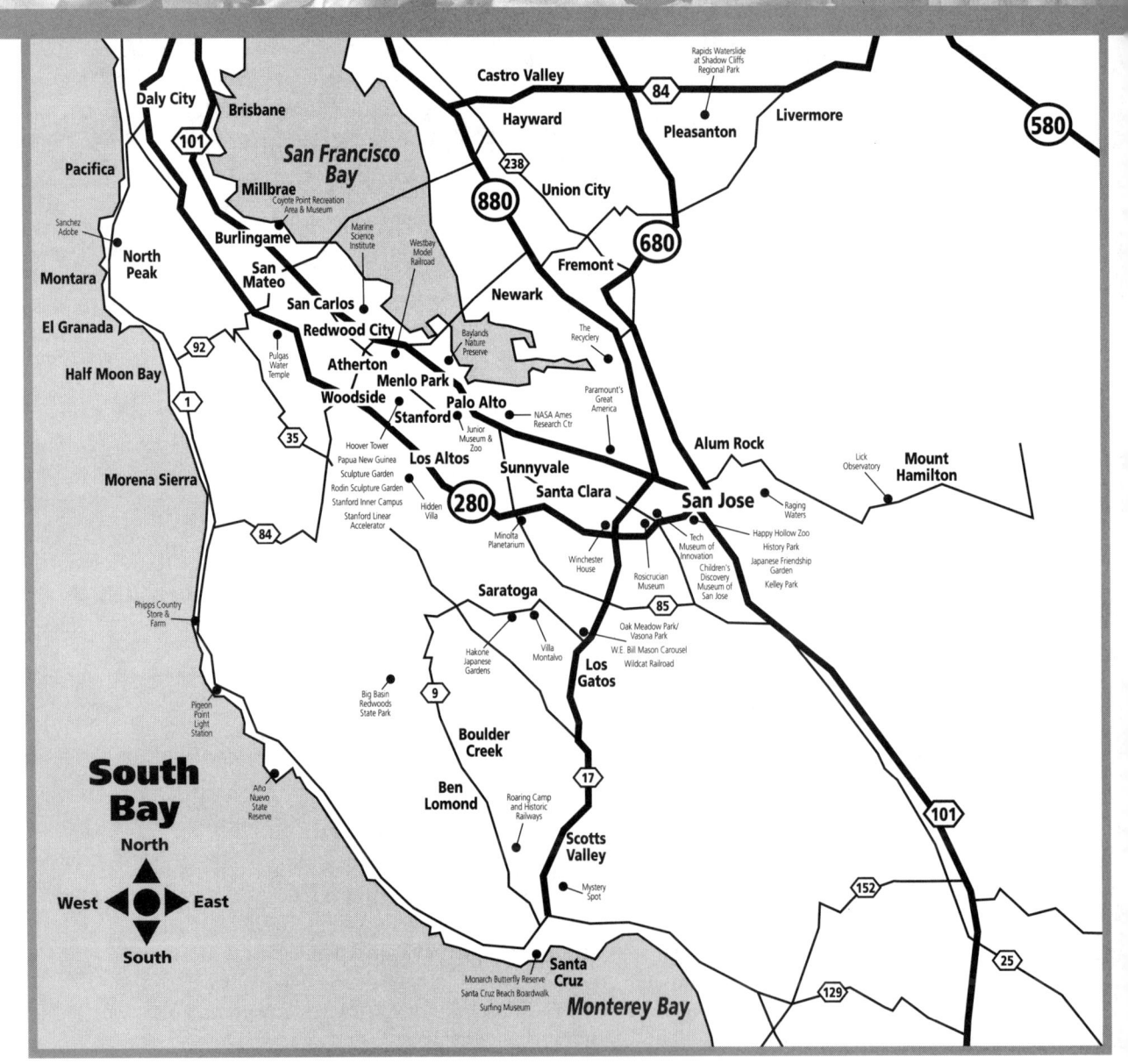

A Parent's Guide to San Francisco

Chapter Five
The Peninsula & South Bay

Burlingame

Coyote Point Recreation Area & Museum

Coyote Point Drive, San Mateo
650/573-2592 • www.eparks.net, www.coyotepointmuseum.org

Hours: The recreation area opens daily at 8:00 a.m. The closing time varies as follows: 6:00 p.m. in March, 7:00 p.m. before Daylight Savings Time starts in April, 8:00 p.m. from the start of Daylight Savings Time through Labor Day, 7:00 p.m. from Labor Day through the end of Daylight Savings Time in October, and 5:00 p.m. from that date through February.

Museum open Tuesday – Saturday, 10:00 a.m. to 5:00 p.m., and Sunday noon to 5:00 p.m. Call for holiday and special Monday openings.

Admission: Museum admission is $3 for adults, $2 for seniors and ages 13–17, $1 ages 4–12, under 4 free. Free the first Wednesday of every month.

Directions: Coming from the north on US-101, take the Poplar Avenue exit, take a quick right on Humboldt, then right on Peninsula, around the loop, and left into the park. Coming from the south on US-101, take the Dore Avenue exit, take an immediate left on N. Bayshore Boulevard, then right into the park.

This waterfront park offers a great chance for recreation on the upper peninsula, as long as you don't mind an endless stream of jets flying over your head on their final approach to the San Francisco International Airport (it's not that bad). There's a bit of a beach, picnic areas, walking and biking paths, playgrounds, restrooms, and other typical facilities. A small marina offers boat launch facilities. Coyote Point Park and Coyote Point Recreation Area are essentially the same thing. Some picnic areas are reservable for parties and such (call 650/363-4021).

Of special interest to families is the Coyote Point Museum, which offers "…exciting educational experiences that enhance curricula from pre-school to college levels." The kids will enjoy live animals while the exhibits teach them about the San Francisco Bay ecosystem and related environmental issues. Recent temporary exhibits included "Side by Side," featuring landscape artworks and poetry, and one designed for 5- to 8-year-olds called, "Recycling: Making Trash into Something New." The museum grounds host a walk-through aviary, theme gardens, and wildlife habitats.

A Parent's Guide to
San Francisco

Chapter Five
The Peninsula & South Bay

San Carlos

Pulgas Water Temple

Cañada Road from I-280, San Carlos

Hours: Temple and grounds open Monday – Friday during daylight hours.

Admission: Free.

Directions: From I-280, take the CA-92 West exit and immediately turn left on Cañada Road. The temple access road is on the right, about 2 miles down, at the south end of the reservoir.

High in the Sierra Nevada, the snowmelt in parts of the Stanislaus National Forest and Yosemite National Park ends up in the Hetch Hetchy Reservoir. Four hydroelectric power plants and 150 miles of pipe and tunnel later, the water emerges in the hills above San Carlos. Here, it is stored in the two Crystal Springs Reservoirs before flowing to the taps of San Francisco, providing the city with 85% of its drinking water—some of the highest quality water in the nation.

The Pulgas Water Temple marks the spot where the water comes up from beneath the ground. It is comprised of a pillared ring (the actual "temple"), a clear pool of water, and a round portal where you can look at the incoming flood. Once upon a time, bold adolescents would dive into the portal and shoot through the last of the tunnel, emerging in the canal that leads to the reservoir. Now the portal is covered by a grid that admits light, but not people.

Few people come here, but I think it's a somewhat magical place to explore and learn. There's plenty of grassy space for play and snacks, as well as access to a poor trail that runs along the reservoir and road.

A Parent's Guide to San Francisco

Chapter Five
The Peninsula & South Bay

Redwood City

Marine Science Institute

500 Discovery Parkway, Redwood City
650/364-2760 • www.sfbaymsi.org

Hours: Call or check the web site for Discovery Voyage times (only a few open to the public every year).

Admission: Discovery Voyage prices for individuals are $35 for adults, $25 ages 10-18.

Directions: Exit at Woodside Road/Seaport Boulevard, head east toward the bay on Seaport, left on Chesapeake Drive through the business park to the Cargill Salt gate, left on the road in front of the gate, around the salt pile, follow signs to MSI.

The main asset of Marine Science Institute (MSI) is the *R/V Robert G. Brownlee*, a 90' boat designed specifically to take kids on "Discovery Voyage" trips through the San Francisco Bay and Sacramento River Delta. MSI serves thousands of kids from schools throughout the south bay, giving them a hands-on appreciation of bay and delta marine life and ecosystems. A few times a year, the institute schedules trips open to the public—investigate your options well ahead of time. MSI also hosts guided nature walks and slide shows about local marine ecology.

MSI is developing a marine science center, which will eventually be open to the public.

Menlo Park

Westbay Model Railroad

1090 Merrill Street, Menlo Park
650/322-0685 • scofolks.ocston.org/~leo/westbay.htm

Hours: The rail layout is open to the public on the fourth Wednesday of the month from 7:00 p.m. to 10:00 p.m.

Admission: Free.

Directions: Turn northwest on Santa Cruz Avenue from El Camino Real in the center of Menlo Park. Go one block to Merrill Street.

It's only open one evening every month, but if your young one is interested in model railroading, this is a place you won't want to miss. The Westbay Model Railroad Association formed in 1947, and they've been upgrading their layout ever since. Housed in a Southern Pacific freight depot, the layout features "O," "S," and "HO" scale lines, intermingled in a U-shaped layout viewable from several angles.

A Parent's Guide to San Francisco

Chapter Five
The Peninsula & South Bay

Stanford University

Hoover Tower

Stanford University, Palo Alto
650/723-2053 • www.stanford.edu/home/visitors

Hours: Observation Deck open daily, 10:00 a.m. to 4:30 p.m., closed during finals and academic breaks.

Admission: $2, $1 kids and seniors.

Directions: From US-101 in Palo Alto, take the Embarcadero Road exit west toward Palo Alto, go 2 miles, cross El Camino Real, becomes Galvez, right on Campus Drive, left on Palm Drive, park along or near loop and walk. Inner campus is straight ahead; tower can be seen from many points.

Like others of its type, the Hoover Tower offers basically only one attraction to kids—going up to the top in an elevator and seeing for miles. Once on top, you can look north along the bay lowlands toward San Francisco, east over the bay at Fremont (the bridge in view is the Dumbarton), south across the economically incomparable Silicon Valley, and west at the lush hills of the Coast Range. And then, down, out, and on to your next adventure. This visit is good for a half-hour, tops.

Stanford Inner Campus

Stanford University, Palo Alto
650/723-2560 • www.stanford.edu/home/visitors

Hours: Public access at all times.

Admission: Free.

Directions: See Hoover Tower above.

This is a great place to be riding bikes, but even kids on foot will have a blast. Play hide-and-seek among the colonnaded walks. Make your way up and down steps, and through archways and tunnels, until you emerge in the beautiful central quad where it's almost impossible not to run. Round the corner to find a chattering fountain, an interesting sculpture, a charming garden, a bench for sitting, or a lawn for tumbling. Students are likely to be about almost any time of year, studying, chatting, or walking hurriedly between classes. Jugglers and musicians sometimes express themselves in an inviting courtyard. In all, it's a great place to walk and play with the kids while letting them come to love the feel of a higher education environment.

A Parent's Guide to San Francisco

Chapter Five
The Peninsula & South Bay

Papua New Guinea Sculpture Garden

Lomita and Santa Teresa Drives, Stanford University, Palo Alto
650/723-2560 • www.stanford.edu/home/visitors

Hours: Public access at all times.

Admission: Free.

Directions: From US-101 in Palo Alto, take the Embarcadero Road exit west toward Palo Alto, go 2 miles, cross El Camino Real, becomes Galvez, left on Campus Drive and follow it around campus, right on Mayfield or Lane W, right on Lomita.

So you're walking along, having parked your car a block away from the sculpture garden, and suddenly your 6-year-old spots tall totems looming through the trees like giants. "Mom, look!" You smile, having set up another moment of discovery and wonder for that little one who was sleeping in a crib such a short time ago—just yesterday it seems. The totems are authentic to the native people of Papua New Guinea (at least one of them was carved on site). The kids can play all about since the totems are not set in any formal garden like the Rodin sculptures across campus.

Rodin Sculpture Garden

Lomita Drive and Museum Way, Stanford University, Palo Alto
650/723-3469 • www.stanford.edu/home/visitors

Hours: Public access at all times. Tours offered Saturdays at 11:00 a.m. and Sundays at 3:00 p.m., rain or shine.

Admission: Free.

Directions: From US-101 in Palo Alto, take the Embarcadero Road exit west toward Palo Alto, go 2 miles, cross El Camino Real, becomes Galvez, right on Campus Drive, left on Palm Drive, right on Museum Way.

You might think that appreciating sculpture is a stretch for your bunch, but Rodin has impressed plenty of young people for a lot of years. His figures are bold, intense, and muscular, not to mention often nude. The writhing, anguished figures around the portal on his *Gates of Hell* could be the stuff of bad dreams if you weren't there to offer perspective. Rodin's *Thinker*, of course, is a classic that all kids should know.

The sculpture garden itself is fun to walk and run (and climb) around. It's set immediately adjacent to the renovated art museum, which I don't list here but might be right for your older artists. All around are the lawns, walks, groves, and other inviting wonders of the largest campus in the world.

A Parent's Guide to San Francisco

Chapter Five
The Peninsula & South Bay

Stanford Linear Accelerator

2575 Sand Hill Road, Palo Alto
650/926-2204 • www2.slac.stanford.edu

Hours: Two-hour tours are by appointment, or by signing on to one of a varying slate of available tour dates.

Admission: Free.

Directions: From I-280, take the Sand Hill Road exit in Palo Alto, head east a half-mile to the entrance on the right.

Can your science buff get excited about a perfectly straight, 2-mile long tunnel to the quantum realm? While it has always seemed strange to me that this precision, atom-smashing facility is located a stone's throw from the San Andreas Fault, it is a technical marvel and a major center for research into the vanishingly small. With its millions of dollars worth of ultra-high tech equipment, the facility is impressive.

A few monthly tour dates are scheduled several weeks in advance—call in and sign up. You may also be able to schedule a tour by appointment, especially if you can put together a small group with some kind of a science theme. How about the Hometown Neighborhood Science Club, composed of your middle school child and four of her friends?

Palo Alto

Baylands Nature Preserve

Embarcadero Road, Palo Alto
650/329-2506 • www.city.palo-alto.cw.us/ross

Hours: The preserve is open from 8:00 a.m. to sunset daily. Baylands Interpretive Center is open 10:00 a.m. to 5:00 p.m. Tuesday and Wednesday, 2:00 p.m. to 5:00 p.m. Thursday and Friday, 1:00 p.m. to 5:00 p.m. Saturday and Sunday. Ecology workshops are offered Saturday and Sunday at 4:00 p.m.

Admission: Free.

Directions: Take the Embarcadero Road exit from US-101 in Palo Alto, head east, toward the bay, turning left where the road hits the marsh to road's end.

Your first stop at Baylands should be the Lucy Evans Baylands Nature Interpretive Center, located where you'll park at the end of Embarcadero Road. If it's open, you can sample the offerings inside, but it is also the place to get oriented any time. Outside, you can take the boardwalk out over Harriet Mandy Marsh to the edge of the bay.

Marked paths head off in three directions from the Center, leading to a total a 14 miles of designated trail. Expect to see plenty of resident waterfowl and migratory birds in season, including Canada geese, mallards, coots, avocets, stilts, gulls, egrets, and more. The endangered clapper rail and salt-marsh harvest mouse both have a home here.

Check with the center to find out about family-oriented events. "Birds, Bikes and Binoculars," and "Beginning Birdwatching" are two that are offered during the winter. Guided interpretive walks go out every weekend afternoon and ecology workshops are offered on Sunday. The preserve has restrooms, drinking water, and picnic tables with barbecues.

A Parent's Guide to San Francisco

Chapter Five
The Peninsula & South Bay

Junior Museum & Zoo

1451 Middlefield Road, Palo Alto
650/329-2111 • www.artcom.com/museums/nv/mr/94301.htm

Hours: Open Tuesday – Saturday, 10:00 a.m. to 5:00 p.m., and Sunday 1:00 p.m. to 4:00 p.m.

Admission: Donations are accepted.

Directions: Located in Rinconada Park. Take the Embarcadero Road west exit from US-101 in Palo Alto, go west toward the hills on Embarcadero, turn right on Middlefield, go 1 block, turn right into parking area.

The goal of the aptly named Junior Museum & Zoo is, "… to provide process oriented experiences that allow young people to develop good observational skills, to learn to ask provocative questions and to understand that they have the capacity within themselves to take action based on their questions and observations." What that means is that your pre-school and elementary kids will have cool things to play with and gentle animals to get excited about. Inside are several themed interactive exhibits with new ones introduced periodically to keep things fresh. Outside is the wonderful little zoo, home to several birds, reptiles, and mammals that are safe enough for close encounters.

129

A Parent's Guide to San Francisco

Chapter Five
The Peninsula & South Bay

Los Altos Hills

Hidden Villa

26870 Moody Road, Los Altos Hills
650/949-8650 • www.hiddenvilla.org

Hours: You can visit Hidden Villa Tuesday – Sunday during daylight hours, except during much of the summer when it becomes a summer camp. Events and camps have varying schedules.

Admission: Parking is $5 per vehicle. Camps and events have various fees.

Directions: Take the El Monte Road exit from I-280 in Los Altos Hills, head southwest on El Monte toward Foothill College, go about 1/3 mile, turn left on Moody by the fire station, follow Moody 1 3/4 miles to Hidden Villa.

Located on 1,600 acres of farm and wild land in the Los Altos Hills, Hidden Villa is, as they say, "a place like no other." They offer multi-cultural summer camp programs for kids ages 6 through 18, environmental education for school groups, community programs, guided hikes, and cultural performances. There's even a hostel, which offers budget, dorm-style lodging to travelers from around the globe.

You'll probably be most interested in the weekend activities for kids and families. You can sign on for events such as a stargazing party, campfire sing-along, overnight wilderness adventure, "Halloween Haunt," or "Saturday on the Farm for Kids." All involve participation and are guided by the mission of connecting kids with the planet and each other. Or, you can just stop up for a walk through the woods and hills.

A Parent's Guide to San Francisco

Chapter Five
The Peninsula & South Bay

Mountain View

NASA Ames Research Center

Moffett Field, Mountain View
650-604-6274 • www.arc.nasa.gov

Hours: The Visitor Center is open Monday – Friday from 8:00 a.m. to 4:30 p.m.

Admission: Free.

Directions: Take the Moffett Field exit from US-101 in Mountain View, turn left in front of the Moffett Field main gate, and follow the signs to the visitor center.

Formerly a Naval Air Station, sprawling *Moffett Field* now hosts several federal, military, and civilian agencies involved in various projects. Public access to the facilities is less than it once was, with only the *Ames Visitor Center* of the NASA Ames Research Center offering regular hours. Even so, it is well worth a visit with your middle years and young teen science kids. Exhibits include a moon rock, a 1/3-size mock space shuttle, a model of the international space station, and the backup Mercury capsule for Alan Shepard.

At this time, it's not possible to visit the amazing wind tunnel (the world's largest), or any of the other interesting Moffett facilities. Watch for the opening of a new public science center in an old hangar in a couple of years.

Cupertino

Minolta Planetarium

21250 Stevens Creek Boulevard, Cupertino
408/864-8814 • planetarium.deanza.fhda.edu

Hours: Schedule varies, shows typically presented on Saturday night at 7:00 p.m., sometimes with a second showing at 8:30 p.m. Summer schedule and offerings differ. Call for current information.

Admission: $6 for adults, $4 for seniors and kids under 12.

Directions: Take CA-85 south from US-101 in Mountain View or from I-280 in Cupertino, take Stevens Creek Boulevard exit, turn left (east) to De Anza College and planetarium.

When the houselights dim, the 50' dome of the Minolta Planetarium comes alive with thousands of stars. If bedtime can be stretched until 9:00 or so, bring the kids out to stretch their horizons. Once a week, shows for children are on the slate with titles like, "Space Bus," "Our Place in Space," "Endless Horizons," "Magic Sky," "Space Elves," and "Winter Wonders." Each is targeted to a specific age range, including a few for those as young as 3. Call ahead or check the web site for the current lineup. If the weather cooperates, the family can enjoy telescope viewing of the real thing outside, after the show.

A Parent's Guide to San Francisco

Chapter Five
The Peninsula & South Bay

Los Gatos

Oak Meadow Park/Vasona Park

Blossom Hill Road at University Avenue, Los Gatos
408/399-5781

Hours: The parks are open from 8:00 a.m. to sunset. Carousel and train operate weekends year round, and daily from March 15 through October 31. Hours are 11:00 a.m. to 3:00 p.m. in winter, 10:30 a.m. to 4:30 p.m. the rest of the year.

Admission: Park entry is free. Rides on carousel and train are $1, under 3 or disabled free.

Directions: From CA-17 south of San Jose, take the CA-9/Saratoga Road exit west, turn right on North Santa Cruz, go 2/3 mile, turn right on Blossom Hill to the park.

One of the nicer kid parks in the San Jose suburbs is Los Gatos' Oak Meadow. There's a good playground, reservable and drop-in picnic spots with barbecues, and a huge meadow for all sorts of run and tumble play. Best of all are the two options described below—how can you miss with a train and a merry-go-round?

Oak Meadow is really just a city-owned corner of the much larger Vasona Lake County Park, which, as you might guess, features Vasona Lake. While completely surrounded by housing areas, the park retains a wild feeling. The lake plays host to ducks, egrets, and other waterfowl. A trail that runs the length of the park is part of the much longer Los Gatos Creek Trail that follows a narrow greenbelt from west San Jose nearly 10 miles to Lexington Reservoir (much of it, unfortunately, right along the freeway).

Billy Jones Wildcat Railroad

Blossom Hill Road at University Avenue, Los Gatos
408/395-RIDE • www.losgatosx.com/business/nonprofit/billyjones

Not too long ago, when the foothills hosted farms instead of million-dollar homes, Billy Jones grew apples. He built a small rail line to move goods around the orchard and used to give the local kids free rides behind the miniature locomotive. When the days of Billy and the orchard passed, dedicated enthusiasts saved the railroad, relocating it to Oak Meadow Park for all to enjoy. Now you and the family can add a leisurely ride through meadow and grove to your day in the park. The 1/3-scale diesel engine can pull over 100 riders at a time. A food stand offers refreshments. The train is wheelchair accessible.

W.E. Bill Mason Carousel

Blossom Hill Road at University Avenue, Los Gatos
408/395-RIDE • www.losgatosx.com/business/nonprofit/billyjones

Originally built in Britain for San Francisco's 1915 Panama-Pacific Exposition, the carousel was fully restored in a 15-year project by the "Billy Jones volunteers." Riders will enjoy music from a replicated Wurlitzer organ. Each of the 36 horses is lovingly maintained; they're bound to enchant the tot set.

A Parent's Guide to San Francisco

Chapter Five
The Peninsula & South Bay

Milpitas

The Recyclery

1601 Dixon Landing Road, Milpitas
408/945-2807

Hours: Call for current hours and tour reservations.

Admission: Free.

Directions: Take the Dixon Landing Road exit from I-880, north of San Jose in Milpitas, head west toward the bay.

How about taking the kids to the dump? Okay, so it's not exactly Disneyland, but if you want to give them a vivid understanding of what happens after that truck drives away on trash day, this is the place.

It's actually a lot of fun. The education center has exhibits on waste and recycling, featuring the rather famous Wall of Garbage—a 100 foot-long construction of the trash thrown out by an average family of four in a year. The kids can see a bit of the operation of the landfill from a safe, clean distance, as well as learning about how much of their trash is recycled back to usefulness, and how it is done. You will need to put a small group together and call to reserve a tour date.

Saratoga

Hakone Japanese Gardens

21000 Big Basin Way, Saratoga
408/741-4994 • www.hakone.com

Hours: Open weekdays from 10:00 a.m. to 5:00 p.m., weekends and holidays from 11:00 a.m. to 5:00 p.m. Docent-led tours are offered April – September on Saturday and Sunday from 1:00 p.m. to 4:00 p.m. The gardens are closed on Christmas and New Year's Day.

Admission: Donations welcomed.

Directions: From CA-17 south of San Jose, take the CA-9/Saratoga Los Gatos Road exit, go north toward Saratoga, turn left on Big Basin Way, the gardens are on your left.

Rules rule here. No pets, radios, musical instruments, food, or drink allowed. Kids under 10 must be with an adult at all times. Toss nothing into the koi pond, including food. Take no cuttings and don't pluck leaves or otherwise damage the plants. The gardens are so discouraging of playfulness in their publicity that I'm not sure why I list them at all, except that kids seem to love it here. I think it's because the artfulness involved in the creation of such a wonderful, peaceful garden taps something deep in all humans, old, young, and younger. Children delight in the winding paths, the bamboo garden, and the cool pond.

Leave your football bruiser at home this time—make this visit a special trip for you and the sensitive, curious one who has an eye for beauty.

Chapter Five
The Peninsula & South Bay

Villa Montalvo

15400 Montalvo Road, Saratoga
408/356-2729 (park), 408/956-5800 (villa)
www.parkhere.org, www.villamontalvo.com

Hours: Park open to public daily until dusk. Event schedule varies, call or check the web site for a current calendar.

Admission: Access to the grounds and county park are free. Most events for kids are about $8 for children, $16 for adults. Adult prices for regular events range from about $30 to $75.

Directions: From I-280 in San Jose, take CA-17 south, exit onto CA-9 toward Saratoga, go about 3 1/2 miles, left on Montalvo Road.

Nestled in the foothills of Saratoga is the lovely, Mediterranean-styled Villa Montalvo. It's the home of Montalvo—an organization with the mission, "…to inspire a love of the arts in everyone through creation, education, and presentation in extraordinary ways and settings." The villa offers a busy calendar of events to the public, including gallery exhibitions, concerts, literary readings, and more.

While many of the events aimed at adults will enrich the lives of your children, a fair number are specifically targeted toward the young and young-at-heart. At the time of publication, the upcoming line-up included the Czechoslovakian-American Marionettes, the Tears of Joy Puppets presenting the *Adventures of Perseus*, Theaterworks performing vignettes from *Reading Rainbow*, California Theater Center's *Beauty and the Beast,* and the Bayshore Lyric Opera with *Hansel und Gretel*.

Much of the 175 acres of land surrounding the villa and performance area comprise a county park and arboretum, offering daily, free opportunities for hiking and outdoor fun. It's a wonderful setting to take your young ones during the day, even if a pricey show isn't on the menu.

A Parent's Guide to San Francisco

Chapter Five
The Peninsula & South Bay

Big Basin

Big Basin Redwoods State Park

21600 Big Basin Way, Boulder Creek
www.bigbasin.org

Hours: Day use hours 6:00 a.m. to 10:00 p.m. Visitor center is always open in season and generally staffed from about 10:00 a.m. to 5:00 p.m.

Admission: Day use parking $3, camping $12.

Directions: CA-236 loops through the heart of the park and is your only good choice for access. From San Francisco and the northern Peninsula, take I-280 to CA-84. Follow CA-84 west to the crest of the ridge, CA-35 south, and CA-9 west to CA-236. From the San Jose area, take CA-17 to CA-9, then CA-9 to CA-236. From Santa Cruz, follow CA-9 north to CA-236. No matter how you approach, expect a long, winding trip of as much as an hour.

Successfully isolated from the masses by long, winding access roads, this gem of a park has been long in the making. Pieced together parcel by parcel, Big Basin preserves some magical spots, not all clearly advertised in the park literature. Eighty miles of trail thread through the park's 18,000 acres, stretching from the Pacific Ocean to the 2,000' ridgecrests of the Santa Cruz Mountains.

Don't waste Big Basin on your littlest ones unless they can easily weather the long minutes of slow curves on the park access road—or unless you check out the park's western tip along CA-1. Instead, save this for your 10-and-ups who can manage a 5-mile or longer hiking loop. You can see some nice big trees and enjoy nature right around the visitor center and campground, but you have to hoof it a good way to visit the nicest groves and waterfalls.

My favorite area is the stretch along Waddell Creek, a mile and more below the visitor center, where huge redwoods, sparkling stream, and steep valley walls create a magical scene that will make the kids (and you) feel like hobbits. A longer hike accesses some lovely waterfalls.

Reserve campsites or tent cabins well in advance.

A Parent's Guide to San Francisco

Chapter Five
The Peninsula & South Bay

Santa Clara

Paramount's Great America

4699 Great America Parkway, Santa Clara
408/988-1776 • www.pgathrills.com

Hours: Open from late spring through early fall. Hours vary widely—check the web site or call for details.

Admission: Prices tend to creep up every year, but there are often well-advertised promotional discounts that can make things much cheaper. The regular rate is about $45 for ages 7 – 59, $40 for over 59, $35 for ages 3 – 6, under 3 free.

Directions: Take the Great America Parkway exit from US-101 in Santa Clara, head north to the park.

As one of the Bay Area's two big time amusement parks, Great America offers everything you'd expect, including scream-provoking rides and long lines of potential screamers waiting to try them out. Among the wilder options, you'll find Stealth—a "flying" roller coaster—and the twisting stomach-churner known as Psycho Mouse. Modern, high-tech rides include a 3-D simulation ride called 7th Portal, and Smash Factory, which satisfies those with a lust for crashing cars. A seven-story IMAX theater offers a variety of features throughout the season while high-energy live shows elsewhere offer a vicarious sugar rush. A couple of the fancier rides involve extra fees.

Great America also has a decent set of milder rides for younger folk (and older folks who have become too sane for the screamers).

San Jose

Children's Discovery Museum of San Jose

180 Woz Way, San Jose
408/298-5437 • www.cdm.org

Hours: Open Memorial Day through the end of September, Monday – Saturday, 10:00 a.m. to 5:00 p.m.; Sunday noon to 5:00 p.m. Hours are the same the rest of the year, but the museum is closed on Mondays.

Admission: $9 for ages 18 – 59; $7 ages 1 – 17; $6 ages 60 and up; under 1 free. Expect to spend from $2 to $8 to park in the public lots most convenient to the facility.

Directions: From San Francisco, follow US-101 south to San Jose, use CA-87/Guadalupe Parkway exit, merge onto Guadalupe Parkway. From the East Bay take I-880 south to San Jose, 1st Street exit towards downtown, bear left, left on 1st, right onto Hedding, left on Guadalupe Parkway. Guadalupe Parkway becomes CA-87. Take the Park Avenue exit toward CA-82/San Carlos Street, left on Park. Turn right onto Woz Way for the Discovery Museum or right onto South Market for The Tech.

You'll spot this purple, architectural wonder of a museum from a distance, as will your kids who will suddenly want to be here after all. The facility was designed from scratch for pre-teens, offering a broad range of interactive exhibits on the arts, sciences, technology, and humanities, with an added focus on community.

Individual exhibits stress creativity and open-ended exploration. In Streets, visitors learn all that it takes to keep a city moving, from traffic lights to city services. Kids can experiment with bubbles in Bubbalogna and try brain teasers in ZOOMzone. They learn about how the postal service works in Post Office, about rhythms in Rhythm, and about electricity in Current Connections. Many more exhibits spread throughout the 50,000 square foot space.

A Parent's Guide to San Francisco

Chapter Five
The Peninsula & South Bay

The Tech Museum of Innovation

201 South Market Street, San Jose
408/294-8324 • www.thetech.com

Hours: Open every day from 10:00 a.m. to 5:00 p.m. except Thanksgiving, Christmas, and an occasional closure for maintenance (often in mid-September).

Admission: The pricing structure is a bit complex (a "triple" is 2 IMAX shows plus exhibits): Ages 13–64: Exhibits $9, IMAX $9, both $16, "triple" $22. Ages 3–12: Exhibits $7, IMAX $7, both $13, "triple" $18. Over 64: Exhibits $8, IMAX $8, both $15, "triple" $21. Under 3: free.

Directions: See Children's Discovery Museum above.

"The Tech," as it's known, features almost 250 high-technology exhibits in four themed galleries. When your kids get too old for the purple architecture and little-kid contents of the Children's Discovery Museum, they can come over to the mango-colored box that is The Tech. Exhibits have included everything from the "Spirit of American Innovation" to one on caving and bats, to "The Lost Spacecraft—Liberty Bell 7 Recovered." The Tech also reaches out via the web with on-line exhibits like the recent "2001: Destination Space." IMAX theater features have included "Mysteries of Egypt," "Journey into Amazing Caves," and "Wild California."

In all, it's *the* place in the South Bay for your science-minded ten-through-teen.

Raging Waters

2333 S. White Road, Lake Cunningham Park, San Jose
408/238-9900 • www.rwsplash.com

Hours: Open mid-May through mid-September at 10:00 a.m. When school is in session, the park is open Saturday and Sunday only, closing at 7:00 p.m. Closing times vary throughout the summer. Call or check the website for the current schedule.

Admission: $25 for adults ($20 after 3:00 p.m.); $15 for adults over age 54; $20 for kids 48" and under ($16 after 3 p.m.); under 3 free. Parking is $4.

Directions: Take the Tully Road exit from US-101 south of downtown San Jose, go east on Tully to the park.

When it's hot, wet them down. Located with Lake Cunningham Park, Raging Waters is the Bay Area's largest water theme park, featuring waterslides and a wave pool set amid 16 acres of tropically-themed grounds. All the rides are included in the admission price, though if you want to rent an innertube for a leisurely float down the Endless River, it will cost you an extra $4. Their signature ride is a twisting, 500-foot long trough/slide that sends an entire family group through banked turns and steep drops with a final plunging splash at the end. There are some non-water activities and mild attractions for the littlest of your bunch.

A Parent's Guide to San Francisco

Chapter Five
The Peninsula & South Bay

Kelley Park

1300 Senter Road, San Jose
408/277-5254 • www.ci.san-jose.ca.us/cae/parks/kp

Hours: Open 8:00 a.m. until a half-hour after sunset.

Admission: Park access is free, though the attractions in it may have a small fee.

Directions: From I-280 between its junctions with I-880 and US-101 in San Jose, take the 10th/11th Street exit, turn south on 10th, left on Keyes, right on Senter.

At 156 acres, Kelley Park is one of the largest parks in the city and is home to several family-friendly attractions. These are lawns, play areas, shady groves, and pleasant walks. Two nice gardens—the Rose Garden and Overfelt Garden—are great places to watch the bees and butterflies at work. You can see a show at the Greek-style amphitheater where no amplification is permitted to disturb the peace of the park. Sinuous Coyote Creek Park stretches southeast from Kelley Park farming a miles-long watercourse preserve.

The three attractions that follow will be of particular interest to you and the kids.

Happy Hollow Zoo

1300 Senter Boulevard, Kelley Park, San Jose
408/295-8383 • www.happyhollowzoo.org

Hours: Open daily, 10:00 a.m. to 5:00 p.m. Open until 6:00 p.m. on Saturday and Sunday in July and August. Closed Christmas Day.

Admission: Ages 2–64 get in for $4.50; 65–74 for $4; under 2 and over 75 for free. Parking is $4.

Here's a guaranteed winner for your toddler through grade schoolers—one that's not too hard on your pocketbook. Happy Hollow features a small zoo with a petting section known as the "Animal Contact Area." Here, children can get close to alpacas, goats, guinea pigs, and miniature horses (a favorite of all). There are also a good playground and several rides geared toward the younger set. The kids can even explore a replica of a riverboat and climb around in a neat tree house. A few rare and endangered animals are here as well, offering the opportunity for awakening your young ones to the ugly realities of habitat destruction and poaching.

A Parent's Guide to San Francisco

Chapter Five
The Peninsula & South Bay

Japanese Friendship Garden

1300 Senter Road, Kelley Park, San Jose
408/277-5254 • www.ci.san-jose.ca.us/cae/parks/kp

Hours: Open daily, 10:00 a.m. to sunset.

Admission: Free.

The beautiful Friendship Garden was dedicated in 1965 to symbolize the relationship between the sister cities of San Jose and Okayama, Japan. Enjoy the sculpted foliage and pleasant walks. The kids will love the koi swimming placidly in their big pond, some of them reaching 30" in length and living to the ripe old age of 40 years. Feeding stations sell koi food for a nominal fee—your kids can feed the seemingly insatiable fish as long as the food supply holds out. Unlike some others of its type, this is a spacious garden with a casual atmosphere. A little noise and some running won't be frowned upon, and there are some swaths of lawn for stretching out.

History Park

1650 Senter Road, Kelley Park, San Jose
408/287-2290 • www.historysanjose.org

Hours: Grounds, candy store, gift shop, and ice cream parlor open Tuesday – Sunday, noon to 5:00 p.m. On weekends, the historic buildings are open and docents lead tours.

Admission: $6, seniors $5, ages 6-14 $4, under 6 free. No fee to enter grounds on weekdays.

The past comes alive on a grand scale at the south end of Kelley Park. History Park features 27 original and replica homes and buildings that have been moved or re-constructed on site, and which exemplify the early days of Santa Clara County. The structures are placed along period-style paved streets with an operating trolley line. An old-fashioned ice cream parlor sells just what you'd expect. On weekends, buildings are opened and staffed with docents, making a self-guided tour fun and informative. Permanent collections of artifacts are joined by touring exhibits to offer a rich slice of history.

The kids should love a walk through the village. They can stretch their legs in an essentially traffic-free zone, marvel at how people could live without Pokémon, and anticipate the pleasure of their scoop of choice at walk's end.

A Parent's Guide to San Francisco

Chapter Five
The Peninsula & South Bay

Rosicrucian Museum

1342 Naglee Avenue, San Jose
408/947-3636 • www.rosicrucian.org

Hours: Open Tuesday – Friday, 10:00 a.m. to 5:00 p.m., Saturday and Sunday from 11:00 a.m. to 6:00 p.m. Call to check on the status of the planetarium.

Admission: General admission is $9, students and seniors $7, ages 5 – 10 $5, under 5 free. Tours are available for an additional fee.

Directions: From I-880 north of I-280 junction in San Jose, take the Alameda exit, left onto Alameda, right at second light on Naglee, left on Park Avenue.

Welcome to San Jose's most popular attraction! The Rosicrucians are an order dedicated to the pursuit of knowledge and education, and they've developed an outstanding facility worth visiting. As more of an educational institution than a museum, the Rosicrucians have made liberal use of models and replicas, assuring that visitors get an idea of how it really was when ancient Egypt was at its height.

There's a full-scale replica of a rock tomb that you can walk through. A life-size replica of the Rosetta Stone lets children understand how the secret of ancient language was unlocked. What kid wouldn't love a room full of animal and human mummies? Outside, even the buildings and grounds of the museum are designed in imitation of the ancients along the Nile.

Winchester House

525 South Winchester Boulevard, San Jose
408/247-2000 • www.winchestermysteryhouse.com

Hours: Open every day of the year except Christmas at 9:00 a.m. Closing times vary annually, but expect something like 5:00 p.m. from October – April, 5:00 p.m. weekdays and 7:00 p.m. weekends from May through mid-June and September, and 7:00 p.m. mid-June through August.

Admission: A regular Mansion Tour runs $16, over 64 $13, ages 6 – 12 $10. The Behind-the-Scenes Tour is $13, over 64 $12, under 13 not permitted. The combined Estate Tour goes for $23, over 64 $20, under 13 not permitted.

Directions: Take the Stevens Creek Boulevard exit from I-880 just north of the junction with I-280, go west on Stevens Creek, left on Winchester, mansion is on the right.

Sarah L. Winchester was an odd one. Heiress of the Winchester Rifle fortune, she became obsessed with continuing construction on her mansion, by some accounts believing that if it was never completed, she would never die. The result is an opulent, 160-room Victorian palace full of all sorts of strange features. Sure, there are the inlaid parquet floors, gold chandeliers, and Tiffany windows. But you'll also find stairs that climb to (but not through) the ceiling, doors that open to reveal walls, a window built into a floor, and features installed upside down.

The "Mansion Tour" covers 110 of the rooms and is the only tour open to kids under 13. The "Behind the Scenes Tour" explores some remaining areas, including an unfinished ballroom, a basement, and stables. A combined tour offers the total package.

A Parent's Guide to San Francisco

Chapter Five
The Peninsula & South Bay

Lick Observatory

Mount Hamilton Road summit, San Jose
408/274-5061 • www.ucolick.org

Hours: The gift shop is open from 12:30 p.m. to 5:00 p.m. daily for much of the year, 10:00 a.m. to 5:00 p.m. on weekends. Tours of the old 36" refracting telescope are given on the hour and half-hour until 4:30 p.m. Self-guided tours of the 120" telescope are an option from 10:00 a.m. to 5:00 p.m. daily.

Admission: Free.

Directions: From US-101 or I-680 on the east side of San Jose, take the Alum Rock Road exit (CA-130). Head east up into the foothills on Alum Rock, turning right on Mount Hamilton Road. The road is good but narrow and winding—allow up to an hour to reach the summit from central San Jose.

Once or twice every winter, local newspeople drive up the Mount Hamilton road for live coverage of that rare Bay Area phenomenon: *snow*. As the highest peak in the region at 4,209' above sea level, a few inches of the white stuff usually crowns the higher reaches for a couple weeks a year. That same snow caps the domes of Lick Observatory, perched precariously atop Hamilton's summit. What the news folks don't tell you is how long it took them to reach the snow on the slow, winding road up the mountain. This trip is probably only appropriate for your science-loving, over-8s who don't get carsick.

Once on top, however, the observatory facilities offer a worthy reward. Scientists researching the cosmos actively use the modern reflecting telescopes. Photographs and other items are exhibited in the halls. When the intrigue of the interiors wears out, head outside for long views and short ventures into the wild land around the crest. There's very little traffic on the road, and few other visitors wandering about, so you can't help but feel "out there." It's a great place to tell kids about the behavior of mountain lions or the trail-blazing exploits of Kit Carson.

The real prize at Lick is a ticket to one of the six summer visitor evenings open to the public. Only 250 people get tickets for each of these exceedingly popular nights out. Attendees are treated to an astronomy and history lecture, followed by the chance to view the heavens through both the 120-inch reflecting and 36-inch refracting telescopes. Outside the domes, volunteers operate smaller telescopes. Good behavior is expected, things go late, and there's that long drive home—think twice before entering the ticket lottery (see below).

You can head to the summit any time you wish for a look about the grounds. Building doors and hallways may be open for exploring, and you may have the chance for a peep into the domes. Remember, though, that this is a working observatory, and most of the work occurs at night. It's essential to call ahead (during gift shop hours) to see what's in store for you.

A Parent's Guide to San Francisco

Chapter Five
The Peninsula & South Bay

Pacifica

Sanchez Adobe

1000 Linda Mar Boulevard, Pacifica
650/359-1462 • www.ci.pacifica.ca.us/history/adobe.html

Hours: Open Tuesday, Wednesday, and Thursday from 10:00 a.m. to 4:00 p.m., weekends 1:00 p.m. to 5:00 p.m.

Admission: Donations accepted.

Directions: From CA-1, turn away from the ocean (east) on Linda Mar Boulevard. Go about 1 mile and turn right into the parking lot just past Adobe Drive.

The oldest building in San Mateo County occupies a site long occupied by the native Ohlone people. Crops grown here supplied Mission Dolores in San Francisco for many years. After that, it was a cattle ranch, the home of the Mexican alcalde (mayor) of San Francisco, a hotel, a bar, and an artichoke storage facility. Now fully restored, it's a great place for kids to get a taste of the region's early years.

Besides regular docent-led tours of the site, Sanchez Adobe offers a schedule of historic shows.

Peninsula Coast

Phipps Country Store and Farm

2700 Pescadero Creek Road, Pescadero
650/879-0787

Hours: Open daily, 10:00 a.m. to 7:00 p.m. in summer, 10:00 a.m. to 5:00 p.m. in winter. Call about berry-picking seasons (usually June for the best strawberries and all summer for lolla-berries).

Admission: $2 for ages 10 – 60, under 10 and over 60 free.

Directions: From CA-1, take Pescadero (Creek) Road inland almost 3 miles. Store and farm are close to the intersection with North Street, about a 1/2 mile from the heart of little Pescadero.

This wonderful, quiet ranch is the perfect place for city-weary Bay Area residents to enjoy a touch of rural life. The store is open year round selling home grown goodies, but you should try to come in season when the strawberries and lolla-berries (a.k.a. olallieberries) are ripe. For $1 a pound, you and the young ones can head out through the rows and pick your own. Afterwards, spend some time at the petting zoo where the array of critters includes pigs, donkeys, chickens, turkeys, ducks, geese, pheasants, and more. You can explore 50 pleasant acres for a while, then pick a spot to enjoy a picnic lunch, hopefully with the addition of something tasty you picked up in the country store.

Courtesy: Frank Spadarella/ San Mateo County Historical Museum

A Parent's Guide to San Francisco

Chapter Five
The Peninsula & South Bay

Peninsula Beaches

CA-1, Peninsula Coast
www.cal-parks.ca.gov

Hours: Public access at all times.
Admission: A few beaches have parking fees of $5; many are free.
Directions: Look for the brown sign with the barefoot or other more explicit signage indicating beach access as you drive CA-1 between Pacifica and Santa Cruz.

A number of nice state beaches dot the coast along CA-1 between Pacifica and Santa Cruz. A few of them have adjacent parking areas and easy access to food and lodging. Others are reached by short, usually downhill hikes via coastal access trails designated by the brown sign with the bare foot. Most are sandy, some feature nice tide pools, all represent a chance for family fun with a touch of education. Beware undertow and rip tides—heed all warning signs. Remember, too, that the coastal waters in this region are usually quite chilly, and that summer fogs can change the scene from blazing, hot sunshine to a dank, chilly blanket in moments.

Heading from north to south, great beaches include: *Montara State Beach* (650/726-8819) just north of Montara; the modestly sheltered *Half Moon Bay State Beach* (650/726-8819) in Half Moon Bay; *San Gregorio, Pomponio,* and *Pescadero State Beaches* (650/879-2170), all close together just north of Pescadero; and little *Bean Hollow State Beach* (650/879-2170). The southern half of the peninsula features more isolated spots with coastal access across private grazing land.

Pigeon Point Light Station

CA-1, 25 miles south of Half Moon Bay
650/879-2120 • www.pigeonpointlighthouse.org

Hours: You can enjoy a self-guided tour of the grounds and point from 8:00 a.m. to sunset. Docent-led tours on Saturday or Sunday depart every 45 minutes, 11:00 a.m. to 4:00 p.m. from April – September; 10:00 a.m. to 3:00 p.m. the rest of the year.
Admission: Guided tours are $2 for adults, $1 for children.
Directions: Pigeon Point is reached from CA-1, about 25 miles south of Half Moon Bay, 8 miles south of Pescadero.

At 110' tall, the Pigeon Point lighthouse is one of the tallest in the country. Though the original Fresnel lens with its thousand prisms is no longer in use, the station is still active and has served coastal mariners since 1872.

Tours take interested visitors up the 144 steep steps to the top of the tower. Younger tour takers must be at least 40" tall and capable of handling the ascent and descent. Even if you don't go up, there is plenty to see and enjoy around the base, including a nice boardwalk that offers a good vantage for whale-viewing in season (January – April). There is access to tidepools and the rocky shore nearby.

A Parent's Guide to San Francisco

Chapter Five
The Peninsula & South Bay

Consider making a night of it with a stay in Hostelling International's Pigeon Point Hostel. You can book a family room, or join the other budget hostellers in one of the dorms. The kids will get the chance to rub elbows with interesting, energetic young people from around the world, many of whom are seeing the wonders of California and the U.S. for the first time. Be careful, though, or they'll be infected with a wanderlust that will stick with them for years to come. Are you ready to hear, "I'm going to India for 6 months," from your soon-to-be-collegian?

Año Nuevo State Reserve

CA-1, 13 miles south of Pescadero
650/879-2025, 800/444-4445 (tour reservations) • **www.cal-parks.ca.gov**

Hours: Open daily year round from 8:00 a.m. to dusk. Seal viewing areas are closed to all access from December 1 – 15, and open only to reserved, guided walking tours from December 15 – March.

Admission: Tours are $4 per person. Parking is $5 per car, seniors $4.

Directions: Accessible from CA-1, 13 miles south of Pescadero.

Time it right and your older kids will get an education in the wonders of nature they'll never forget. A sizable herd of elephant seals has adopted the beaches at Año Nuevo as their chosen site for harem-building, mating, and birthing. It's impressive to witness any of these activities, especially the vicious battling of 2,000 pound males vying for the right to sire the next round of offspring.

While the schedule may vary a bit, fighting and birthing take place in December, mating in January. These are also the times when reservations are necessary to join the tightly controlled tours to seal viewing spots. Elephant seals may be seen in smaller numbers through much of the rest of the year, including the molting season from April through August. California and Steller's sea lions frequent an island just offshore that also hosts the eerie ruins of an old lighthouse.

Plan on walking about a mile to get from the parking area to the main seal viewing spot and back. There are a number of other nice trails in this large park and only a few have controlled access during the peak winter birthing and mating times.

144

A Parent's Guide to San Francisco

Chapter Five
The Peninsula & South Bay

Felton

Roaring Camp and Historic Railways

Mount Hermon Road, 1 mile east of Felton
831/335-4484 • www.roaringcamprr.com

Hours: The train schedule is a bit complex. For up-to-date information, call or visit the web site.

Admission: A small vehicle fee is required to enter the grounds. The Roaring Camp Railroad fare is $15, ages 3-12 $10, under 3 free. A one-way run between Roaring Camp and Santa Cruz goes for $16.50, ages 3-12 $11.50, under 3 free.

Directions: From CA-17, take the Mount Hermon Road exit. Follow Mount Hermon Road north and west about 5 miles, through Scott's Valley, to Roaring Camp. From Santa Cruz, head 7 miles north on CA-9 to Felton and turn right on Mount Hermon Road.

Here's a guaranteed winner for a half-day adventure. Less than a mile from the center of Felton, you'll find Roaring Camp, site of the historic Southern Pacific depot and home base of two historic narrow gauge rail lines. The Roaring Camp Railroad takes a 75-minute, round-trip run through redwood country from the station to Bear Mountain. Heading the other direction, the Santa Cruz, Big Trees, and Pacific Railway chugs from Roaring Camp right down to the Beach Boardwalk amusement park in the heart of Santa Cruz. The run takes an hour each way.

If your kids are old enough or there are at least two adults involved, you can set up the Santa Cruz, Big Trees, and Pacific Railway ride to be a one-way trip. One hour is plenty of train riding for most kids, and you'll save the cost of return fare. Drop the travelers off at Roaring Camp, drive back to town on CA-9, park in one of the Beach Boardwalk lots, and meet them when they arrive. If possible, don't let the kids know where they are headed and surprise them with a half-day of rides, amusements, and beach play. There are changing rooms for the beach so they can trade cool-morning-in-the-redwoods clothes for swim suits.

Roaring Camp itself features several attractions besides the trains. There are historic buildings with living history activities, various displays of rail-related hardware, sprawling lawns for play, and picnic areas. In summer, various types of entertainment are scheduled to coordinate with rail arrival and departure times. A couple of shops sell snacks and gifts.

A Parent's Guide to San Francisco

Chapter Five
The Peninsula & South Bay

Santa Cruz

Santa Cruz Beach Boardwalk

400 Beach Street, Santa Cruz
831/423-5590 • www.beachboardwalk.com

Hours: Beach accessible at all times. Boardwalk open daily from Memorial Day through Labor Day, weekends and holidays in spring and fall. Some rides open weekdays in spring. Indoor arcades and miniature golf open daily year round, except for Christmas Day. Hours vary; summer hours are 11:00 a.m. to 11:00 p.m. (until 10:00 p.m. Sundays).

Admission: Free access to beach and boardwalk. Buy 60-cent individual tickets for rides, which range from 3 to 6 tickets each. There's an $8 discount on a strip of 60 tickets.

Directions: Take CA-17 south to Santa Cruz from I-280 or I-880 in San Jose, exit onto CA-1 north, continue straight onto Chestnut where the freeway ends, left on Laurel, right on Center to the water, left on Beach.

An amusement park on a beach—how can you lose? Ride the roller coaster, buy some cotton candy, and bask in the sand, all within a hearty walk or 5-minute drive of the still-hip Santa Cruz downtown. Rides include the wonderful 1924 Giant Dipper wooden roller coaster, offering thrills that are only indirectly related to speed and height. There's also the classic 1911 Looff Carousel for those who aren't quite ready for the climbs and plunges of the coaster. Thirty more rides and attractions fill out the slate. Don't expect a Six Flags or Great America sized park—this is a medium-sized venture with a lot of history.

Oh, and that boardwalk? It's mostly asphalt now.

A Parent's Guide to San Francisco

Chapter Five
The Peninsula & South Bay

Monarch Butterfly Reserve

At Natural Bridges State Park, West Cliff Drive, Santa Cruz
831/423-4609 • www.cal-parks.ca.gov (link to Natural Bridges SB)

Hours: The reserve is accessible from 8:00 a.m. to sunset. Monarchs are generally present from October – April.

Admission: Small parking fee.

Directions: Take CA-17 south to Santa Cruz from I-280 or I-880 in San Jose, exit onto CA-1 north, stay on CA-1 as it exits right on city streets to become Mission Street, left on Swift, right on West Cliff Drive to end.

At a few select spots along the California coastline, monarch butterflies come by the thousands to wait out the winter before fanning out across the land again in spring. When the air is chill, they crowd the branches, hanging motionless like dead, brown leaves. But when the sun comes out and the day warms, many will stretch their wings, drop from the trees, and flutter about the groves.

Natural Bridges State Beach in Santa Cruz hosts as many as 100,000 monarchs in a beautiful grove of eucalyptus trees. Typically, the monarchs begin to arrive in mid-October, departing again at the end of February. The park maintains a demonstration patch of milkweed where a number of monarchs lay eggs. The eggs eventually hatch into caterpillars that form cocoons, emerging as adult butterflies and completing the life cycle right on site.

Access to the grove is via a designated boardwalk and observation platform. The butterflies cannot be touched or harassed. Quiet is requested.

A Parent's Guide to San Francisco

Chapter Five
The Peninsula & South Bay

Mystery Spot

465 Mystery Spot Road, Santa Cruz
831/423-8897 • www.mysteryspot.com

Hours: Just like the gravity it defies, the Mystery Spot is in business 365 days a year. It's open 9:00 a.m. to 7:00 p.m., Memorial Day through Labor Day; 9:00 a.m. to 4:30 p.m. the rest of the year.

Admission: $5 for adults, $3 for kids.

Directions: Take CA-17 south to Santa Cruz from I-280 or I-880 in San Jose, cross CA-1 into Santa Cruz, becomes Ocean Street, left on Water, left on Market, becomes Branciforte Drive, left on Mystery Spot Road.

All kids should get the chance to experience an old-style illusion attraction like the Mystery Spot at least once in their lives. Children love it—whether they are gullible 6-year-olds with noses dripping and mouths agape, or sharp, science-savvy, skeptical 11-year-olds ready to debunk the world. Heck, I still enjoy watching a ball roll uphill.

Surfing Museum

Lighthouse Point, West Cliff Drive, Santa Cruz
831/420-6289

Hours: Open daily except Tuesday, noon to 4:00 p.m. (closed both Tuesday and Wednesday in winter).

Admission: Free.

Directions: Take CA-17 south to Santa Cruz from I-280 or I-880 in San Jose, exit west on CA-1, where freeway ends, continue straight on Chestnut, left on Laurel, 2 blocks to right on Center, right on Beach and continue onto West Cliff Drive to Lighthouse Point.

Is your young hipster bored with the world? Well, he or she can't help but be impressed by the stories and paraphernalia of surfdom. Adding to its appeal, the Surfing Museum is located in the Mark Abbott Memorial Lighthouse, perched high above the water on the west edge of Santa Cruz. A favorite surfing break is below, giving the kids a chance to see live action after the museum's static history.

Within 100 Miles...

There are simply too many great, kid-friendly places in Northern California—too many, that is, for average humans who can't spend every weekend of junior's growing years on the road. In trying to choose what to list, I decided to keep it geographically simple. All the entries in this chapter are located within 100 miles of San Francisco's City Hall as the crow flies (your driving route may be longer). Some choices might work as half-day or day-trip destinations, but most should be thought of as worthy stops on longer journeys to or from the Bay Area. It all depends on your starting point and how your kids handle long stints in the car.

It turns out that most of the following options are located in three good overnight or weekend destinations. The *Monterey Peninsula* is close enough to reach on Friday evening and rich enough in options to leave you wanting more when it's time to join the stream of Sunday traffic heading back to the Bay. The *Russian River Valley* and near *North Coast* offer several enclaves, but are perfect for that drive-a-little, stop-awhile type of weekend exploration. While people rarely decide to spend a weekend in *Sacramento*, it's a good place to break up the long drive to the mountains for a fun lesson in civics or history.

Don't let my 100-mile limit blind you to possibilities further afield! Continue north to find the best state and national redwood parks, the cool coastal town of Mendocino, and the amazing volcano country around Mount Shasta and Mount Lassen. Wander east and explore Yosemite, Lake Tahoe, the Gold Country, Owens Valley, and the High Sierra. Travel south to find Pinnacles National Monument, the Big Sur coast, Hearst Castle, Hollywood, Guatemala, Macchu Picchu, and Antarctica! Lead your kids while you can; open their minds to the planet.

The listings ahead begin in the north and follow a clockwise arc around the Bay Area.

A Parent's Guide to San Francisco

Chapter Six
Within 100 Miles

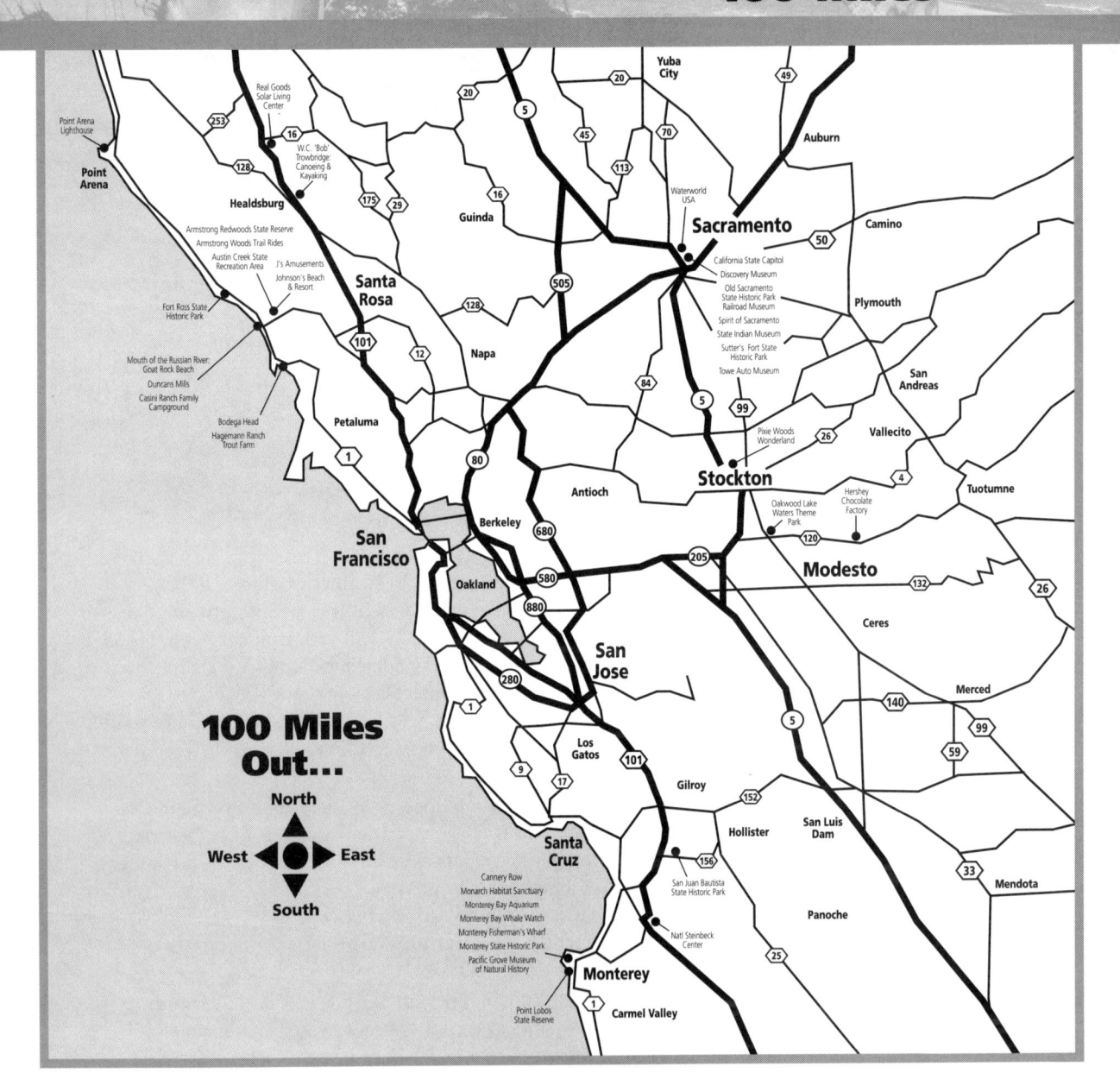

A Parent's Guide to
San Francisco

Chapter Six
Within 100 Miles

North Coast

Bodega Head
End of Bay Flats Road, Bodega Head
707/847-3221 • parks.ca.gov

Hours: Open to public access daily from dawn to dusk.

Admission: The parking fee of $5 per vehicle is good for parking all day at any of the Sonoma Coast parks and beaches.

Directions: Take Eastshore Road west from CA-1, just north of Bodega Bay's main concentration of businesses, turn right on Bay Flats road along the north shore of the harbor to the Bodega Head parking lots. Southbound travelers stay on Bay Flats Road when returning to CA-1.

Need a spot to let your kids stretch their legs on your trip up the coast? Bodega Head is a fine choice. This windy promontory shelters Bodega Bay's harbor from the rough Pacific and is one of the more accessible headlands along the lower North Coast. It's a five-minute drive from CA-1 with good parking and nice trails. Make sure to pack your binoculars if you'll be here during the peak whale migration months of December and March. There is limited access to coastal rocks and tide pools, but you should generally keep the young ones a step or two back from the soft rock of the cliff edges.

Hagemann Ranch Trout Farm
CA-1, Bodega Bay
707/876-3217 • www.sonic.net/~bruceh

Hours: The trout farm is open June – September, Thursday – Sunday, 9:00 a.m. to 4:00 p.m. Call for hours in April, May, October, and November.

Admission: Fishing options begin at $2.25 per fish for fish under 7", up to $9 per fish for 17-inchers, and $3 per inch above that. Bring your own pole in for $1 or rent one for $2.50.

Directions: Watch for the sign on the east side of CA-1 between Bodega and Bodega Bay.

I can't think of an easier way to introduce your kids to the pleasures of fishing than by a visit here. Follow the winding drive in from the highway through the Hagemann's 219-acre sheep ranch to reach a small, stocked lake. If you don't have rods and tackle of your own, you can rent them cheaply at the office. If you are more interested in landing a trout than your young ones, they can hunt for frogs and play in the grass while you fish. It's not catch-and-release; what you catch, you keep. The staff will clean, ice, and bag your catch so it's ready for freezer or broiler. When the time is right, pull out your basket and enjoy the contents in the picnic area. This is basic, no-frills family fun.

A Parent's Guide to San Francisco

Chapter Six
Within 100 Miles

Fort Ross State Historic Park

CA-1, 12 miles north of Jenner
707/847-3286 • parks.ca.gov

Hours: Park grounds open from a half-hour before sunrise to a half-hour after sunset. Fort compound and other facilities open 10:00 a.m. to 4:30 p.m. daily.

Admission: $6 day-use parking fee.

Directions: The entrance to the park is on CA-1, 12 miles north of Jenner. The main attractions are west of the highway.

Russia established Fort Ross as a base of operations in 1812 to support their relentless pursuit of otter pelts. Thirty years later, the otters were virtually gone from the region and the fort was abandoned. Today, visitors can enjoy an accurate reconstruction of the fort and surrounding compound, getting a taste of a long gone world. The visitor center features a library and historical exhibits to round out the educational value of the place, but it's the fort that will impress the kids.

Fort Ross also features several good hiking trails on the coast, as well as in the hills above the highway. You can't buy food in the park, but there are several picnic spots, including a couple inside the fort compound itself. Remember that warm, sunny days can become chilly, foggy days in a moment, and that the rocks along the coast can be hazardous places for unsupervised play.

Point Arena Lighthouse

Lighthouse Road from CA-1, Point Arena
707/882-2777, 877/725-4448 (overnight reservations) • www.mcn.org/1/palight

Hours: Open daily April – September, 10:00 a.m. to 3:30 p.m., guided tours offered from 11:00 a.m. to 2:30 p.m. Open daily October – March, 11:00 a.m. to 3:30 p.m. weekdays, 10:00 a.m. to 3:30 p.m. weekends. Open weekends only in December and January, except open weekdays between Christmas and New Year's. Closed Thanksgiving Day and Christmas Day. ...I'd call ahead in winter!

Admission: $4, children under 12 free.

Directions: Take Lighthouse Road from CA-1, just north of the village of Point Arena.

The Point Arena light began operation in 1870, but had to be rebuilt when it was damaged in the 1906 San Francisco earthquake. At 115' from base to cap, it's one of California's tallest. The kids should get a kick out of ascending to the top of the tower for a look around, though it's not for the fainthearted. The narrow, spiral stairs are safe enough, but are steep and confining.

Next to the lighthouse, there's a nice museum with a terrific set of historic photographs and several impressive pieces of equipment used in the operation of a light station. There are a couple of good trails, but access to the shore is limited outside the lighthouse due to concerns about safety and erosion.

An added attraction here is the chance to spend one or more nights in one of the three original station keepers' homes. Each has kitchen and dining facilities, a wood-burning stove for heat, satellite TV and VCR, two baths, and three bedrooms. Rates are a coastal bargain at $155 to $170. There is a 3-night minimum on holiday weekends.

A Parent's Guide to San Francisco

Chapter Six
Within 100 Miles

Sonoma Coast State Beaches

Several locations along CA-1, Sonoma County
707/847-3221 • parks.ca.gov

Hours: All of the beaches are open from dawn to dusk.

Admission: The $5 parking fee is good for a full day, even if you try more than one beach.

Directions: As you drive north from Bodega Bay on CA-1, you'll pass quite a few beach access points and parking areas.

So you're heading to Mendocino along the beautiful coast highway, soaking in the splendid views, when you notice a strange silence in the back seat. Investigating, you discover that those endless, winding curves north of Jenner have taken their toll and junior is car sick. What can you do? Don't worry! Sonoma County residents have anticipated your problem and peppered their coastline with public beaches. Just pull over at one of them and let sea, sand, and sun work their magic.

It's hard to recommend one beach over another—they are all excellent. Most feature a modest-sized cove with a broad swath of sand, framed by mild headlands and dotted with rocky outcrops and tide pools. Shells and driftwood may be thick or rare. The water will be chilly, and you should always be aware of the power of undertow and rip tides—heed all warning signs!

Russian River Valley

Mouth of the Russian River

CA-1, just south of CA-116, Jenner
707/875-3483 • parks.ca.gov

Hours: Open to public access from dawn to dusk.

Admission: Free for people, but you'll pay $5 to park. The pass is good for a full day for all of the Sonoma Coast State Beaches.

Directions: Look for the Goat Rock Beach turnout along CA-1, high on the ridge south of the river and Jenner.

The Russian River anchors one of the major road and activity corridors of the California coast. Originating high in the Coast Range, it passes through redwood forests in the north, wine-growing country further downstream, and resort and recreation areas near its end.

The mouth of the Russian is blocked by the sprawling expanse of Goat Rock Beach—part of the Sonoma Coast State Beaches system. You'll find acres of sand, shells, and driftwood. Following the long breakwater, you can walk out to the point where river meets sea.

A Parent's Guide to San Francisco

Chapter Six
Within 100 Miles

Best of all, harbor seals and sea lions frequently bask on the shore of the Russian, just inside the river mouth. While it is both illegal and unwise to get too close, you and the kids can enjoy a terrific wildlife experience in a natural setting. To locate the vociferous sea mammals, just follow your ears. For a guided walk to view harbor seal pups from March – September, call 707/874-3013.

Remember that distances are deceiving on long beach walks, and that plodding through the sand can fatigue young legs more quickly than similar distances on lawns and walks—older legs, too, for that matter. It can be quite a trek out to the river mouth and seals. Break it up into stages on a leisurely visit with a couple of hours to spend.

Duncans Mills

CA-116, Duncans Mills
707/865-2024 • www.duncansmillscamp.com

Hours: Opening hours vary.
Admission: Free.
Directions: CA-116 meets CA-1 where the Russian River meets the Pacific. Duncans Mills is 4 miles inland from the junction on CA-116.

After a windy, wild experience out on the sand, consider a short stop in the small enclave of Duncans Mills, about 4 miles in from the coast on CA-116. What at first looks like a tiny town is actually a tourist stop-off with several shops all owned by the same company. The kids may like a look inside the museum. There are also a couple of old rail cars, including Caboose #2—a relic from the days when a narrow gauge rail line ran from here to San Francisco to haul redwood timber. Buy them some juice and travel on.

Casini Ranch Family Campground

CA-116, Duncans Mills
800/451-8400

Hours: Open year round.
Admission: Sites range from $22 to $29 a night.
Directions: Follow CA-116 inland from CA-1 about 4 miles, watch for signs for the campground.

Looking for an overnight or weekend stay in family heaven? The Casini Ranch Family Campground is a sprawling, 120-acre facility on the Russian River floodplain featuring a full mile of river frontage. The 225 sites tend to be fairly well spaced, and include regular tentsites as well as RV pull-throughs. You'll find a store, recreation hall, duck pond, canoe rental, fishing sites, beaches, playgrounds, and Saturday night hayrides. Let the older kids go while you sit in a lawn chair reading a fat paperback.

A Parent's Guide to San Francisco

**Chapter Six
Within
100 Miles**

Armstrong Redwoods State Reserve

**Armstrong Woods Road, north of Guerneville
707/869-2015 • www.cal-parks.ca.gov**

Hours: The redwood grove is open daily from 8:00 a.m. until one hour after sunset.

Admission: Parking is $5 per vehicle.

Directions: To reach Guerneville, take CA-116 west from US-101 in Cotati or east from CA-1 at Jenner. In Guerneville, go 2 miles north on Armstrong Woods Road to reach the redwood reserve, recreation area, campground, and pack station.

One of the reasons a huge area of San Francisco burned to the ground after the 1906 earthquake is that so many buildings were constructed of redwood—beautiful, fine-grain, old-growth redwood, harvested from northern coastal valleys. Fortunately, the saws and axes missed a few spots like Armstrong Woods. On your excursion to the Russian River region, head two miles north of Guerneville for a walk among the giants, a couple of which are over 300' tall. If you wish, make a weekend of it, camping in adjacent Austin Creek State Recreation Area, riding horses through the cool trees and hot hills with Armstrong Woods Trail Rides, and driving into town for some water play at Johnson's Beach.

Austin Creek State Recreation Area

**Armstrong Woods Road, north of Guerneville
707/869-2015 • www.parks.sonoma.net/austin.html**

Hours: Open to public access at all times, including overnight camping.

Admission: Parking is $5 per vehicle. Austin Creek campsites are $12, available on a first come, first served basis.

Directions: See Armstrong Redwoods State Reserve above.

The Austin Creek area protects 5,600 acres of wildlands adjacent to Armstrong Redwoods State Reserve. About 20 miles of trails thread through the rugged terrain, offering access to narrow, forested valleys, and views from open, high slopes.

One nice choice is to spend the night in the 24-site campground, located near the aptly named Bullfrog Pond. The campground offers flush toilets, potable water, tables, and fire rings, but is closed to vehicles with trailers and those over 20' long. You'll see why when you drive the winding, narrow, 2.5-mile campground access road. How about a quiet night under the stars, not too far from civilization? Do you remember how to make a 'smore?'

A Parent's Guide to San Francisco

Chapter Six
Within 100 Miles

Armstrong Woods Trail Rides

Armstrong Woods Road, north of Guerneville
707/887-2939 • www.redwoodhorses.com

Hours: Scheduled rides October – May, departing 9:30 a.m., 10:30 a.m., 11:00 a.m., and 2:00 p.m. Custom rides available year round. Various and custom rides of 1.5 hours to all day. Overnights and longer rides possible. You must call ahead.

Admission: 1.5 hour ride with lunch stop $50, 2.5 to 3 hour ride $75, full-day ride $125 to $150.

Whether or not you've ever ridden a horse, Armstrong Woods Trail Rides has an option for you. If you wish, you and your young ones can perch on mild-mannered beasts that stroll along through the redwoods, following the guide like sleepy sheep. More experienced riders can take the reins a bit. There's a rough schedule of rides during the warmer half of the year, but the owners will do what they can to match your plans and preferences. Ask about the "Kids Horse Camp Program" and naturalist-guided rides. Fully-guided overnight and multi-day options are available. Dress for your ride by wearing sturdy, long pants and shoes (no sandals). Bring a bag lunch or snack. No drop-ins—call ahead and speak to a human to reserve your ride.

J's Amusements

16101 Neeley Road, Guerneville
707/869-3102 • www.sterba.com/river/j

Hours: Open late March through fall; March weekends from noon to 6:00 p.m., daily during school spring vacation from noon to 6:00 p.m., weekends after that from 11:00 a.m. to 6:00 p.m., daily during summer school break from 11:00 a.m. to 10:00 p.m. Extended hours during Memorial Day weekend.

Admission: Most rides $2, go-karts $4, Pee Wee Golf $3.75, all day waterslide pass $7.50.

Directions: From US-101, take the Guerneville/River Road/Russian River Resort exit at the north edge of Santa Rosa, turn left on Mark West Springs/River Road, go about 20 miles on River Road to Guerneville. Turn left on Guerneville Highway (CA-116) and cross the river to J's Amusements, or continue one more block on River Road before turning left onto Church Street to the beach.

Just south of the Russian River on the Guerneville Highway (CA-116), you'll find a mild, old-timey amusement park. J's offers go-karts, bumper cars, a waterslide, and other rides, all moderately priced. The miniature golf course features big animal models sure to be popular with the young ones. There are picnic tables with grills.

A Parent's Guide to San Francisco

Chapter Six
Within 100 Miles

Johnson's Beach & Resort

16241 First Street, Guerneville
707/869-2022 • www.johnsonsbeach.com

Hours: Open daily, mid-May through early October, 10:00 a.m. to 6:00 p.m.

Admission: Free. Innertubes rent for $3 a day. Boats go for about $7 an hour or $20 per day.

Directions: See J's Amusements above.

The Russian River between Guerneville and the Pacific has been a vacation and resort area for decades. Johnson's Beach has been in business for a long time and reminds me of those long lost days of low-key family amusements. You'll definitely find other families here, along with that feeling of supervision you get when there are a lot of watchful eyes about. If you'd like to get off the sand and out of the shallows, you can rent a canoe, kayak, paddleboat, or inner tube. Beach chairs and umbrellas can also be had. A roped-off area is designated for the littlest bathers. The beach hosts several events throughout the year, including both a jazz and a blues festival.

The "Resort" part of the business involves cabins and a campground. Camping is first come, first served; rooms are rented by the week.

W.C. "Bob" Trowbridge: Canoeing and Kayaking the Russian

20 Healdsburg Avenue, Healdsburg
800/640-1386 • www.trowbridgecanoee.com

Hours: Open April – October. Trips length and departure times vary. Call ahead to reserve.

Admission: A half-day paddle runs $40 per canoe, plus a $2 shuttle fee. The full-day version is $55 per canoe, plus a $3 shuttle fee. 2-day trips are $75 with each additional day costing $20.

Directions: Take the Healdsburg Avenue exit from US-101 in Healdsburg, head east to the river.

Enjoy a canoe trip on a lovely stretch of the Russian River in a W.C. "Bob" Trowbridge canoe or kayak. They will drop you off at a launch point for a downstream paddle back to Healdsburg. The full-day route is about 11 miles and takes about 5 hours. As you might expect, the half-day route is about half that. The company also offers shuttles to launch points for overnight or multi-day paddles. They'll set you up with camping.

Consider booking a trip with a company like Petaluma-based Getaway Adventures (800/499-2453, www.getawayadventures.com). Expert guides lead a variety of outdoor trips, some of which finish with a relaxing paddle in a Trowbridge canoe.

A Parent's Guide to San Francisco

Chapter Six: Within 100 Miles

Real Goods Solar Living Center
US-101, Hopland
707/744-2100 • www.solarliving.org

Hours: Open Monday – Saturday, 10:00 a.m. to 6:00 p.m., and Sunday from 10:00 a.m. to 5:00 p.m. 50-minute tours offered Friday – Sunday at 11:00 a.m. and 3:00 p.m.

Admission: Free. Donations welcome. $1 donation requested for tour.

Directions: The Real Goods Center is on the east side of US-101, 95 miles north of San Francisco at the south edge of Hopland.

The Solar Living Center began as an outgrowth of the *Real Goods Trading Company*, which offers solar energy devices and technology for sale, along with other items, related to renewable energy and environmentally friendly lifestyles. Every year or two on a trip up north, I'd stop by the center for a look, only to find even more of their 12-acre site developed to show the hows, whys, and wonders of sustainable living. You can still buy Real Goods' goods, but the center is now part of the full-fledged educational non-profit *Institute for Solar Living*.

As you zoom up or down US-101 between redwoods and suburbs, don't miss the chance to stop in—it's right on the highway. You and the children will get a look at the latest in sustainable living, including solar and wind power generators, environmentally friendly building materials, energy-efficient architecture, organic gardening, and more. The grounds feature walks and a pond. The store sells all sorts of cool stuff, including some inexpensive items that can give the kids something to focus their attentions for sustainable living at home.

A Parent's Guide to San Francisco

Chapter Six
Within 100 Miles

Sacramento

Old Sacramento State Historic Park

Front Street between L and I Streets, Sacramento

Hours: Area open to public access at all times. Shops have varying hours. Restaurants stay open for evening dining.

Admission: Free, though there are many places to spend money.

Directions: Take I-80 west from the Bay Area to Sacramento and stay left at the fork onto US-50/Business I-80. Take Capitol Mall exit and turn left just after crossing the river into Old Sacramento.

During the gold rush of 1849, Sacramento was a good deal smaller than the sprawling metropolis it is today. Back then, commerce was centered on the banks of the Sacramento River, just below its confluence with the American River. Today, Old Sacramento preserves what's left of the original commercial district and offers several excellent diversions for families. Best of all is the Railroad Museum, though the kids may be most impressed by the riverboats moored along the waterfront.

It's fun just to roam the streets in this compact zone, ducking into the touristy shops behind the historic storefronts. There are plenty of places that will take your money, including restaurants, candy stores, gift shops, and the like. If sugar and t-shirts aren't what you had in mind, the following trio offers more substantial experiences.

Spirit of Sacramento Cruise

Front Street, Old Sacramento, Sacramento
800/433-0263, 916-552-2933 • www.spiritofsacramento.com

Hours: Call or check the web site for the current schedule.

Admission: 1-hour sightseeing tours are $10 for adults, $5 for children under 12. Lunch, brunch, happy hour, and dinner cruises range from $15 to $35.

Directions: See Old Sacramento State Historic Park above.

It was a sad day when the original *Spirit of Sacramento* riverboat burned in 1996 and a landmark of Old Sacramento was lost forever. Things took another bad turn when Hurricane Oscar damaged the vessel purchased to replace the *Spirit*—the *Becky Thatcher* out of Cincinnati—which then languished in a shipyard that went bankrupt. Eventually, the boat was released for its long trip through the Gulf of Mexico and Panama Canal, up the coast to the Golden Gate, then on up the Sacramento River to its current home. Re-christened *Spirit of Sacramento,* the fully refurbished boat now takes visitors on dining and sightseeing cruises. There are nice open decks for viewing.

A Parent's Guide to
San Francisco

Chapter Six
Within 100 Miles

Railroad Museum and Train Rides

2nd and I Streets, Sacramento
916/445-6645 • www.cmrsf.org

Hours: The museum is open every day from 10:00 a.m. to 5:00 p.m. Trains depart the station every hour from 10:00 a.m. to 5:00 p.m., Saturday and Sunday, April – September. Call to confirm the schedule.

Admission: Adults $6, kids ages 6–12 $3, under 6 free. The admission price covers both museum and station. Train rides are $6, ages 6-12 $3, under 6 free.

Directions: See Old Sacramento State Historic Park.

Old Sacramento's top attractions are a train trio that includes the California State Railroad Museum, the Central Pacific Passenger Station, and historic trains of the Sacramento Southern Railroad. The museum features 21 historic railcars and locomotives, all creatively displayed in a modern, indoor facility. Kids can even enter an old car, push a button, and experience the sounds and motions of past rail travel.

Nearby, the restored rail station is particularly interesting if you are waiting for an historic train ride. Steam trains run on weekends from April through September, following the Sacramento River on a 6-mile, 40-minute route. Half way through, the kids can watch as the engine unhooks from the cars then loops around to reconnect at the other end. Be there 20 minutes early to buy tickets.

Discovery Museum: History Center

101 I Street, Old Sacramento, Sacramento
916/264-7057 • www.thediscovery.org

Hours: Open daily, 10:00 a.m. to 5:00 p.m., closed Mondays during the winter.

Admission: $5 for adults; $4 for seniors and ages 13–17; $3 ages 6–12; under 6 free.

Next door to the rail museum, the Discovery Museum offers exhibits on California history, technology, and science. You'll find a working newspaper print shop dating to the days of manual typesetting, as well as a million-dollar display of gold from the mother lode. The museum successfully utilizes a number of display techniques to entice the interest of young ones, offering a number of hands-on, interactive exhibits. Give it 1/2-hour then head out for the boats, trains, and shops.

The science unit of the museum (3615 Auburn Boulevard, Sacramento, 916/575-3941) features a wildlife gallery, planetarium, and nature trail. It also hosts the Challenger Learning Center, one of several nationwide that offer a space and science learning experience to area kids.

A Parent's Guide to San Francisco

Chapter Six
Within 100 Miles

California State Capitol

L Street at 10th Street, Sacramento
916/324-0333 • www.assembly.ca.gov/museum

Hours: Guided tours are offered daily, on the hour, 9:00 a.m. to 4:00 p.m. Museum open daily from 8:30 a.m. to 5:00 p.m. The capitol is closed Thanksgiving, Christmas, and New Year's Day.

Admission: Free. Tour tickets are available in the Capitol Museum, which is open from 9:00 a.m. to 5:00 p.m. and is located in room B-27 of the Capitol basement.

Directions: The beautiful Capitol is easy to spot at L and 10th Streets in the heart of town. Capitol Park is bounded by L, N, 10th, and 15th Streets. Take Business I-80 from I-80, exit at the 15th Street or 16th Street exit (CA-160), follow 16th (one way), turn left on "L" Street.

Here's where the greats of the state hobnob and deliberate, contemplating the important issues of the day. Whether or not your kids will be impressed is another story. If you want to give them a dose of civics, you'll find a lovely rotunda and dome, legislative chambers, restored offices, beautiful murals, stern statues, and various historic displays. You may be heading back out to the wide and pleasant Capitol Park sooner than you'd hoped—though if you're there at a likely time, ask if there's a committee or legislative body in session. Whether you're a California citizen or not, you and the kids can sit in on any public proceeding where there's an open chair.

Waterworld USA

1600 Exposition Boulevard, Sacramento
916/924-0556 • www.sixflags.com/parks/waterworldsacramento

Hours: Open 10:30 a.m. to 6:00 p.m. daily, Memorial Day weekend through Labor Day.

Admission: Adults get in for $18, but you get half back when you leave if you are only observing. Kids under 48" tall get in for $13, ages 2 and under free. Expect to shell out more for parking ($5), lockers, inner tubes, and snacks.

Directions: Take Business I-80 from I-80, exit on Exposition Boulevard, and go one block east.

This popular, pricey escape has all sorts of great rides, including water slides, river tubing, wave pool, water luge, and kids' area with wading pool and giant playhouse. With attraction names like "Shark Attack," "Cannonball Falls," and "Cliffhanger Speed Slide," your older kids will be in heaven. The slow and lazy "Calypso Cooler" is more my speed—just park everyone in an innertube and float along. As with all such parks, lifeguards and other personnel keep an eye on the frolickers. Waterworld is located within the California Exposition grounds along the American River north of downtown Sacramento.

A Parent's Guide to
San Francisco

Chapter Six
Within 100 Miles

Towe Auto Museum

2200 Front Street, Sacramento
916/442-6802 • www.toweautomuseum.org

Hours: Open 10:00 a.m. to 6:00 p.m. daily.

Admission: $6 for adults; ages 14-17 $2.50; ages 5-13 $2; under 5 free.

Directions: From Capital Mall in the heart of town, take Front Street south. It's between I-5 and the Sacramento River.

I have a soft spot in my heart for really nice cars—cars that aren't sticky with spilled juice and have no footprints on the seats. But while a Lexus dealership might be a snooze for kids, the Towe Museum features 150 beauties of several other eras that will seem like a fleet of alien spaceships. The colors, curves, and shine will dazzle your less discriminating youngsters. Your teen may be inspired by different aspects of the collection (the one who will be able to get a learner's permit in 1 year, 2 months, 14 days, 3 hours, and 6 minutes). Tours are offered.

Sutter's Fort State Historic Park

27th and L Streets, Sacramento
916/445-4422 • parks.ca.gov/

Hours: Sutter's Fort and the Indian Museum are open daily, 10:00 a.m. to 5:00 p.m.

Admission: The admission price gets you into one or both: adults $3, ages 6 – 12 $1.50, under 6 free. Prices are slightly higher on scheduled living history days.

Directions: Sutter's Fort and the State Indian Museum are both located in a large park between K and L Streets, fifteen blocks east of the capitol building. Coming from the Bay Area, take the US-50 east/Business I-80 exit from I-80, then the Business I-80 exit north to the "N" Street exit. Bear left on 30th. Turn left on "L" Street.

Captain John Sutter was one of California's founding fathers. It was in his sawmill on the American River that James Marshall first spotted gold in 1848. Sutter, however, failed to capitalize on his gold rush opportunity and soon faded from importance.

Originally constructed in 1839, Sutter's Fort was the first real non-native center established inland from the mission centers of coastal California. Today's reconstruction includes little of the original adobe, but is true to the design and well worth a tour. The fort stands as the oldest restored fort in the West. The self-guided audio tour leads you through the fort for a look at period-furnished rooms and artifacts.

The best time to take kids to this California landmark is when living history activities are underway. There's nothing like humans to bring an old pile of logs and mud to life. Periodically throughout the year, volunteers and school children participate, dressing in period clothing and performing common tasks with the tools of the time: cooking, weaving, candle-making, etc. If your schedule is flexible, call ahead to see what's on the calendar.

Sutter's Fort sits in the corner of a large park that's good for squirrel-chasing, snacking, and a nap. The State Indian Museum is right next door (see below).

A Parent's Guide to San Francisco

Chapter Six
Within 100 Miles

State Indian Museum

26th and K Streets, Sacramento
916/324-0971 • parks.ca.gov/

Hours: Sutter's Fort and the Indian Museum are open daily, 10:00 a.m. to 5:00 p.m.

Admission: The admission price gets you into one or both: adults $3, ages 6 – 12 $1.50, under 6 free. Prices are slightly higher on scheduled living history days.

Directions: Sutter's Fort and the State Indian Museum are both located in a large park between K and L Streets, fifteen blocks east of the capitol building. Coming from the Bay Area, take the US-50 east/Business I-80 exit from I-80, then the Business I-80 exit north to the "N" Street exit. Bear left on 30th. Turn left on "L" Street.

Located right next to Sutter's Fort, the Indian Museum offers the chance to get two stops out of one parking spot. Exhibits include cultural and historic artifacts from many of California's native tribes, along with contemporary art works by native artists. In 1999, a new permanent exhibit opened that showcases the effects of the Gold Rush on native populations in the region. The museum offers a variety of special events throughout the year, including Ishi Day, Acorn Day, and a gathering of Indian Elders.

Central Valley

Pixie Woods Wonderland

Occidental Avenue and Monte Diablo Boulevard, Stockton
209/937-8206 • www.ci.stockton.ca.us/Parks/Pixie.htm

Hours: Open Saturday, Sunday, and holidays, weather permitting.

Admission: $1.25 for kids 12 and under, $1.75 for everyone else. Rides are 60 cents each.

Directions: Take the Monte Diablo exit from I-5 in Stockton, head west to Occidental. Pixie Woods is in Stockton's Louis Park.

Let your small ones loose in a fairy tale land, complete with a toadstool puppet theater, water-spouting dragon, and pirate ship play structure. They can ride the Pixie Express Train through Indian Country, or float along through "mysterious" lagoon on the Pixie Queen II Paddle Wheel Steamer. There's plenty of shade for snacks on a blanket, and lots of like-minded little ones to play with. Once they hit a certain age, however, interest in this cutesy fairyland will disappear in a hurry. Enjoy it while it lasts.

A Parent's Guide to San Francisco

**Chapter Six
Within
100 Miles**

Oakwood Lake Waters Theme Park

**874 East Woodward, Manteca
209/239-9566 • www.oakwoodlake.com**

Hours: Open from May – September. When school is in session, it's open weekends from 10:00 a.m. to 5:00 p.m. Summer hours are 10:00 a.m. to 6:00 p.m. daily. Check the website or call for the current schedule.

Admission: All areas ticket $21; kids from 42" to 48" tall $14; under 42" tall free (teach your kids to slump). Admission to the children's area and wading pool only is $10.

Directions: Take the CA-120/Manteca exit form I-5, turn south on Airport Way, go 1/2 mile, turn right onto Woodward and go 2 miles to the park.

Interested in frying eggs in the Central Valley on a summer afternoon? Just toss them on the hood of your car, the street, the sidewalk, or the foreheads of your cranky children. Better yet, forget your cooking experiment and take the kids and a couple of their friends to a water park. You can sit in the shade and read a Stephen King while they enjoy marginally supervised splashing and soaking.

Oakwood Lake Waters Theme Park encompasses a 75-acre lake, campground, picnic area, and over 30 "rides." The latest is Thunder Falls, which offers various ways to shoot down three stories into the pool below. There's even a children's area with wading pool for the tykes. If you wish, you can make an overnight or weekend out of it and stay at Oakwood's campground, which offers everything from RV sites with full hook-ups to basic tent sites.

Hershey Chocolate Factory

**120 South Sierra Avenue, Oakdale
209/848-8126 • www.hershey.com/visit/oakdale**

Hours: You can visit Monday – Friday, except for Good Friday and standard holidays. Tours are offered from 8:30 a.m. to 3:00 p.m., the visitor center stays open until 5:00 p.m.

Admission: Free.

Directions: Take CA-120 west from I-5, 28 miles to Oakdale. Follow CA-120 left around the corner from N. Yosemite Avenue onto East "F" Street, take the first right on South Sierra.

Need a diversion on your drive to Yosemite? Hershey's Oakdale plant is just the thing (unless your child is allergic to chocolate). A 30-minute walking tour follows the chocolate-making process from cocoa beans to wrapper. At the end, everyone is treated to a tasty sample of this American original. You won't be discouraged from buying plenty more at the factory store.

Drive to the visitor center at 120 South Sierra Street. From there, you'll ride a shuttle bus to the plant.

A Parent's Guide to San Francisco

Chapter Six
Within 100 Miles

Salinas Valley

San Juan Bautista State Historic Park

Centered at Second and Mariposa Streets, San Juan Bautista
831/623-4528 (mission), 831/623-4526 (park)

Hours: Open daily from 10:00 a.m. to 4:30 p.m.
Admission: Mission admission is $2 for adults, $1 ages 6-12, under 6 free.
Directions: From US-101 in the Salinas Valley, head east into San Juan Bautista on CA-156. All park facilities are easily found above 3rd Street in the heart of town. The San Juan Bakery is at 319 3rd Street.

Every California school student studies state history, including the fascinating Mission Period. In 1769, Father Junipero Serra and Gaspar de Portola headed north from Mexico to begin establishing Catholic missions. By 1823, 21 missions had been established, each located a "hard day's travel" from one another along the El Camino Real (king's road).

Today, you can visit mission sites and restored facilities up and down the coast, as far north as Sonoma. The best and most interesting to kids is the Mission San Juan Bautista. The outer walls of the 3-aisle mission church came down in the 1906 earthquake, but a complete restoration in 1976 returned the building to its former glory. The church, grounds, graveyard, and wing of the original mission are open for self-guided tours.

The young ones may be more interested in other nearby options. Across the historic Old Plaza from the mission are several historic Spanish-colonial buildings, all protected as part of San Juan Bautista State Historic Park. Check out the old horse-drawn carriages at the 1868 Zaneta House. The feel of yesteryear is unmistakable, with plenty of history to see, touch, and climb on.

Of special note is the fact that park and mission are perched literally on the edge of the San Andreas Fault. Down a short bank from the mission ground, an old path traces the faultline along the edge of the broad Salinas River valley. If they are old enough to appreciate it, spice up your children's experience with a walk on the fault. A sign on the edge of the plateau near the front entrance to the church offers some geological background.

To complete your trip, take the family on a short walk down historic 3rd Street. Make sure to visit the San Juan Bakery, the oldest bakery in the West.

A Parent's Guide to San Francisco

Chapter Six: Within 100 Miles

National Steinbeck Center

One Main Street, Salinas
831/775-4720 • www.steinbeck.org

Hours: Open daily, 10:00 a.m. to 5:00 p.m. The Steinbeck House is open for lunch only, Monday – Saturday.

Admission: Adults $8; seniors and students $7; ages 13-17 $6; ages 6-12 $4; under 6 free.

Directions: Approaching from the north on US-101, take the Salinas Main Street exit, follow Main 3 lights to the Center. Coming from the south, take the John Street exit from US-101, right on South Main, 5 blocks to the Center.

While you might expect this one to be a stretch for all but your not-too-little bookworms, the creators of this outstanding facility did a wonderful job of bringing John Steinbeck's work to life. Even kids who can't pronounce "Steinbeck" will enjoy the lights, colors, and animation of the multimedia exhibits, each of which corresponds to one of his books. The facility also includes a library and gift shop.

The plaza in front of the center looks down the historic Main Street of Salinas. While the district isn't nearly as vibrant as similar zones in more popular destinations, there are some interesting shops and eateries, including a couple of "antiques" emporia crammed full of all sorts of goodies.

To complete their literary experience, you might want to treat your more mature children to a dignified lunch at The Steinbeck House—Steinbeck's birthplace and the home of his youth. You'll find it a 132 Central Avenue, 3 blocks from the Center. Lunch runs about $9; there's no special children's menu.

A Parent's Guide to
San Francisco

Chapter Six
Within
100 Miles

Monterey/Big Sur

Monterey Bay Aquarium

886 Cannery Row, Monterey
831/648-4800, 800/756-3737 • www.montereybayaquarium.com

Hours: Open daily, 9:00 a.m. to 6:00 p.m. from June 15 through Labor Day; 10:00 a.m. to 6:00 p.m. the rest of the year.

Admission: $16 for adults; $13 seniors and students ages 13–17 or with college ID; $8 ages 3– 2 and disabled; kids under 3 free.

Directions: From CA-1, take the Pacific Grove/Del Monte Avenue exit (avoid the other Del Monte exits), bear right onto Lighthouse Avenue through the tunnel, turn right on David Avenue to the aquarium.

Considered one of the world's premiere facilities for the display of marine life, the Monterey Bay Aquarium is a must-visit for Bay Area families. Unlike Marine World and its counterparts, the aquarium is designed from scratch to be educational. It features the life of Monterey Bay exclusively, presented in the most naturalistic ways possible.

The *Outer Bay* is a favorite of mine. Visitors view this million-gallon "indoor ocean" through an expanse of glass that qualifies as the largest window in the world. Within, sharks, rays, barracudas, sea turtles, and numerous other species swim languidly along, waiting for their next feeding.

Kids can view otters and the other denizens of the Kelp Forest through a 6" acrylic window that's three stories tall. At the surface, the otters pop up onto the rocks for a look about before diving in again. "Playful" is word that seems to fit these delightful creatures.

Other exhibits include a wonderful group of endangered seahorses, big tanks of jellyfish lit in a way that showcases their alien forms, pools with touchable bat rays, an astonishingly close encounter with shorebirds, and Splash Zone—a favorite of kids for all the reasons you might expect.

Note that the aquarium is very popular and can be packed on weekends from late spring through early fall. That's not so bad inside the spacious facility, but if you don't have reservations, you might wait in line a long time to get in, and you know how the kids will love that. Call ahead, or check with your hotel—many lodgings sell aquarium tickets directly.

A Parent's Guide to San Francisco

Chapter Six
Within 100 Miles

Cannery Row

Monterey
www.canneryrow.com

Hours: Public access at all times. Business hours vary.

Admission: Free to visit, but many places to part with your cash.

Directions: From CA-1, take the Pacific Grove/Del Monte Avenue exit (avoid the other Del Monte exits), bear right onto Lighthouse Avenue through the tunnel, turn right on Drake Avenue to Cannery Row.

In the mid-1900s, Monterey Bay was a major sardine fishery and Cannery Row was just that—a row of bustling sardine canneries. As was typical with many coastal fisheries, the sardines were over-fished, the canneries went bust, and the row went to seed. Monterey's version got a jump on a renaissance, however, thanks to John Steinbeck and his book, *Cannery Row*.

Today, the touristy businesses of the Row milk Steinbeck for all he's worth and the area is main destination for the t-shirt and cotton candy set—which means the kids will love it. Consider spending a half-hour in Steinbeck's Spirit of Monterey Wax Museum (700 Cannery Row, Suite II, 831/375-3770) where you'll find over 100 wax figures set in a variety of scenes that trace the history of the region.

In addition to typical tourist places, you'll get a decent dose of history and find several nice shops and galleries. Best of all is the wonderful *Monterey Bay Aquarium* (see above).

Monterey State Historic Park

Central Monterey
831/649-7118, 831/649-7173 (tours), www.cal-parks.ca.gov

Hours: Plaza open to public access at all times, gardens open 10:00 a.m. to 4:00 p.m. Basic walking tours offered daily at 10:00 a.m., 11:00 a.m., and 2:00 p.m., departing from Stanton House visitor center in Custom House Plaza. Most other tours follow the same schedule, but call ahead.

Admission: Free.

Directions: From CA-1, take the Pacific Grove/Del Monte Avenue exit (avoid other Del Monte exits), go west on Del Monte about 1 1/2 miles, turn right at Washington to park or continue straight on Del Monte to Pacific, then turn right and park. If you bear right onto Lighthouse, you'll go through a tunnel and will have to turn around and come back at the first opportunity.

Some of the oldest California buildings are preserved in Monterey, which three times served as the state's capital (under Spanish, Mexican, and U.S. rule). Monterey State Historic Park preserves these structures in several small units, centered by the waterfront Custom House Plaza. The buildings include the 1827 Custom House, California's first theater, the Cooper Molera Adobe, a whaling station, and the house where Robert Louis Stevenson may have penned *Treasure Island*.

A Parent's Guide to San Francisco

Chapter Six
Within 100 Miles

It's fun to just pick up a map and walking tour pamphlet at the visitor center in Custom House Plaza and do a short walkabout. The plaza itself hosts a few of the structures, as well as a good maritime museum with items including excellent model ships. Fisherman's Wharf is nearby while Cannery Row and the Monterey Bay Aquarium are less than a mile away along the waterfront walk.

The best way to get a really good look at things is to take one of the tours offered by rangers and docents. Year round offerings include individual tours of Casa Soberanes, the Larkin House, Cooper Molera Adobe, or the Stevenson house. From April through October, you can opt for the "Secret Gardens Tour," "Night Time Garden Tour," "Monterey Presidio Tour," or a basic walking tour.

It's hard to say what the kids will like; home and garden tours might be a poor choice for those with short attention spans and active attitudes. To be safe, consider the Custom House Plaza area as part of a general 2-hour, tourist-style exploration of the Monterey waterfront area. Try blending an historic walkabout with a museum or house visit, some play on beach or rocks, and a trip to the end of Fisherman's Wharf.

Monterey Fisherman's Wharf

From Del Monte Avenue and Washington Street, Monterey
www.montereywharf.com

Hours: Open to public access, shop hours vary, restaurants open through evening dining hours.
Admission: Free to walk the wharf, lots of places to spend money.
Directions: See Monterey State Historic Park.

Is every "Fisherman's Wharf" the same? Just as in San Francisco, the Monterey Fisherman's Wharf caters to tourists, not to fishing professionals. Wander along the pier and you'll find dozens of places to buy a t-shirt, souvenir, or snack. At the end, you can climb the steps to a deck that gives you a bit of a view.

Several Monterey Bay tour companies are based on the pier. Among other things, you can opt for a glass-bottom boat ride (Sea Life Tours, 831/372-7151), fishing trip (Sam's Fishing Fleet, 831/372-0577), or sailing charter (Olympus Sailing Charters, 831/647-1957).

A Parent's Guide to San Francisco

Chapter Six: Within 100 Miles

Monterey Bay Whale Watch

Fisherman's Wharf, Monterey
831/375-4658 • www.montereybaywhalewatch.com

Hours: Offered at various times, trips last from 3 to 6 hours.

Admission: Six-hour trips: adults $42, under 13 $33. Three-hour trips: adults and teens $25, under 13 $18.

Directions: See Monterey State Historic Park above.

If you think your older kids can handle a few hours on the open sea without getting seasick or bored, consider treating them to the rare thrill of a close encounter with a whale. The hours of driving, waiting, and queasiness will be forgotten as soon as the first behemoth is spotted.

Gray whales are the most commonly seen. They migrate annually between the Gulf of California to the waters of Alaska, passing northward along the coast from February through April, southward in December and January. At other times of the year, giant blue whales and other species can be encountered.

Make sure everyone in your party has a cap, sunglasses, and sunscreen. Dress the kids in layers that can keep them warm, dry, and comfortable in the wind if needed. Reserve your tour in advance and check to see whether you should bring snacks and water. Most of all, remember your camera and binoculars!

Excursions are offered through much of the year. Blue and humpback whales are seen in summer and fall, grays in winter and spring. Marine biologists are your guides. Trips depart from Sam's Fishing at Monterey Fisherman's Wharf.

Pacific Grove Museum of Natural History

Forest Avenue and Central Avenue, Pacific Grove
831/648-5716 • www.pgmuseum.org

Hours: Open Tuesday – Sunday, 10:00 a.m. to 5:00 p.m.

Admission: Free.

Directions: From CA-1, take the Del Monte/Pacific Grove exit (avoid the other Del Monte exits). Follow Del Monte for about 1 1/2 miles, then bear right onto Lighthouse Avenue and through the tunnel to Pacific Grove, right on Forest to Central.

Dedicated to educating visitors in the natural history of Monterey County, museum exhibits interpret the native plants, animals, geology, and aboriginal populations of the region. Special, temporary exhibits come and go throughout the year, including the annual wildflower show, which is up for one weekend only. The museum also has a strong involvement in the preservation of monarch butterflies and their habitat, and has a good exhibit that can help prepare young people for a visit to the Monarch Sanctuary.

A Parent's Guide to San Francisco

Chapter Six: Within 100 Miles

Monarch Habitat Sanctuary

Ridge Road from Lighthouse Avenue, Monterey
831/375-0982 • www.pgmonarchs.org/fomh.html

Hours: Always open.

Admission: Free.

Directions: See Pacific Grove Museum of Natural History.

In the chill of early morning, the casual observer might not even realize that all those dead leaves hanging from the trees are really butterflies awaiting the sun. As the morning heats up, the leaves begin to flicker from bland to bright as wings are tested. Soon, some of the livelier specimens flutter about the grove, and perhaps out into the surrounding area, though most are content to wait for a change of seasons before leaving town.

Only a small piece of the monarchs' original Monterey Peninsula wintering habitat is still intact. All that remains is a 2.4-acre park behind the Butterfly Grove Inn, though restoration of Monterey's Washington Park habitat may be bearing fruit when you visit. The monarchs arrive in October, apparently glad for the moist, frost-free winters of the coast. They join the spring migration in March, fanning out north and east in search of the milkweed plants they use exclusively for laying their eggs. To experience this wonder of nature with the kids, plan on a visit between these months.

This is another one of those spots where you might try to surprise the kids. See how long it takes them to notice that that leaf is a butterfly, and then that there are hundreds—no, thousands of butterflies all around. Discovery and awe are a great team to fuel the imagination of young minds.

A Parent's Guide to San Francisco

Chapter Six
Within 100 Miles

Point Pinos Lighthouse

End of Lighthouse Avenue, Pacific Grove
831/648-5716 • www.pgmuseum.org/Lighthouse.htm

Hours: Open Thursday – Sunday from 1:00 p.m. to 4:00 p.m., though you can walk around the outside at any time.

Admission: Free.

Directions: From CA-1, take the Del Monte/Pacific Grove exit (avoid the other Del Monte exits). Follow Del Monte for about 1 1/2 miles, then bear right onto Lighthouse Avenue and through the tunnel to Pacific Grove, to the end of Lighthouse, right on Asilomar, left to the lighthouse.

Surrounded by the fairways of a Pacific Grove golf course, Point Pinos is the oldest continuously operating lighthouse on the west coast. The point itself is the northernmost tip of the Monterey Peninsula and offers a distinct hazard to ships entering or exiting Monterey Bay. Fortunately for sailors, the Point Pinos Light has served to keep ships on course since February 1, 1855.

As a small light set back from the rocky coast, the light isn't really much of an attraction for anyone but lighthouse buffs. It's only open 12 hours a week, making it difficult to tour unless you plan your visit with some care. I wouldn't bother—treat it casually, stopping by for walk around the outside on your way to the aquarium, beach, museum, coast walk, or historic park.

Point Lobos State Reserve

CA-1, South of Carmel
831/624-4909 • parks.ca.gov

Hours: Open 9:00 a.m. to 5:00 p.m. daily, until 7:00 p.m. in the summer.

Admission: Day-use parking is $7 per vehicle.

Directions: The Reserve entrance is along CA-1, 3 miles south of Carmel.

Among California's many excellent coastal parks, Point Lobos is a particularly good choice for families. The reserve concentrates the best of the coast in a relatively small area. Waves explode against craggy headlands while California and Steller's sea lions lounge in the shallows just around the bend. Trails pass through open coastal meadows one minute, wind-sculpted forests of pine and cedar the next. Migrating whales are easily spotted in season, which peaks in March and December.

If you are in the park around high tide, take the kids to see Devil's Cauldron— a blowhole that can send up an impressive gush of water. When the conditions are right, the waters of incoming swells are forced into a narrow chute, naturally accelerated, and directed more or less upward. The ensuing blast elicits shrieks of delight from young watchers. Of course, conditions aren't always right for the best display. Ask the ranger at the entrance gate what you should expect to see.

Point Lobos is a popular park. If you come on a weekend, you might find it hard to park near the main coastal spots, necessitating walks of a few hundred yards.

Appendices

Every year, the Bay Area hosts hundreds of events that attract kids and parents—far more than I could ever list here, or even know about. Your best bet is to check print, radio, television, and web media regularly so you don't miss out on something great. As you might expect, certain holidays bring similar events in many communities—like fireworks on the 4th of July, egg hunts on Easter, and tree-lighting ceremonies after Thanksgiving. Other events are new or randomly scheduled, and so don't make it onto the annual calendar.

Below you'll find some good sources for events news, followed by a calendar of some yearly happenings that are worth checking out:

Area Newspapers That Lists Events

- *Contra Costa Times* (Contra Costa County, including much of the East Bay)
- *Marin Independent Journal* (Marin County)
- *Oakland Tribune* (Oakland, Berkeley, and the southern East Bay)
- *San Francisco Chronicle* (The "Pink Section" in the Sunday edition of the Chronicle/Examiner is the top print source for Bay Area Events)
- *San Jose Mercury News* (South Bay)

A Parent's Guide to San Francisco

Appendices
Calendar

Helpful Web Sites

www.sfgate.com (Great resource for the entire Bay Area)
www.sfvisitor.org (San Francisco's visitors' bureau site)
www.eastbayexpress.com/calendarlist/lkids.html
www.bayarea.com/entertainment/calendar (The web arm of several area newspapers, including the San Jose Mercury News—click on "Family")
www.ci.san-jose.ca.us/upcoming.html (San Jose and vicinity)
www.parentspress.com (find links to resources like Mother's Clubs where you can get event and activity ideas from other parents)
www.sonoma.com/events.html (Sonoma County)
www.napavalley.com/events.html (Napa Valley)
www.craigslist.org/sfo/eve/ (One of my favorite sites and sources, though not much for kids)

Calendar of Annual Events

January

Vietnamese New Year, San Jose, 408/295-9210, www.lienhoi.com
Whalefest, Monterey, 831/644-7588, www.monterey.com/mc2/whalefest

February

Chinese New Year Parade, San Francisco, 415/391-9680, www.chineseparade.com

March

Junior Grand National Livestock Expo, San Francisco

April

Apple Blossom Festival, Sebastopol, 707/823-3032, www.sebastopol.org
Asparagus Festival, Stockton, www.asparagusfest.com
Earth Day, Berkeley, 510/654-6346, www.bayareaearthday.net
Earth Day, San Francisco, www.bayareaearthday.net
Kite Festival, Carmel
Fisherman's Festival, Bodega Bay, 707/875-3866, www.sonomacoastguide.com
Good Old Days Celebration, Pacific Grove, 831/373-3304, www.pacificgrove.org
Log Race, Petaluma
Nikkei Matsuri Festival, San Jose, 408/241-0900, www.scu.edu/diversity/nikmatsu.html

A Parent's Guide to San Francisco

Appendices
Calendar

May

Chamarita Festival and Parade, Half Moon Bay, 650/726-5701, **halfmoonbaychamber.citysearch.com**

Cinco de Mayo, San Francisco and other communities, 415/826-1401, 877/203-1703, **www.latinbayarea.com/meca.htm**

Contra Costa County Fair, Antioch, 925/757-4400, **www.ccfair.org**

Festival of Greece, Oakland, 510/531-3400, **www.ascensioncathedral.org/Pages/festinfo.html**

Living History Days, Petaluma Adobe State Historic Park, 707/762-4871, **parks.sonoma.net/adobe.html**

Salinas Valley Fair, King City, 831/385-3243, **www.salinasvalleyfair.com**

San Francisco Examiner Bay to Breakers, San Francisco, 415/808-5000 ext. 2222, **www.baytobreakers.com**

Stump Town Days and Rodeo, Guerneville

West Coast National Antique Fly-in, Watsonville, 831/763-5600, **www.watsonvilleflying.org**

June

Alameda County Fair, Pleasanton, 925/426-7600, **www.alamedacountyfair.com**

Bear Flag Day, Sonoma

Fathers Day Fun Fly (kite festival), San Francisco, **www.kitefest.com**

The Great Cannery Row Sardine Festival and Frog Jump, Monterey, 831/648-6690, **www.mty.com**

Hot Air Balloon Classic, Sonoma, 707/837-1884

Juneteenth Celebration, Oakland/Berkeley, 510/286-8041, **www.juneteenth.com**

Merienda, Monterey, **users.depot.com/mchs/pacifichouse.html**

Solano County Fair, Vallejo, 707/644-4401, **www.scfair.com**

Sonoma-Marin Fair, Petaluma, 707/283-3247, **www.sonoma-marinfair.org**

July

Asian Festival, Oakland Museum, Oakland

California Rodeo, Salinas, 800/757-5134, **www.carodeo.com**

ESPN X Games, San Francisco, **expn.go.com**

Feast of Lanterns, Pacific Grove, 831/649-7837, **www.pacificgrove.org**

Fiesta Rodeo de San Juan Bautista, San Juan Bautista, 831/623-2127

Garlic Festival, Gilroy, 408/842-1625, **www.gilroygarlicfestival.com**

Marin County Fair, San Rafael, 415/499-6400, **www.marinfair.org**

Napa County Fair, Calistoga

Native American Big-Time Celebration, Point Reyes Station, 415/663-1092
Obon Festival, Monterey,
    www.gomonterey.com/special_interests/current_events/sul.html
Sacramento Water Festival, Sacramento
San Mateo County Fair, 800/338-EXPO, 650/574-3247,
    www.sanmateoexpo.org/fair.html
San Jose America Festival, San Jose, 408/294-2100 ext.444, www.americafestival.com
Scotts Valley Days, Scotts Valley
Sonoma County Fair, Santa Rosa, 707/545-4200, www.sonomacountyfair.com
Strawberry Festival, Watsonville, 831/724-3945, www.infopoint.com/sc/msw/strawberry.html
Water Carnival, Monte Rio, www.monterio.org/historypage.htm

August

California State Fair, Sacramento, 916/263-3247, www.bigfun.org
Children's Fairytale Birthday Week, Oakland
Chinatown Streetfest, Oakland, 510/893-8979, www.oakland-business.com/chinatown
Gem and Mineral Show, San Francisco, 415/564-4230,
    www.sfgrs.org/august_show/august_show.html
Monterey County Fair, www.montereycountyfair.com
Gilroy Garlic Festival, Gilroy, 408/842-1625, www.gilroygarlicfestival.com
Gravenstein Apple Fair, Sebastopol, 800/207-9464, 707/571-8288,
    www.farmtrails.org/gravfair.htm
Monterey County Fair, Monterey
Nihonmachi Street Fair, Japantown, San Francisco, 415/771-9861, www.nihonmachistreetfair.org
Old Adobe Days, Petaluma Adobe State Historic Park
Renaissance Pleasure Fair, 800/52-FAIRE, www.renfaire.com
Santa Clara County Fair, San Jose, 408/494-3185, www.thefair.org
Steinbeck Festival, Salinas, 831/775-4720, www.steinbeck.org

A Parent's Guide to San Francisco

Appendices
Calendar

September

California State Fair, Sacramento, 916/263-3247, www.bigfun.org
Celtic Festival, Sebastopol, 707/823-1511, www.monitor.net/celtic
LEAP Sand Castle Contest, San Francisco
Moon Festival, Chinatown, San Francisco, 415/982-6306, www.moonfest.org
Pageant of Fire Mountain, Guerneville
Renaissance Pleasure Fair, 800/52-FAIRE, www.renfaire.com
Santa Cruz, County Fair, Watsonville, 831/724-5671, www.santacruzcountyfair.com
Sofa Festival, San Jose, 408/279-1775, www.sj-downtown.com
Solano Avenue Stroll, Berkeley/Albany, 510/527-5358, www.solano-ave.com/stroll
Valley of the Moon Vintage Festival, Sonoma, www.sonomavinfest.com
Walnut Festival, Walnut Creek
Worldfest, Berkeley

October

Black Cowboys Parade, Oakland, www.oaklandnet.com/community
California International Airshow, Salinas, 888/845-7469, www.ca-airshow.com
Chinese Double Ten Celebration, San Francisco
Columbus Day Carnival and Parade, Martinez
Columbus Day Festival, San Francisco, 415/434-1492
Dia de Los Muertos (Day of the Dead), San Jose, San Francisco, Oakland, 415/821-1155
Fleet Week, San Francisco, 415/621-2325, www.fleetweek.com
Grand National Rodeo, Horse, and Stock Show 415/469-6065, www.grandnational-rodeo.com
Great Pumpkin Weigh Off, Half Moon Bay, 650/726-9652, www.miramarevents.com/pumpkinfest
Great Sandcastle Building Contest, Carmel, 831/372-6527, www.aiamb.org/pubevents.htm
Harvest Fair and Pumpkin Fest, Healdsburg, 707/545-4203, 707/431-1956
Marin Grape Festival, San Rafael, 415/256-1580
Old Mill Days, Bale Grist Mill State Historic Park, St. Helena, 707/942-4575
Sonoma County Harvest Festival, Santa Rosa, 707/545-4203, www.sonomacountyfair.com
Welcome Back Monarchs Day, Santa Cruz, 831/423-4609, www.lighthousedogs.com/monarchsday.html

November

Holiday Parade, San Jose, 408/277-3303, www.sanjoseholidayparade.com
Embarcadero Center Holiday Lights Celebration, San Francisco, 415/772-0253

December

Christmas at the Mission, Sonoma Mission State Historic Park, 707/938-1519
Christmas At Sea, San Francisco, 415/561-6662
Christmas Balloon Parade, San Jose, 408/277-4191, www.sanjoseholidayparade.com
Festival of the Trees, Monterey
Festival of the Trees, San Rafael
Lighted Yacht Parade, Oakland, 510/814-6000, www.jacklondonsquare.com/events.html
Lighting of the Tree of Lebanon, Santa Rosa
Nutcracker Ballet, San Francisco and other communities, 415/865-2000,
    www.sfballet.com/nutcracker
Pioneer Christmas, Bale Grist Mill State Historic Park, 707/942-4575
Rice-pounding Ceremony, Japantown, San Francisco
San Juan Bautista Candlelight Procession, San Juan Bautista, 831/623-2454,
    www.san-juan-bautista.ca.us/calendar.htm
Santa Cruz Holiday Lights Train, Santa Cruz, www.roaringcamp.com/schedule.html

A Parent's Guide to San Francisco

Appendices
Index

Name	City/Region	Chapter	Page
Animal Experience			
Año Nuevo State Reserve	Peninsula Coast	South Bay & Peninsula	144
Armstrong Woods Trail Rides	Russian River Valley	Within 100 Miles	156
Buffalo Enclosure	Golden Gate Park	San Francisco	46
Happy Hollow Zoo	San Jose	South Bay & Peninsula	138
Junior Museum & Zoo	Palo Alto	South Bay & Peninsula	129
Lindsay Wildlife Museum	Walnut Creek	East Bay	116
Marine Mammal Center	Marin Headlands	Marin County	63
Monterey Bay Aquarium	Monterey / Big Sur	Within 100 Miles	167
Monterey Bay Whale Watch	Monterey / Big Sur	Within 100 Miles	170
Mouth of the Russian River: Goat Rock Beach	Russian River Valley	Within 100 Miles	153
Oakland Zoo	Oakland	East Bay	108
Point Reyes Bird Observatory	Point Reyes National Seashore	Marin County	69
Pony Rides	Tilden Regional Park	East Bay	102
Randall Museum	Castro / Upper Market	San Francisco	50
San Francisco Zoo	Sunset District	San Francisco	51
Steinhart Aquarium	Golden Gate Park	San Francisco	45
Tomales Point and the Tule Elk Reserve	Point Reyes National Seashore	Marin County	73
UnderWater World	Fisherman's Wharf	San Francisco	25
WildCare	San Rafael	Marin County	79
Art			
Balmy Alley	Mission District	San Francisco	53
Cartoon Art Museum	South of Market	San Francisco	55
Coit Tower	Chinatown / North Beach	San Francisco	20
Jewish Museum of San Francisco	South of Market	San Francisco	56
Mural Walk	Mission District	San Francisco	52
Museo Italo-Americano	Fort Mason	San Francisco	32
Museum of Craft and Folk Art	Fort Mason	San Francisco	32
Museum of Modern Art	South of Market	San Francisco	55
Oakland Museum of California	Oakland	East Bay	107
Papua New Guinea Sculpture Garden	Stanford University	South Bay & Peninsula	127
Rodin Sculpture Garden	Stanford University	South Bay & Peninsula	127
San Francisco African American Historical & Cultural Society	Fort Mason	San Francisco	33
University Museum	University of California	East Bay	99
Beaches			
China Beach	Seacliff	San Francisco	38
McClure's Beach	Point Reyes National Seashore	Marin County	74
McNears Beach	San Rafael	Marin County	78
Mouth of the Russian River: Goat Rock Beach	Russian River Valley	Within 100 Miles	153
Muir Beach	Marin Coast	Marin County	65
Ocean Beach	Outer Richmond	San Francisco	41
Peninsula Beaches	Peninsula Coast	South Bay & Peninsula	143
Point Reyes Beaches	Point Reyes National Seashore	Marin County	71
Rodeo Lagoon & Beach	Marin Headlands	Marin County	64
Santa Cruz Beach Boardwalk	Santa Cruz	South Bay & Peninsula	146
Sonoma Coast State Beaches	North Coast	Within 100 Miles	153
Stinson Beach	Marin Coast	Marin County	67

A Parent's Guide to San Francisco

Appendices
Index

Big Rides: By Air, Land & Water

Alcatraz	Fisherman's Wharf	San Francisco	25
Balloon, Glider & Vintage Plane Rides	Napa Valley	Marin County	85
Bay Boat Tours and Ferries	Fisherman's Wharf	San Francisco	26
Cable Car Ride	Chinatown / North Beach	San Francisco	18
Niles Canyon Railway	Sunol	East Bay	113
Railroad Museum and Train Rides	Sacramento	Within 100 Miles	160
Roaring Camp and Historic Railways	Felton	South Bay & Peninsula	145
Spirit of Sacramento Cruise	Sacramento	Within 100 Miles	159

Culture, Food & Shopping

Cliff House	Outer Richmond	San Francisco	39
Embarcadero Center	Financial District	San Francisco	17
Ghirardelli Square: Chocolate!	Fisherman's Wharf	San Francisco	31
Golden Gate Fortune Cookie Company	Chinatown / North Beach	San Francisco	22
Grant Street	Chinatown / North Beach	San Francisco	22
Sproul Plaza	University of California	East Bay	97
Telegraph Avenue	Berkeley	East Bay	96
Town of Bolinas	Marin Coast	Marin County	68
Winery Visit	Napa & Sonoma Valleys	Marin County	83

Entertainment, Recreation & Sports

Baby Brigade Night at the Parkway	Oakland	East Bay	103
Casini Ranch Family Campground	Russian River Valley	Within 100 Miles	154
Crissy Field	The Presidio	San Francisco	36
Hagemann Ranch Trout Farm	North Coast	Within 100 Miles	151
Iceland	Berkeley	East Bay	96
J's Amusements	Russian River Valley	Within 100 Miles	156
Johnson's Beach & Resort	Russian River Valley	Within 100 Miles	157
Lake Merritt Boating Center	Oakland	East Bay	105
Metreon	South of Market	San Francisco	54
Pacific Bell Park	South of Market	San Francisco	59
Villa Montalvo	Saratoga	South Bay & Peninsula	134
W.C. "Bob" Trowbridge: Canoeing and Kayaking the Russian	Russian River Valley	Within 100 Miles	157
Yerba Buena Gardens/Moscone Center	South of Market	San Francisco	56
Yerba Buena Ice Skating and Bowling Center	South of Market	San Francisco	57

Environmental Education

Hidden Villa	Los Altos Hills	South Bay & Peninsula	130
Lake Merritt Rotary Nature Center	Oakland	East Bay	105
Marine Science Institute	Redwood City	South Bay & Peninsula	125
Phipps Country Store and Farm	Peninsula Coast	South Bay & Peninsula	142
Real Goods Solar Living Center	Russian River Valley	Within 100 Miles	158
Slide Ranch	Marin Coast	Marin County	66
Sulphur Creek Nature Center	Hayward	East Bay	110
WildCare	San Rafael	Marin County	79

A Parent's Guide to San Francisco

Appendices
Index

Gardens, Grounds & Ponds

Hakone Japanese Gardens	Saratoga	South Bay & Peninsula	133
Japanese Friendship Garden	San Jose	South Bay & Peninsula	139
Japanese Tea Garden	Golden Gate Park	San Francisco	48
Palace of Fine Arts	Marina District	San Francisco	34
Papua New Guinea Sculpture Garden	Stanford University	South Bay & Peninsula	127
Spreckels Lake	Golden Gate Park	San Francisco	46
Stanford Inner Campus	Stanford University	South Bay & Peninsula	126
Strawberry Creek	University of California	East Bay	98
Strybing Arboretum	Golden Gate Park	San Francisco	49

Government, Civics & Libraries

California State Capitol	Sacramento	Within 100 Miles	161
City Hall	Civic Center	San Francisco	16
San Francisco Public Library	Civic Center	San Francisco	17

Hands-on Museum

Bay Area Discovery Museum	Fort Baker	Marin County	74
Chabot Space & Science Center	Oakland	East Bay	106
Children's Discovery Museum of San Jose	San Jose	South Bay & Peninsula	136
Exploratorium	Marina District	San Francisco	34
Habitot Children's Museum	Berkeley	East Bay	94
Hall of Health	Berkeley	East Bay	95
Lawrence Hall of Science	University of California	East Bay	100
Randall Museum	Castro / Upper Market	San Francisco	50
Tech Museum of Innovation, The	San Jose	South Bay & Peninsula	137
Zeum	South of Market	San Francisco	57

Hiking and Wildlands

Angel Island State Park	Tiburon	Marin County	77
Austin Creek State Recreation Area	Russian River Valley	Within 100 Miles	155
Bear Valley	Point Reyes National Seashore	Marin County	70
Big Basin Redwoods State Park	Big Basin	South Bay & Peninsula	135
Black Diamond Mines Regional Preserve	Antioch	East Bay	119
Bodega Head	North Coast	Within 100 Miles	151
Borges Ranch	Walnut Creek	East Bay	116
Drakes Estero	Point Reyes National Seashore	Marin County	71
John Muir National Historic Site	Martinez	East Bay	120
Mount Diablo State Park	Walnut Creek	East Bay	117
Mount Tamalpais State Park	Marin Coast	Marin County	64
Palomarin Trail	Point Reyes National Seashore	Marin County	69
Rodeo Lagoon & Beach	Marin Headlands	Marin County	64
Tomales Point and the Tule Elk Reserve	Point Reyes National Seashore	Marin County	73

181

A Parent's Guide to San Francisco

Appendices
Index

Historic Sites & Parks

Alcatraz	Fisherman's Wharf	San Francisco	25
Ardenwood Farm	Fremont	East Bay	111
Bale Grist Mill State Historic Park	St. Helena	Marin County	83
Black Diamond Mines Regional Preserve	Antioch	East Bay	119
China Camp State Park	San Rafael	Marin County	78
Fort Point National Historic Site	The Presidio	San Francisco	36
Fort Ross State Historic Park	North Coast	Within 100 Miles	152
History Park	San Jose	South Bay & Peninsula	139
Hyde Street Ships Pier	Fisherman's Wharf	San Francisco	29
John Muir National Historic Site	Martinez	East Bay	120
Monterey State Historic Park	Monterey / Big Sur	Within 100 Miles	168
Old Sacramento State Historic Park	Sacramento	Within 100 Miles	159
Petaluma Adobe State Historic Park	Petaluma	Marin County	82
San Juan Bautista State Historic Park	Salinas Valley	Within 100 Miles	165
Sanchez Adobe	Pacifica	South Bay & Peninsula	142
Sutro Baths Ruins	Outer Richmond	San Francisco	39
Sutter's Fort State Historic Park	Sacramento	Within 100 Miles	162

History Museums

Cable Car Barn Museum	Chinatown / North Beach	San Francisco	19
Discovery Museum: History Center	Sacramento	Within 100 Miles	160
Fire Department Museum	Laurel Heights	San Francisco	38
Marin Museum of the American Indian	Novato	Marin County	80
Musee Mechanique	Outer Richmond	San Francisco	40
National Steinbeck Center	Salinas Valley	Within 100 Miles	166
Oakland Museum of California	Oakland	East Bay	107
Rosicrucian Museum	San Jose	South Bay & Peninsula	140
San Francisco National Maritime Museum	Fisherman's Wharf	San Francisco	30
Seymour Pioneer Museum	South of Market	San Francisco	53
Sharpsteen Museum	Calistoga	Marin County	88
State Indian Museum	Sacramento	Within 100 Miles	163
Surfing Museum	Santa Cruz	South Bay & Peninsula	148
Wells Fargo History Museum	Financial District	San Francisco	18

Nature Experience

Armstrong Redwoods State Reserve	Russian River Valley	Within 100 Miles	155
Audubon Canyon Ranch	Marin Coast	Marin County	68
Bay Audubon Center & Sanctuary	Tiburon	Marin County	76
Baylands Nature Preserve	Palo Alto	South Bay & Peninsula	128
Bolinas Lagoon	Marin Coast	Marin County	67
Coyote Point Recreation Area & Museum	Burlingame	South Bay & Peninsula	123
Don Edwards San Francisco Bay National Wildlife Refuge	Fremont	East Bay	112
Monarch Butterfly Reserve	Santa Cruz	South Bay & Peninsula	147
Monarch Habitat Sanctuary	Monterey / Big Sur	Within 100 Miles	171
Muir Woods National Monument	Marin Coast	Marin County	65
Nature Area	Tilden Regional Park	East Bay	102
Old Faithful	Calistoga	Marin County	86
Petrified Forest	Calistoga	Marin County	87
Shorebird Nature Center	Berkeley	East Bay	93
Sulphur Creek Nature Center	Hayward	East Bay	110

A Parent's Guide to San Francisco

Appendices
Index

Oceanside: Parks, Piers & Lighthouses

Año Nuevo State Reserve	Peninsula Coast	South Bay & Peninsula	144
Aquatic Park	Fisherman's Wharf	San Francisco	30
Baylands Nature Preserve	Palo Alto	South Bay & Peninsula	128
Berkeley Marina Pier	Berkeley	East Bay	93
Bodega Head	North Coast	Within 100 Miles	151
Cesar Chavez Park	Berkeley	East Bay	94
China Camp State Park	San Rafael	Marin County	78
Coyote Point Recreation Area & Museum	Burlingame	South Bay & Peninsula	123
Crissy Field	The Presidio	San Francisco	36
Don Edwards San Francisco Bay National Wildlife Refuge	Fremont	East Bay	112
Fort Funston	Sunset District	San Francisco	51
Fort Ross State Historic Park	North Coast	Within 100 Miles	152
Marina Green	Marina District	San Francisco	35
Monterey Fisherman's Wharf	Monterey / Big Sur	Within 100 Miles	169
Pier 39	Fisherman's Wharf	San Francisco	24
Pigeon Point Light Station	Peninsula Coast	South Bay & Peninsula	143
Point Arena Lighthouse	North Coast	Within 100 Miles	152
Point Bonita Lighthouse	Marin Headlands	Marin County	63
Point Lobos State Reserve	Monterey / Big Sur	Within 100 Miles	172
Point Pinos Lighthouse	Monterey / Big Sur	Within 100 Miles	172
Point Reyes Lighthouse	Point Reyes National Seashore	Marin County	72
Sutro Baths Ruins	Outer Richmond	San Francisco	39
Wave Organ	Marina District	San Francisco	35

Old Planes, Ships, Cars & Trains

Blackhawk Auto Museum	Danville	East Bay	115
Cable Car Barn Museum	Chinatown / North Beach	San Francisco	19
Cable Car Ride	Chinatown / North Beach	San Francisco	18
Hyde Street Ships Pier	Fisherman's Wharf	San Francisco	29
Liberty Ship Jeremiah O'Brien	Fisherman's Wharf	San Francisco	28
Niles Canyon Railway	Sunol	East Bay	113
Pier 45 and the USS Pampanito	Fisherman's Wharf	San Francisco	27
Railroad Museum and Train Rides	Sacramento	Within 100 Miles	160
Roaring Camp and Historic Railways	Felton	South Bay & Peninsula	145
Towe Auto Museum	Sacramento	Within 100 Miles	162
U.S.S. Hornet Museum	Alameda	East Bay	109
Western Aerospace Museum	Oakland	East Bay	108

183

A Parent's Guide to San Francisco

Appendices
Index

Parks & Lakes

Golden Gate Park and How to Get There	Golden Gate Park	San Francisco	42
Kelley Park	San Jose	South Bay & Peninsula	138
Knowland Park	Oakland	East Bay	108
Lafayette Reservoir	Lafayette	East Bay	118
Lake Anza	Tilden Regional Park	East Bay	101
Lake Merritt Boating Center	Oakland	East Bay	105
Lake Temescal	Oakland	East Bay	107
Music Concourse	Golden Gate Park	San Francisco	48
Oak Meadow Park/Vasona Park	Los Gatos	South Bay & Peninsula	132
Pulgas Water Temple	San Carlos	South Bay & Peninsula	124
Rapids Waterslide at Shadow Cliffs Regional Park	Pleasanton	South Bay & Peninsula	114
Stow Lake	Golden Gate Park	San Francisco	47
Strawberry Hill	Golden Gate Park	San Francisco	47

Playgrounds, Kiddie Parks & Rides

Adventure Playground	Berkeley	East Bay	92
Billy Jones Wildcat Railroad	Los Gatos	South Bay & Peninsula	132
Children's Fairyland	Oakland	East Bay	104
Children's Play Area	South of Market	San Francisco	58
Children's Playground and Carousel	Golden Gate Park	San Francisco	43
Looff Carousel	South of Market	San Francisco	58
Merry-go-round	Tilden Regional Park	East Bay	101
Pixie Woods Wonderland	Central Valley	Within 100 Miles	163
Pixieland Park	Concord	East Bay	118
Sonoma Traintown	Sonoma	Marin County	82
Steam Train	Tilden Regional Park	East Bay	103
W.E. Bill Mason Carousel	Los Gatos	South Bay & Peninsula	132

Science

Academy of Sciences	Golden Gate Park	San Francisco	44
Bay Model	Sausalito	Marin County	75
Camera Obscura	Outer Richmond	San Francisco	40
Chabot Space & Science Center	Oakland	East Bay	106
Children's Discovery Museum of San Jose	San Jose	South Bay & Peninsula	136
Exploratorium	Marina District	San Francisco	34
Lawrence Hall of Science	University of California	East Bay	100
Lick Observatory	San Jose	South Bay & Peninsula	141
Minolta Planetarium	Cupertino	South Bay & Peninsula	131
Morrison Planetarium	Golden Gate Park	San Francisco	45
NASA Ames Research Center	Mountain View	South Bay & Peninsula	131
Natural History Museum	Golden Gate Park	San Francisco	44
Oakland Museum of California	Oakland	East Bay	107
Pacific Grove Museum of Natural History	Monterey / Big Sur	Within 100 Miles	170
Paleontology Museum	University of California	East Bay	98
Recyclery, The	Milpitas	South Bay & Peninsula	133
Stanford Linear Accelerator	Stanford University	South Bay & Peninsula	128
Steinhart Aquarium	Golden Gate Park	San Francisco	45
Tech Museum of Innovation, The	San Jose	South Bay & Peninsula	137
UnderWater World	Fisherman's Wharf	San Francisco	25

A Parent's Guide to San Francisco

Appendices
Index

Special or Strange

Basic Brown Bear Factory	South of Market	San Francisco	54
Camera Obscura	Outer Richmond	San Francisco	40
Crookedest Street in the World	Chinatown / North Beach	San Francisco	21
Golden Gate Bridge	The Presidio	San Francisco	37
Hershey Chocolate Factory	Central Valley	Within 100 Miles	164
Hidden Stairways	Chinatown / North Beach	San Francisco	21
Musee Mechanique	Outer Richmond	San Francisco	40
Mystery Spot	Santa Cruz	South Bay & Peninsula	148
Rosicrucian Museum	San Jose	South Bay & Peninsula	140
Wave Organ	Marina District	San Francisco	35
Westbay Model Railroad	Menlo Park	South Bay & Peninsula	125
Winchester House	San Jose	South Bay & Peninsula	140

Summits & Views

Coit Tower	Chinatown / North Beach	San Francisco	20
Hoover Tower	Stanford University	South Bay & Peninsula	126
Mount Diablo State Park	Walnut Creek	East Bay	117
Mount Tamalpais State Park	Marin Coast	Marin County	64
Sather Tower	University of California	East Bay	99
WWII Gun Emplacements	Marin Headlands	Marin County	62

Theme & Water Parks

Oakwood Lake Waters Theme Park	Central Valley	Within 100 Miles	164
Paramount's Great America	Santa Clara	South Bay & Peninsula	136
Raging Waters	San Jose	South Bay & Peninsula	137
Rapids Waterslide at Shadow Cliffs Regional Park	Pleasanton	South Bay & Peninsula	114
Santa Cruz Beach Boardwalk	Santa Cruz	South Bay & Peninsula	146
Scandia Family Fun Center	Fairfield	Marin County	81
Six Flags Marine World	Vallejo	Marin County	81
Waterworld USA	Sacramento	Within 100 Miles	161

Tourist Areas & Attractions

Cannery Row	Monterey / Big Sur	Within 100 Miles	168
Duncans Mills	Russian River Valley	Within 100 Miles	154
Fisherman's Wharf Area and How to Get There, The	Fisherman's Wharf	San Francisco	23
Monterey Fisherman's Wharf	Monterey / Big Sur	Within 100 Miles	169
Pier 39	Fisherman's Wharf	San Francisco	24
Ripley's Believe it or Not!	Fisherman's Wharf	San Francisco	28
UnderWater World	Fisherman's Wharf	San Francisco	25
Wax Museum	Fisherman's Wharf	San Francisco	29

A Parent's Guide to San Francisco

NOTES

West Coast or East Coast?
America's greatest cities are waiting.

A Parent's Guide™ to
Los Angeles

ISBN 0-9675127-1-9
UPC 679762060029
$14.95
7.375"x9.125"
192 pages.

A Parent's Guide™ to
New York City

ISBN 0-9675127-0-0
UPC 679762060012
$14.95
7.375"x9.125"
192 pages.

MARS®
PUBLISHING

**6404 Wilshire Blvd
Los Angeles CA 90048**

800-549-6646

www.marspub.com

Parent's Guides — The Best Books Are From Mars.™

Chicago Attracts Families.

parent's guide press

6404 Wilshire Boulevard, Suite 1200
Los Angeles, CA 90048
phone: 800-549-6646
fax: 323-782-1775